HISTORY IN CONTEMPORARY ART AND CULTURE

Paul O'Kane

Routledge
Taylor & Francis Group
LONDON AND NEW YORK

Cover image: Folkert de Jong, *The Dance – Balthazar G*, 2008, Styrofoam, pigmented polyurethane foam, artificial gemstones. With kind permission of the artist. Photographed by Aatjan Renders.

First published 2023
by Routledge
4 Park Square, Milton Park, Abingdon, Oxon OX14 4RN

and by Routledge
605 Third Avenue, New York, NY 10158

Routledge is an imprint of the Taylor & Francis Group, an informa business

British Library Cataloguing-in-Publication Data
A catalogue record for this book is available from the British Library

Library of Congress Cataloging-in-Publication Data
Names: O'Kane, Paul, author.
Title: History in contemporary art and culture / Paul O'Kane.
Description: Abingdon, Oxon: Routledge, 2022. |
Includes bibliographical references and index.
Identifiers: LCCN 2021062118 (print) | LCCN 2021062119 (ebook) |
ISBN 9781032137384 (hardback) | ISBN 9781032137360 (paperback) |
ISBN 9781003230632 (ebook)
Subjects: LCSH: Art and history. | Arts, Modern–21st century–Themes, motives.
Classification: LCC N72.H58 O39 2022 (print) | LCC N72.H58 (ebook) |
DDC 709–dc23/eng/20211231
LC record available at https://lccn.loc.gov/2021062118
LC ebook record available at https://lccn.loc.gov/2021062119

ISBN: 978-1-032-13738-4 (hbk)
ISBN: 978-1-032-13736-0 (pbk)
ISBN: 978-1-003-23063-2 (ebk)

DOI: 10.4324/9781003230632

Typeset in Bembo
by Newgen Publishing UK

ual: central saint martins

HISTORY IN CONTEMPORARY ART AND CULTURE

This unique book offers guidance for contemporary art practices in dialogue with history, story, memory, and tradition.

Artist and lecturer Paul O'Kane uses innovative and creative means, informed by a storytelling tradition as well as academic research, to make connections between contemporary art, history, and the past. The aim of this book is to give readers a sense of the profundity of historical questions, while making the challenge inviting, welcoming, and manageable. It is designed to set out an expansive, inclusive, and diverse range of potential directions, and speculations from which students can develop personal paths of enquiry. This is achieved by writing and designing the text in an accessible way and providing a range of 'ways-in'. A series of carefully chosen references, examples, key texts, and possible essay questions are chosen and pitched at various levels and can be close-read, discussed, digested, and responded to either verbally or in the form of a presentation or essay.

Written primarily for a broad range of fine arts students, this book encourages readers to reconsider their studies and art practices in light of a historical perspective, enhanced by creative contributions from artists, imaginative philosophers, and influential cultural commentators.

Paul O'Kane is a lecturer in Critical Studies at Central St. Martin's College, University of the Arts, London. He specialises in histories and theories of art and popular culture.

This book is dedicated to the memory of my recently departed friend and colleague Dr. Kate Love, one of a few people in my life who gave me such a significant break that it became a break-through to the kind of recognition that truly changed my life for the better and allowed me to finally find a way to do the work that I do, that I always wanted to do, and always believed I could do. Kate's is a kindred spirit, as someone also from a working-class background and thus also taking the strange, difficult and often vertiginous journey of class migration, while learning along the way that we have to tip the cultural table in our direction; to write and do our history and theory, and make our art, in our way, not as imitators of more dominant, confident, and established voices. I hope and believe that Kate would have agreed with the way in which I have written this book, which is always intended to be generous and accessible to the widest range of potential readers and students; to those newly emerging voices and perspectives who live and work in hope and thereby offer hope of a better world.

CONTENTS

FIGURES

INTRODUCTION

How to use this book

What I would most like this book to pass on is the conviction that history is ever-present, once we attune to it, look for it, and seek a dialogue with it. Once we have nurtured a certain historical consciousness (that I hope to example if not define here), history is perceived wherever we look, not just in books, archives, or museums. We might start out by taking a statement made by Rolf Tiedman in relation to Walter Benjamin as our axiom here, when Tiedman says: "… In this way the historian should no longer try to enter the past; rather, he should allow the past to enter his life".[1]

I hope to show ways in which many kinds of receipts, finds, and observations (small, local, incidental, anecdotal, and unexpected) can be drawn into a potentially profound or dauntingly philosophical discussion without hierarchy. Apparently banal or un-promising events, objects, ideas or connections can contain historical value, if pressed, probed, turned over, and explored in a sufficiently curious manner, thus demonstrating an appropriately equitable approach to gathering and producing knowledge in the 21st century.[2]

It was at art college that I first began to consciously appreciate and write about art's own history, its relation to wider culture, the way art history can lead us into cultural history, or history *per se*. However, I believe that before I ever thought of going to art college a certain historical interest may have been stirring within me, born during adolescence, along with a strong subjectivity, and as part of my passion for listening to pop, rock, reggae, and soul music on the radio.

Quiet, private epiphanies might, like Hansel's pebbles in the fairy tale, enable us to connect up and retrace a (or 'the') story of our life, albeit one whose depths and nuances, memories, and forgettings we can never comprehensively share.

At about age 12, I made myself late for school in order to hear a favourite song on the radio (*Midnight Train to Georgia* by Gladys Knight and the Pips) played through to the end.[3] I remember how that special and valuable connection was so

DOI: 10.4324/9781003230632-1

'now'. The broadcast event could not be missed, it had to be captured, savoured, as it would not come again. It made me feel my life at that moment was special and valuable, as were the choices (to linger and listen or hurry away) that seemed to make my life my own.

We might say that thinking historically is simply taking a thing, an event, or ourselves seriously. That is partially true but does not account for the less serious pleasures to be had in museums, archives, libraries, or in our own historicised lives. Nor does it account for those moments when we might take things, events, or ourselves *too* seriously.

Nevertheless, I still believe that a special regard for the 'now' provides our best access to history, which is, in turn, related to the quality of attention, value, and form that we give to otherwise fleeting experience and evaporating time.

What is a museum collection if not a group of objects that, after being taken from their original context, have been taken seriously (albeit in a newly and peculiarly 'serious' way), re-valued, and awarded a place in a new organisation, order and story? However, rather than just 'taking' things or events seriously, we might also say that thinking and living historically is (as above) to savour them, and the reward for this savouring is what I call 'traction'.

We know that we are living, thinking, feeling, and writing historically when we feel a certain effective engagement – like that of gears, chain, tyres, and road – wherein our own experience meshes with what was once called by chroniclers (according to Walter Benjamin) 'the way of the world'.[4] I'd like to think and to suggest that we have all experienced this 'traction', have perhaps moved towards or away from it, and in what follows I have provided several examples of such experiences of historical 'traction' drawn from my own life.

In this book, anecdotal and biographical elements candidly implicate the particular time and 'culture' of the writer's lived experience. Thus, my very own history is also inscribed here, determining and delimiting the choice of materials (revealing the writer's own way to them and describing a particular life as formed by them), along with a sustained attempt to define and understand history as a collectively understood object, distinct from any particular subjectivity.

This book's origins may lie in a seminar titled *Uses of History in Contemporary Art*, but then, we could ask – if only perversely (but also, in a way, historically) – 'then what was the origin of that seminar title?' The answer to that question may lead only to more, similar questions, stacked one within the other like Russian dolls (a possible model of history), or like the infinite 'why? … why? … why? … ' asked by children (the first historians perhaps?) when playfully challenging their parents to reach the unreachable foundations of things, of events, of grown-up reasoning. Suffice to say, my experiences as a mature undergraduate, introduced simultaneously to T.J. Clark and postmodern theories, may well have been the 'first cut' that has proven 'deepest' and now proudly parades itself as this ever-growing, ever-healing 'scar' of a text.

Many of these essays (which originally varied in length from 1,000 to 12,000 words) have been written, written-up, or cut down for this occasion. They are taken from seminar and lecture notes or from previously unresolved essay and lecture ideas. Others are transformed, enhanced, reduced or extended pieces, previously published in other contexts but which have now been edited for and found their way to this appropriate home and shared context.

A seasoned arts editor once warned me that trying to replicate a seminar in book form was a folly, bound to fail. I couldn't help but see this advice as a gauntlet thrown down and that I have here accepted. I have previously written, designed, and self-published (in collaboration with others) books emerging from seminars, and these have in part proved that editor's advice to be correct, while nevertheless showing that there are also ways to develop creatively in response to this challenge, and that some fusion of the book and seminar formats might even be a promising model for further accessible-yet-challenging educational books.

One of the significant differences between a seminar and a book is the special air of free-flowing communicative conversation in a seminar that is hard to reproduce in a book. Nevertheless, I have tried to preserve some of this, particularly in what I have called the 'shorter' essays (less than 4,000 words). These provide introductions to, and cameos of relevant artists, thinkers, ideas, writers, and other protagonists qualified to contribute to our theme. Some of these focus on individual artists while others tend towards theories and theorists.

Another significant difference between a book and a seminar is the way in which a seminar conversation and its weekly agenda is relatively free to shift focus and create a particular and un-repeatable journey (an event in fact) determined by the interests of the participants. A traditional book however, necessarily establishes materials in a certain structure, order, and form of organisation. Having experimented with several such structures, I found myself gravitating to a mix of linear and 'holistic' models, i.e., the essays are divided into the shorter and the longer, and are given a particular linear order. However, they are also written and edited in such a way as to be autonomous enough, and 'holistic' enough (in that each detail and each essay should contain something of the whole) to allow the reader to also read them in whichever order they wish.

Some readers might like to 'find their feet' by first reading the shorter essays and then progressing to read the longer essays. These vary in length up to 11,000 words but for the convenience of a broad readership I have divided the longest essays into two parts.

I always wanted to use copious illustrations in this book, and they, along with their captions, plus some generous endnotes, and an index, might also provide alternative paths and ways through and around this book that I hope some readers might follow.

I aspire to the idea that our best writing can and should result in its whole being implicitly present in each of its parts; even within every sentence, and perhaps every word. With a mind to such a holistic model, this book is designed in a way influenced by Gilles Deleuze's reading of Leibniz's model of the 'monad',[5] and by Walter Benjamin's model of the 'constellation'.[6] Thus, each part of this book hopefully contains recognisable elements, not only of the whole within its parts but also of a sense of its writer's undeniable involvement, i.e., my own history, presence, and process in producing it.

I hope that readers will connect and critically evaluate the materials collected here in their own ways; including, of course, ways in which I have not evaluated and connected them myself. I perceive this book not as my own *fait accompli* but rather as a collection of prompts and resources that, here and there, and now and then might be connected and completed by the reader in the act of reading, and simultaneously provide springboards for the reader's own enquiries into and out of the book's title and theme. A set of possible essay questions, derived from teaching, are also provided.

In terms of form and process, every piece of serious writing that I have completed, whether published or unpublished, and since the late 1990s when my writing attained a certain publishable standard and consistency, has sought for, and fortunately in most cases found its final form, style and content as it were from 'within itself'. That is the approach I have taken again here, both in the individual essays and in the book as a whole. Unlike some more scholarly and research-based writing, my own primarily tends to explore itself and use itself, if only to then find a way out of itself to a new and personal thought – and this is the point at which I feel I might make an objective contribution.

Nevertheless, I have of course used the academic tradition of citation where necessary and where useful, often returning to certain key texts that have obviously influenced me strongly. As above, the reader will encounter a relatively small number of key references here, which recur in different essays. These include Walter Benjamin's comments on 'the outmoded'; his '*Theses on the Philosophy of History*' and 'Storyteller' essay; Baudelaire's 1846 salon essay; Deleuze's theorisation of 'event', Bourriaud's geographical description of history, Robert Smithson's 'Passaic' piece and Spiral Jetty, and one or two others).[7] This is yet another echo of my teaching's effects upon my writing, and the influence of the seminar environment that I have tried to retain, emulate, and perpetuate in book form.

There is, however, something both historical and autobiographical about these repeated references, at least in that I find they represent, first my own experience as a mature undergraduate (circa 1992), and then milestones on the journeys I have taken since with regard to this subject. I have subsequently become interested in the way that, given my title, theme and task, these references came, as it were, up and out of my own history, to persistently reassert themselves here. It might therefore prove to be the case that I am sharing the history of my own educational experience with the reader and using these historical references to explore my current perspectives on art, history, and the contemporary.

I have found that, during seminars, a repeated reference that becomes increasingly familiar to participants can help constitute the culture and community of the seminar (like an 'in joke' or *shibboleth*), becoming known and valued in a particular way for the period of the seminar and to those currently involved and most engaged. References repeatedly returned-to can provide a foothold of familiarity, on and around which confidence and camaraderie can develop.

Furthermore, when they recur, in slightly changed contexts and circumstances, such references attract and accumulate different information, and so, using them without prejudice can and does constitute a valuable learning experience and process of consolidation, looking at a single idea or reference, as it were, through several filters or from many different angles.

I hope that the diversity of materials – in terms of themes, styles, lengths, protagonists, eras, and epochs – collected and presented here make this an entertaining collection that keeps the interest of the reader, to whom, as I have said above, I hand over the task, the responsibility, and hopefully the pleasure of utilising all of this, in ways that are beneficial to their own writing, thinking, making, and research.

While the consistent emphasis of this book is history, the almost impossibly expansive term 'culture', used in the title relates to the regular inclusion of social and autobiographical reference, and is included to point to the fact that I discuss novels, popular music and lived experience as much as contemporary fine art and artists.

Fine art's perennially, and increasingly broad audience, readership, and student body will hopefully find in what follows elements of the contemporary balanced by historical example, popular-cultural references meeting fine art, contemporary visual artists rubbing shoulders with movies, 1970s soul encountering 1980s Hip-Hop, and thoughts on Empire subtly alluding to Chinese short stories or movies and novels by Kazuo Ishiguro. Meanwhile, selfie-sticks extend themselves into 17th-century Dutch culture and all of this intercultural and pan-chronic mingling is overseen by a small group of creative theorists, including Walter Benjamin, Nicolas Bourriaud, Gilles Deleuze, Charles Baudelaire, and Ariella Azoulay.

As a reflection of my own 'historical' journeys I find myself, in what follows, repeatedly alluding to, and 'still' (I hope excusably, and usefully) working through what might be called 'modernism and its others', those 'others' being postmodernism, pre-modernism, altermodernism, neo- or perhaps even re-postmodernism, as well as considering a current consideration of ahistorical, geological, or pre-historical time, and what aboriginal Australians call 'The Dreaming'.

Here, partly influenced by the writing of Ariella Azoulay, I prefer to consistently use the term 'modernism', rather than mix it with 'modernity', believing that 'modernism' can do much of the work done by the perhaps overused term 'modernity'. However, I do insist that both modernism and postmodernism be understood as profound and encompassing cultural paradigms rather than as mere styles or fashions.

When speaking of matters as temporal as history, 'event' (sometimes 'eventful' or 'eventual') may be the most appropriate and useful term, and I have therefore tried, influenced by philosopher Gilles Deleuze, to use it frequently to help supplant what might be called a 'thing-based (extensive) paradigm' with an (intensive) event-based paradigm.

Despite writing my PhD as an artist in a history department I do not call myself a historian but do regard myself as an 'artist, writer and lecturer' who enjoys the special sense of responsibility and fascination that comes from working with history, meanwhile finding, writing, and making connections in the special, conceptual, and creative ways that art allows and encourages us to do.

With apologies then to relevant specialists, and despite consistent and significant personal doubts concerning my ability and suitability for the task I here created for myself, I have persisted, and hopefully prevailed in my aspiration to contribute something of value to current and emerging debates regarding art, culture, and history; their overlaps, and their representation in writing.

Ultimately, this book is perhaps most useful as a model or example of how its enquiry might be pursued by others, differently, or better. I thus offer it as a potential resource to readers, students, peers, colleagues and experts working in specialisms to which I have alluded only from their margins, in the hope that others might 'complete' my task in their own and various ways.

Notes

1 Benjamin, W. (1999) p. 935.
2 See current, critical, cultural conversation motivated by Baljeet Sandhu MBE, e.g., here: www.bbc.co.uk/programmes/m000ycvl for a discussion of the values of 'Lived Experience' and 'Knowledge Equity'.
3 Gladys Knight & The Pips (1973).
4 Benjamin, W. (1968) pp. 83–110.
5 Deleuze, G. (2001, 1990).
6 Walter Benjamin famously proposed in the 'Epistemo-Critical Prologue' to *Ursprung des deutschen Trauerspiels* (1928), translated as *The Origin of German Tragic Drama* (1977), that ideas are to objects as constellations are to stars. That is to say, ideas are no more present in the world than constellations actually exist in the heavens, but like constellations they enable us to perceive relations between objects. See www.oxfordreference.com/view/10.1093/oi/authority.20110803095633862.
7 Baudelaire, C. (1992); Benjamin, W. (1968). See https://holtsmithsonfoundation.org/monuments-passaic; https://holtsmithsonfoundation.org/spiral-jetty.

Bibliography

Azoulay, A.A. (2019) *Potential History – Unlearning Imperialism*. London: Verso.
Baudelaire, C. (1992) *Selected Writings on Art & Literature*. London: Penguin.
Benjamin, W. (1968) *Illuminations*. New York: Schocken Books.
Benjamin, W. (1999) *The Arcades Project*. Cambridge, MA: Belknap.
Bourriaud, N. (2009) *Altermodern – The Third Tate Triennial*. London: Tate.
Deleuze G. (1990) *Negotiations*. New York: Columbia University Press.
Deleuze, G. (2001) *The Fold, Leibniz and the Baroque*. London: The Athlone Press.
Gladys Knight & The Pips (Weatherly, J. writer) (1973) *Midnight Train to Georgia* (music recording). Universal Polygram International Publishing Inc.

PART I

Shorter essays

1

COUNTRY LIFE

One night, at the end of the 1990s, I said goodbye to a friend at London Bridge underground station and made my way to the nearby bus terminal. My bus was waiting at the stop. It was the last of the evening before the route switched over to the night bus service. As the driver's first customer I had the privilege of marching up the stairs and claiming what many Londoners regard as the prime seat, i.e., front window, left hand side. Lowering myself into the seat I noticed a magazine abandoned there. I recognised the title as something I would not usually read; in fact it was not the kind of magazine I'd expect to find here on this relatively lowly form of transport. Its title was *Country Life*.[1]

At that time in my own life, I was probably a little more superstitious than I am today, but even now I sometimes wonder just how that copy of the July 1996 issue of that magazine came to rendezvous with me, presumably by means of long chains of chance connections. At first I went to dismiss the journal, to set it apart from me and put it on another seat, but curiosity, the possibility of a boring bus ride, and a kind of holistic relativism that I was then beginning to cultivate in my judgements, all made me counter my initial prejudice and begin to examine the magazine, albeit as a kind of exotic object. 'OK' I thought, 'just what does this magazine contain? Who reads it, and why? And is there anything in this for me?'

I skimmed through the pages, and at first found little to detain me. I was interested and slightly amused by images of landed debutantes posing against the classicist pillars of their family's substantial homes. I was momentarily detained by property pages on which lavish mansions with enormous grounds and luxurious facilities were advertised for sale. However, I only stopped skimming and started reading when I came to a double-page spread titled *Around the Salerooms*.

At this time, I had just published my first pieces of art writing, and it struck me that I should take an interest in this example of a cultural equivalent of a contemporary art review. Here, a connoisseur of some kind was evaluating a series of sales

DOI: 10.4324/9781003230632-3

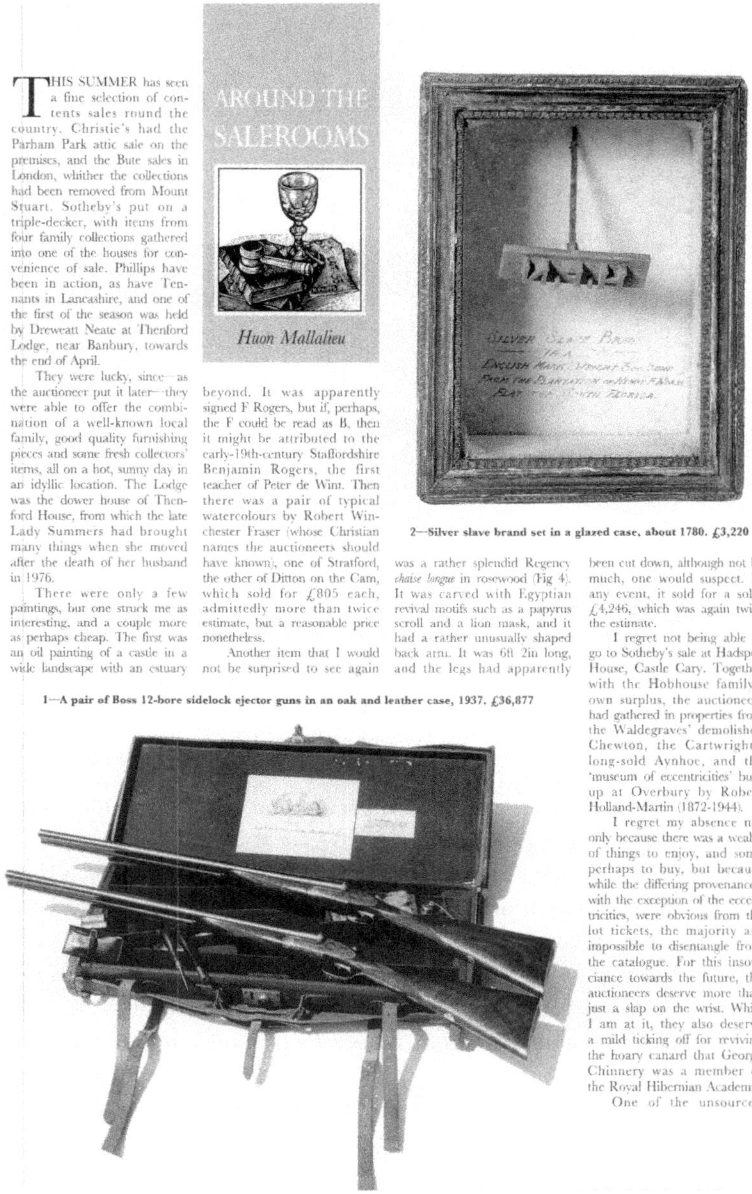

AROUND THE SALEROOMS

Huon Mallalieu

THIS SUMMER has seen a fine selection of contents sales round the country. Christie's had the Parham Park attic sale on the premises, and the Bute sales in London, whither the collections had been removed from Mount Stuart. Sotheby's put on a triple-decker, with items from four family collections gathered into one of the houses for convenience of sale. Phillips have been in action, as have Tennants in Lancashire, and one of the first of the season was held by Dreweatt Neate at Thenford Lodge, near Banbury, towards the end of April.

They were lucky, since—as the auctioneer put it later—they were able to offer the combination of a well-known local family, good quality furnishing pieces and some fresh collectors' items, all on a hot, sunny day in an idyllic location. The Lodge was the dower house of Thenford House, from which the late Lady Summers had brought many things when she moved after the death of her husband in 1976.

There were only a few paintings, but one struck me as interesting, and a couple more as perhaps cheap. The first was an oil painting of a castle in a wide landscape with an estuary beyond. It was apparently signed F Rogers, but if, perhaps, the F could be read as B, then it might be attributed to the early-19th-century Staffordshire Benjamin Rogers, the first teacher of Peter de Wint. Then there was a pair of typical watercolours by Robert Winchester Fraser (whose Christian names the auctioneers should have known), one of Stratford, the other of Ditton on the Cam, which sold for £805 each, admittedly more than twice estimate, but a reasonable price nonetheless.

Another item that I would not be surprised to see again was a rather splendid Regency *chaise longue* in rosewood (Fig 4). It was carved with Egyptian revival motifs such as a papyrus scroll and a lion mask, and it had a rather unusually shaped back arm. It was 6ft 2in long, and the legs had apparently been cut down, although not by much, one would suspect. In any event, it sold for a solid £4,246, which was again twice the estimate.

I regret not being able to go to Sotheby's sale at Hadspen House, Castle Cary. Together with the Hobhouse family's own surplus, the auctioneers had gathered in properties from the Waldegraves' demolished Chewton, the Cartwrights' long-sold Aynhoe, and the 'museum of eccentricities' built up at Overbury by Robert Holland-Martin (1872-1944).

I regret my absence not only because there was a wealth of things to enjoy, and some perhaps to buy, but because while the differing provenances, with the exception of the eccentricities, were obvious from the lot tickets, the majority are impossible to disentangle from the catalogue. For this insouciance towards the future, the auctioneers deserve more than just a slap on the wrist. While I am at it, they also deserve a mild ticking off for reviving the hoary canard that George Chinnery was a member of the Royal Hibernian Academy.

One of the unsourced

2—Silver slave brand set in a glazed case, about 1780. £3,220

1—A pair of Boss 12-bore sidelock ejector guns in an oak and leather case, 1937. £36,877

FIGURE 1.1 'Around the Salerooms', double-age feature from *Country Life* magazine, July 1996 pp. 76–77. Courtesy of Futurenet.

or auctions taking place at various country houses and auction houses. I became interested in the kind of language, writing and judgements being made, and how they might diverge from or compare with the kind of writing with which I was involved – i.e., contemporary art writing for contemporary art magazines.

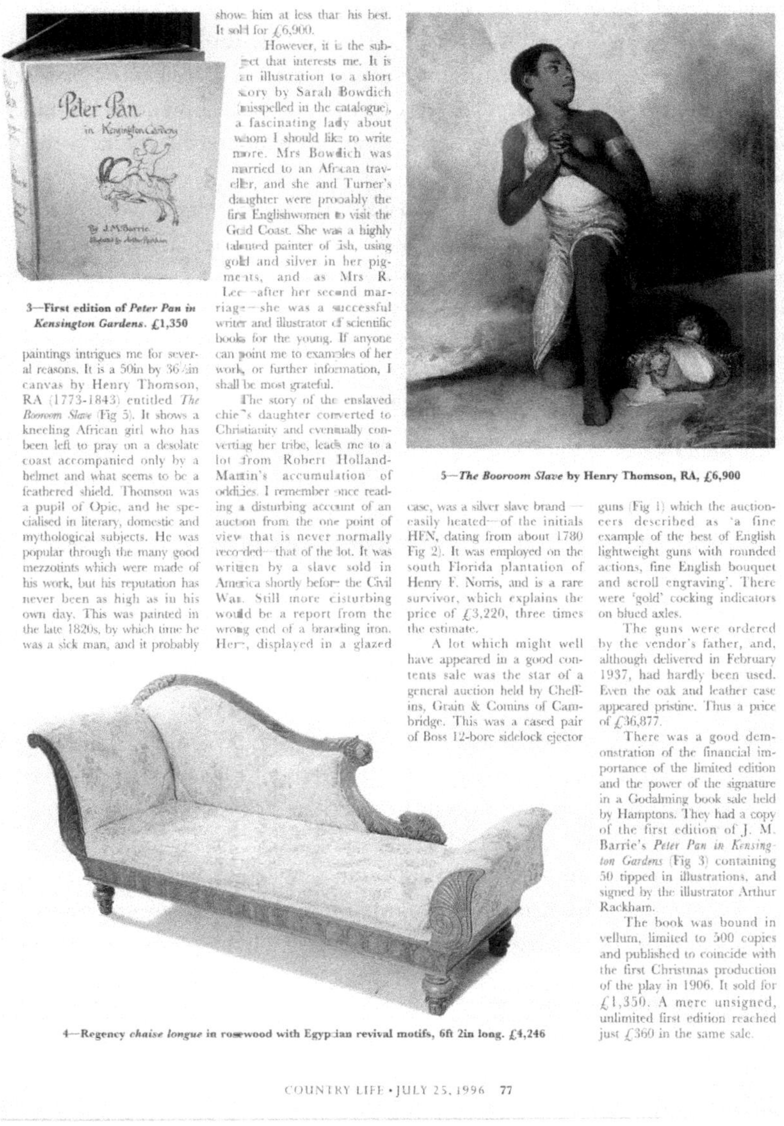

3—First edition of *Peter Pan in Kensington Gardens*. £1,350

paintings intrigues me for several reasons. It is a 50in by 36½in canvas by Henry Thomson, RA (1773-1843) entitled *The Booroom Slave* (Fig 5). It shows a kneeling African girl who has been left to pray on a desolate coast accompanied only by a helmet and what seems to be a feathered shield. Thomson was a pupil of Opie, and he specialised in literary, domestic and mythological subjects. He was popular through the many good mezzotints which were made of his work, but his reputation has never been as high as in his own day. This was painted in the late 1820s, by which time he was a sick man, and it probably shows him at less than his best. It sold for £6,900.

However, it is the subject that interests me. It is an illustration to a short story by Sarah Bowdich (misspelled in the catalogue), a fascinating lady about whom I should like to write more. Mrs Bowdich was married to an African traveller, and she and Turner's daughter were probably the first Englishwomen to visit the Gold Coast. She was a highly talented painter of fish, using gold and silver in her pigments, and as Mrs R. Lee—after her second marriage—she was a successful writer and illustrator of scientific books for the young. If anyone can point me to examples of her work, or further information, I shall be most grateful.

The story of the enslaved chief's daughter converted to Christianity and eventually converting her tribe, leads me to a lot from Robert Holland-Martin's accumulation of oddities. I remember once reading a disturbing account of an auction from the one point of view that is never normally recorded—that of the lot. It was written by a slave sold in America shortly before the Civil War. Still more disturbing would be a report from the wrong end of a branding iron. Here, displayed in a glazed case, was a silver slave brand—easily heated—of the initials HFN, dating from about 1780 (Fig 2). It was employed on the south Florida plantation of Henry F. Norris, and is a rare survivor, which explains the price of £3,220, three times the estimate.

A lot which might well have appeared in a good contents sale was the star of a general auction held by Cheffins, Grain & Comins of Cambridge. This was a cased pair of Boss 12-bore sidelock ejector guns (Fig 1) which the auctioneers described as 'a fine example of the best of English lightweight guns with rounded actions, fine English bouquet and scroll engraving'. There were 'gold' cocking indicators on blued axles.

The guns were ordered by the vendor's father, and, although delivered in February 1937, had hardly been used. Even the oak and leather case appeared pristine. Thus a price of £36,877.

There was a good demonstration of the financial importance of the limited edition and the power of the signature in a Godalming book sale held by Hamptons. They had a copy of the first edition of J. M. Barrie's *Peter Pan in Kensington Gardens* (Fig 3) containing 50 tipped in illustrations, and signed by the illustrator Arthur Rackham.

The book was bound in vellum, limited to 500 copies and published to coincide with the first Christmas production of the play in 1906. It sold for £1,350. A mere unsigned, unlimited first edition reached just £360 in the same sale.

5—*The Booroom Slave* by Henry Thomson, RA, £6,900

4—Regency *chaise longue* in rosewood with Egyptian revival motifs, 6ft 2in long. £4,246

COUNTRY LIFE • JULY 25, 1996 77

FIGURE 1.1 (continued)

The tone of the writing was interesting; it maintained an elevated good humour that seemed politely dispassionate and disengaged from the diverse range of historical artefacts and *objet d'art* it described. In addition to the writer's jaunty tone, I became increasingly interested in the particular array of images of objects that had been chosen to lay out across the article's two pages. These were as follows: a pair of decorated shotguns in a case, a silver slave brand in a frame, a first edition copy of *Peter Pan*, a *chaise longues*, and an oil painting of a slave girl.

As mentioned above, the writer effortlessly threaded all of this and more together with the air of someone whose area of expertise this was. I, however, began to wonder how these same objects might be interpreted and connected by viewers, critics, or curators if transported to a contemporary art context. What kinds of narrative would this assembly suggest to a visitor encountering them in the contemporary art context?

It struck me that while a contemporary art audience or critic would be immediately drawn into a critical and historical, as well as imaginative, interpretation, the writer here seemed able to skate relatively lightly over the social and political implications of this grouping. I suspected that some form of denial or cultural blind spot might be operating here (we all have our cultural blind spots), one that allowed the writer, editor, picture editor, chief editor, and the journal's intended readers to acknowledge that these objects belonged within and emerged from their own *milieu* (every magazine represents a *milieu*), while nevertheless remaining barely aware of the potential critical, political, and historical implications of these objects and their juxtaposition. A Freudian reading might even diagnose some form of repression manifest here on the part of a certain swathe of Britain's famously diverse and highly stratified culture.

Who, I wondered, would want to own, who owned, who sold, and who bought these objects, and for what purposes? I began to imagine scenarios and stories that might unite the objects and make some sense of their proximity and association. Was there a person, for example, who might lie back on this *chaise longues*, reading their first edition copy of *Peter Pan* (a children's story about a child who never grows up), occasionally admiring a painting of a slave girl on one wall and the framed slave brand on another, before taking a break to go out and do some shooting?

Hopefully the reader can begin to see now how incongruous this journal seemed to me on the top deck of a late night 133 bus from London Bridge to Brixton. Now, looking back, it also makes me think about the 'country' in '*Country Life*'. That 'country' is of course aspirational and desirable, as are the houses and the *objets d'art* for sale in the magazine. And yet, while the houses and *objets d'art* are real, particular, and actual, the 'country' is ideal and abstract, it's really a kind of signifier of something to which the buyer of the magazine subscribes or aspires.

As the artist Sigrid Holmwood shows in her performed or painted works (discussed in Chapter 5 of this book), as well as in her recent research and writing, the rural is, in medieval terms, the realm of the peasant as well as that of the landowner. But that peasant class has long been subjected to clearances, enclosures, urbanisation, and industrialisation. While modernism came to emphasise the city as its primary *locus* and breeding ground, and as power drained away from the aristocracy into the hands of the urban bourgeoisie or middle class, the country also took on an increasingly mythic quality, as can be seen first in Romanticism, but also all the way into the present, where SUV cars overpopulate the city as echoes of imaginary country estates on which they might be better suited and more necessary. Even the green Wellington boot has become a symbol of 'landedness', but if so, only as a way of dallying with a rural idyll generally supplanted by the centrality of modern urban culture.

If Georgian Romantics were already making a myth of the countryside, modern artists sometimes escaped to it (e.g. Cezanne, Gauguin, or Van Gogh) or pioneered, with the help of the new railways, the cultivation of new suburban space between city and country, as seen in Impressionism. Today, the 'country' in *Country Life* retains *cache*. It signifies or suggests that the magazine's reader, owner, or contributor approves of and adheres to certain values and standards that both precede and exceed the modern and urban.

As I have said, at the time that I found the copy of *Country Life* on that bus seat, I had just published my first art writings, and those small breakthroughs and successes were helping me to confirm a long, slow, and difficult career change. Since the 1980s I had repeatedly switched my focus back and forth between fine art and popular music, and in 1996–1997 I was letting go of music once again and coming back to fully concentrate on fine art.

While working in Indie music and Hip-Hop I had never been *un*aware of the crucial cultural legacy of black artists and black culture burning away at the root of these musical genres, but when I went back into the fine art world I was dismayed by the dearth of black artists visible there. I have come to believe that it was, in part at least, my encounter with those pages of *Country Life* magazine, and perhaps in particular the framed slave brand for sale as an *objet d'art*, that moved me to a new resolve. Since I was now able to publish my ideas and opinions, judgements, ideas and descriptions of art and culture, and in prestigious and prominent art journals, I would henceforth write only about what I then called 'Black and Asian Artists in London'.[2] That, I thought, would be my noble remit, my parameters, my cause.

Soon I had published reviews, previews, essays, or profiles on Susan Pui San Lok, Sonia Boyce, Johannes Phokela, Ajamu, Godfried Donkor, Rita Keegan, Hew Locke, Sabera Bham, Mayling To, Talawa Theatre Company, Suki Chan, Amanda Francis, Janette Paris, and others. Some of these writings appeared in the journal *Third Text* where my editors included artist and founding editor Rasheed Araeen, unflinchingly flinty critic Jean Fisher, innovative cultural theorist Stuart Hall, ahead-of-his-times internationalist Guy Brett, and maverick academic Sarat Maharaj (who later became my professor).[3]

Meanwhile, I was lucky enough to be asked to contribute small profiles and previews to black woman's lifestyle magazine *Pride*.[4] Here I aimed to reach an audience less familiar perhaps with the contemporary fine art world. In the pages of *Pride*, my writing – introducing one black, usually female, artist, show or group each month – rubbed shoulders with advertisements for hair and skin products, articles on health, beauty, sex, music, relationships, and fashion.

Discovering what at that time felt like a hidden art world within 'the art world' (there are in truth an infinite number of such 'worlds within worlds') was an exciting experience. Always on the lookout for new artists I was passed on from one to another as recommendations were made to me. I felt more of a journalist than a critic in that role and had in fact gained a press card and official National Council for the Training of Journalists (NCTJ) print journalism qualification just prior to getting published for the first time. My new realm and remit of 'Black and Asian Artists in London' not only connected me to artists but also allowed me to discover and piece together a number of often poorly funded yet nobly sustained institutions. Among these were the Institute of International Visual Artists (iniva), African and Asian Visual Arts Archive (AAVAA), the 198 Gallery in Brixton, the Brunei Gallery at the School of African and Oriental Studies (SOAS) University of London, and others.[5]

In this role, and in this realm, I met friendly, helpful, and inspiring people and felt welcomed wherever I went. Soon I was also proud to be asked to contribute to the Routledge publication *Companion to Contemporary Black British Culture* which, then and now, provides a rich and valuable directory of hundreds of artists, events, and organisations pertinent to its title and purpose.[6]

I carried on in this mode for a couple of busy and rewarding years, and I have sometimes wished that I had stayed longer on that particular path, a trajectory on which I felt I could make a difference to perceived inequalities and imbalances in British art and culture.[7] However, fundamental personal and financial challenges, including those of housing and employment, as well as growing ethical doubts concerning my self-assumed role and my academic qualifications, all eventually led me to move on.

As a result of my published writing, I began to be asked to teach, and a corresponding sense of academic insufficiency or inadequacy (early signs of imposter syndrome) led me to believe that now was the time to complete a Master of Arts (MA) course. I could only afford to do that by giving up living in London, returning to live with my family, and commuting into London to attend classes and lectures. Those studies led to an MA in Visual Cultures and then a PhD in History. All these changes pushed me away from my previously focused role as a 'Black and Asian arts' journalist but opened up new avenues and possibilities – including the beginning of a first chance, coming quite late in life, to make my way, and pay my way in the world by means of teaching.

As can be seen above, I have never forgotten those pages from *Country Life*, and they never let go of me, but studying and teaching gave me more ways to think about those pages, those images, and those words, and allowed me to contextualise, deconstruct, interpret, and challenge them, and also to share them with others – as I am doing here.

> As one small example of this newfound intellectual and academic contextualisation, I will conclude this short opening section by drawing those objects, their images and the writing that accompanies them in the July 1996 issue of *Country Life*, into a dialogue with some of the best-known words of Walter Benjamin, taken from his *Theses On The Philosophy of History* – a text that

is, in a way, foundational to this book. I hope the reader can attend to and think about Benjamin's words carefully while revisiting the *Country Life* pages illustrated above.

Those words are:
Every image of the past that is not recognised by the present as one of its own concerns threatens to disappear irretrievably

And:
There is no document of civilisation which is not at the same time a document of barbarism. And just as such a document is not free of barbarism, barbarism taints also the manner in which it was transmitted from one owner to another.[8]

Notes

1 Mallalieu, H. (1996) pp. 76–77.
2 I would not use this terminology now. Discomfort regarding this terminology, and other ethical nuances (some of which I later came to understood under the term 'intersectionality') relating both to my own identity and those of whom I was writing about, eventually meant that I relinquished this reductive and imposing remit.
3 http://thirdtext.org/about-us.
4 www.pridemagazine.com/
5 See
http://thirdtext.org/about-us
www.pridemagazine.com/
https://iniva.org/
https://vads.ac.uk/digital/collection/AAVAA
www.198.org, www.soas.ac.uk/gallery/
6 Donnell, A. (ed.) (2001).
As far as I am aware, the Routledge *Companion To Black British Culture* has not been updated in the form of a new edition, but it would seem to be timely now to do so.
7 However, see footnote 2.
8 Benjamin, W. (1968) pp. 255–256.

Bibliography

Benjamin, W. (1968) *Illuminations*. New York: Schocken Books.
Donnell, A. (ed.) (2001) *Companion to Contemporary Black British Culture*. London: Routledge.
Mallalieu, H. (1996) 'Around the Salercoms' Country Life (Vol CXC No. 30, 25th July).

2

FOLKERT DE JONG

Serious history and black comedy

Is history serious? Is it more serious than other kind of story we might tell? I recall a visit to London's Saatchi Gallery in 2011, with sculpture students, to see a show titled *The Shape of Things to Come: New Sculpture*.[1] More than any other work in this rich and varied show I fixed upon the art of Folkert de Jong. Although de Jong's larger-than-life figures were made of modern materials, they obviously related to history. And although de Jong's figures often appeared to dance, celebrate, and grin, they were also grim – something cynical seemed to emit from them.

Tracking down some interviews with the artist I learned about his content, his processes, and his motives.[2] The experience left a strong impression on me and de Jong became a key example in my seminar. The sculpted dress of his figures seemed to vaguely allude to something 17th century and European; they wore clothes a little like those seen in Dutch or Spanish paintings of that period, e.g. by Velasquez or Gerard Ter Borch. The scale of the figures was, as I say above, larger-than-life and it may be worth briefly discussing this issue of scale here because it alludes to a historical and monumental tradition that will be discussed elsewhere in this book.

According to this tradition, sculptural figures made for public sites are scaled up to appear sufficiently significant in spaces that would otherwise dwarf and deprive them of their necessary sense of importance. One or two other contemporary artists have referred to and perhaps challenged this larger-than-life tradition when making works for the so-called 'Fourth Plinth' in London's Trafalgar Square. Anthony Gormley, with his 2009 work *One and Other* made the plinth available to life-sized members of the public, who took turns in speaking, posing, dancing, protesting, or otherwise performing on the plinth.[3] This immediately illustrated how 'life-size' figures appear inadequate and inappropriate in relation to the scale of the plinth, the surrounding square, and given our familiarity with the scaled-up monumental tradition. Interestingly, the public, unless gathered *en mass*, do not look very significant in the public square.

DOI: 10.4324/9781003230632-4

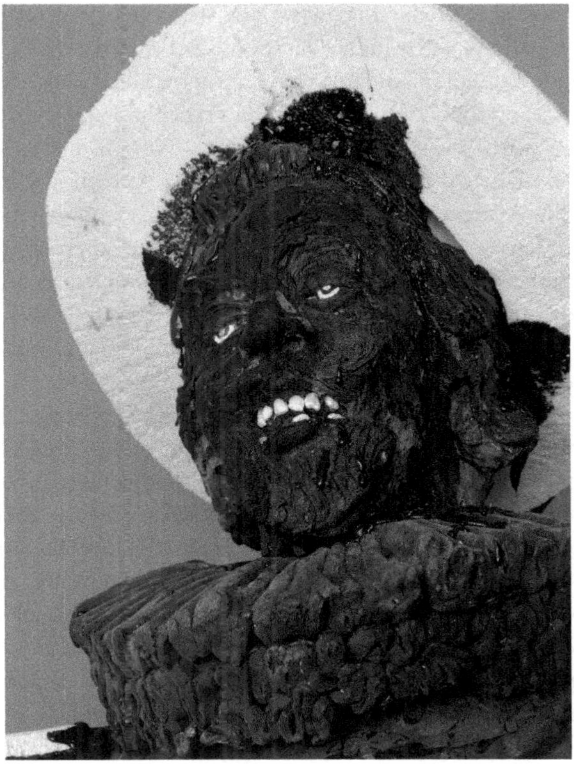

FIGURE 2.1 Folkert de Jong's work at Saatchi Gallery. Folkert de Jong, *The Dance, Balthazar G* (detail), 2008, Styrofoam, pigmented polyurethane foam, artificial gemstones.

Mark Wallinger's *Ecce Homo* (1999) placed a figure of Christ on the plinth which, using life-size rather than the traditionally enlarged scale, resulted in an unusually humane, empathy-inducing scenario wherein the figure of Christ seemed to rely upon the mercy of the viewer, rather than presuming superiority as a saviour looming over the viewer (as do many figures boosted by the inaccurate but nevertheless effective monumental tradition).[4]

But to return to Folkert de Jong: like the size and the dress of his sculptures, their dances and other gestures seemed to allude to another age.[5] Meanwhile, the state of the figures' teeth might provide a pointer to a more accurate and realistic historical rendition than those regularly created in TV costume dramas or Hollywood movies. And this small but significant touch of realism in de Jong's sculptures is likely to transport questioning minds into a more serious consideration of the past.[6]

All of this is important for the dialogue between the present and the past opened up by de Jong within the liberal space of contemporary art. Reading interviews with the artist we may gain more specific details about the works and connect de Jong's Dutch nationality to the scenarios that he has conjured up in the gallery.

We probably know that the Netherlands, along with Spain, Portugal, England, and other European nations, was a highly successful global power in the 17th century, building an empire of colonised lands and an international network of ports, as it traded, navigated, and fought competitively and successfully with its rivals.

One of these ports was what we now know as New York City and the island of Manhattan, which at the time of Dutch rule was known as New Amsterdam before becoming Anglicised to New York following a subsequent exchange of power. Nevertheless, Manhattan's native American name (approximately translated as 'place to gather bow-making materials') has survived centuries of such exchanges and thus remains for us a route between present and past, between Manhattan's famous hyper-modernity and the ancient traditions of the island's original inhabitants.

Another, more indexical trace that brings Manhattan's ancient past and present into dialogue, is the phenomenon of Broadway. On a visit to New York City some years ago, I was lucky enough to discover the surprisingly modest museum of the great city itself. At The Museum of the City of New York I learned how the island was increasingly capitalised and rationalised into saleable plots which resulted in its famously strict grid system of streets and avenues.[7] Interestingly, Broadway is an exception to the rule of this strict grid, progressing, as it does, at a more organic and oblique angle, up from the South to the North of the island. The famously sharp-angled 'Flat Iron' building was an inventive response to an anomalous plot of land shaped by Broadway's eccentric trajectory as it cut through the otherwise regular grid.

Broadway is therefore a much consolidated example of what we today call a 'desire path', i.e., a naturally emerging path created by people living and trading on, and crossing the island, carrying goods by the most convenient and direct route, back and forth between the Southernmost landing place and a Northern crossing point that accessed the mainland. Hence, just as a name can quickly transcend historical time and connect us to the past, so might the mere shape of a road in a city. Personally, living and working in London, I always find that a significant curve in a road makes me think historically.

Folkert de Jong does not in fact concentrate on the architectural issues of Manhattan's street plan but is more interested in a certain modest monument that takes the form of a flagpole with an inscribed base or plinth and is installed on the Southern tip of Manhattan in a public area and park South of Wall Street known as The Battery.[8] This small monument marks an exchange made by Dutch settlers in 1626 with indigenous peoples, according to which the 22,000 acres of the Island of Manhattan became Dutch property in return for – as legend varies – 60 Gilders, or the equivalent of 24 dollars' worth of trinkets. Today the island is valued at 1.74 trillion dollars. So now we begin to understand why de Jong's figures look so happy; why they are dancing, playing stringed instruments, and are perhaps a little drunk. Their dreams of becoming rich in 'the new world' have come true.

In interviews, de Jong refers to the works in the 2011 Saatchi Gallery show as illustrating the then recent and ongoing financial crash caused by dangerous practices in Wall Street and other financial centres around the world. He makes a link between the risk-taking financial adventurers of the 17th century and those of today. Thus, we short-circuit time and history, drawing the present into proximity with the past in a way that gives the present new depths and textures of meaning, and brings the past into the present as something renewed. Folkert de Jong has confronted us with something serious, dark, and cynical, seen through and seen despite the grins of his dancing figures. He has opened swathes of history for us to investigate, albeit by deploying his work in the most contemporary of spaces.

It is also noticeable that de Jong's figures are both finely wrought and messy, both detailed and impressionistic, both charming and grotesque. Now we know a little more about the figures, they seem, though happy, to have also been endowed by their maker with some sense of guilt or shame. There is a dark heart to the work, and this might encourage us to look further and deeper into the history to which the work alludes, and to consider what are, what were, and what could be the ramifications and legacies today of a certain, modestly monumentalised 17th century exchange between two such very different peoples as the original inhabitants of the lands we now call America, and Netherlandish settlers.

While de Jong has incorporated both mess and finesse, impression and detail in his figures, he has also left exposed, in places, the very modern material of bright pink Styrofoam that materially underpins these historical representations. Once

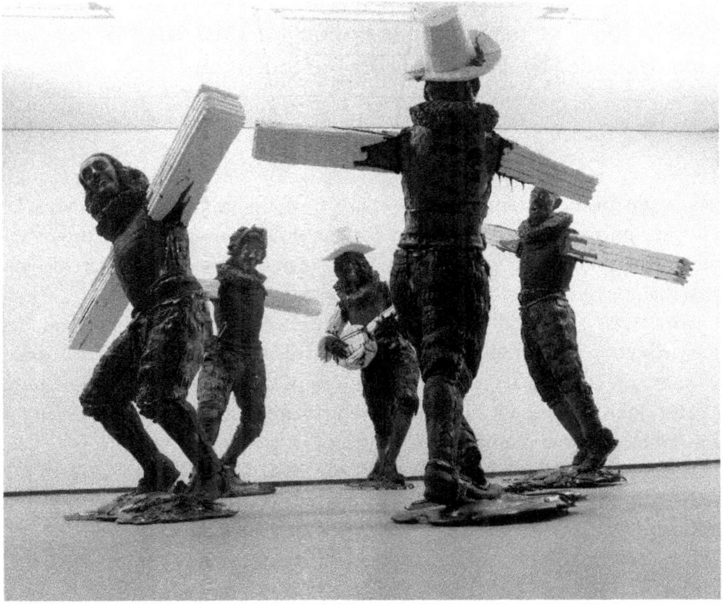

FIGURE 2.2 Folkert de Jong's work at Saatchi Gallery. Folkert de Jong, *The Dance*, 2008, Styrofoam, pigmented polyurethane foam, artificial gemstones.

again, present and past are clapped together disallowing any more habitual and perhaps more convenient separation. There is, after all, no actual separation, no real dividing line or clearly discernible hiatus between the past – no matter how recent or ancient – and the present, though for some reason this is always a slightly disturbing fact for us to acknowledge. We seem to need some (at least imagined) bulwark of form that keeps us feeling that we are inhabiting a present, progressing into a future, and avoiding falling into the past.

Folkert de Jong's Styrofoam includes barcodes attached to the raw materials, just as you might find it in a hardware superstore. Thus, commercial transaction is once again brought to our mind, as the artist, having hooked us with the work's apparent gaiety and levity, refuses to let us disconnect past from present.

So, history is serious, and yet there is still space perhaps for our own dancing and laughter here. In the work of de Jong, as in the work of the artist Jimmie Durham (see Chapter 3 of this book), contemporary art, and the contemporary artist, no matter how serious the ideas with which they become embroiled, often succeed in transmitting their message, most widely and effectively by lacing their work with humour (N.B. Walter Benjamin, influenced by fairy tales, advises us to deploy 'cunning and high spirits' when confronting difficulty and dark forces).[9] If so, it might just be the 'black humour' first defined and determined by surrealist Andre Breton to accommodate a particularly modern and new form of amusement emerging from the modern age.

Yes, history is serious, but there is also a history of humour for researchers to pursue, and there may even be constantly updated demands for new forms of humour. After all, critic and poet Charles Baudelaire, launching modern art in his Salon of 1846, spoke of 'new forms of passion' (also translated as 'new emotions') created and demanded by, and appropriate to modern life.[10]

Notes

1 See www.saatchigallery.com/exhibition/shape_of_things. Núñez-Fernández, L. (2011).
2 See https://burnaway.org/magazine/interview-folkert-de-jong-an-artist-of-spirit-and-styrofoam/; www.dailyserving.com/2011/05/an-interview-with-folkert-de-jong/.
3 See www.antonygormley.com/show/item-view/id/2277.
4 The work was later exhibited at the entrance to St Paul's Cathedral. See www.hauserwirth.com/news/18484-mark-wallingers-ecce-homo-st-pauls-cathedral.
5 Here we might consider research into a history of dance, of dances, and of gestures.
6 The artist John Akomfrah has also shown an interest in making contemporary art influenced by costume dramas (see Chapter 10 of this book).
7 See www.mcny.org/about?gclid=EAIaIQobChMIjOS2z6qA8gIViZWzCh0ygwrhEAAYASAAEgIkQvD_BwE; www.mcny.org/nyatitscore; www.mcny.org/exhibition/greatest-grid-0.
8 See www.nycgovparks.org/parks/battery-park/monuments/1092.
9 Benjamin, W. (1968) p. 102.
10 Baudelaire, C. (1992) p. 106.

Bibliography

Baudelaire, C. (1992) *Selected Writings on Art & Literature*. London: Penguin.
Benjamin, W. (1968) *Illuminations*. New York: Schocken Books.
Núñez-Fernández, L. (2011) *The Shape of Things to Come: New Sculpture*. London: Saatchi Gallery.

3

JIMMIE DURHAM

Spoof museologist, *a*historical dreamer

Some years ago, while teaching a then new seminar titled *Uses of History in Contemporary Art*, I came across the art of Jimmie Durham.[1] I knew a little about the artist already but this was the first time I had engaged directly with his work. My way-in was via what may be called Durham's satirical museology in which he creates spoof anthropological artefacts supposedly alluding to native American culture – to and from which he (controversially, and with increasing complexity) likes to draw part of his own ancestry and identity.[2]

By creating these spoofs and satires, some of which might fool some visitors to museums and galleries, Durham does something in the best traditions of conceptual art (he trained in the 1970s) but also common to postmodern artists (he came to prominence in the 1980s). That is to say that Durham takes minimal means to address monumental issues and uses idea-based art to engage materially with disruptive and disorienting issues of identity, representation, and organisation.

In his work, a simple-looking assemblage set in a museological frame and context (typically a plinth or vitrine), and deployed with satirical, critical intent, quickly comes to implicate the entire museological and anthropological apparatus underpinning the modern, Eurocentric hierarchy of which the American settlers are a part, and which progressive historian Ariella Azoulay refers to as 'Empire'.

Hence, the very notion of a 'native' person or culture might derive from a colonial or otherwise intrusive perspective, i.e., not of course from 'natives' themselves who are merely people forced to adopt this imposed 'native' identity as a legacy of colonisation.[3] We should also note here that 'native', as uttered by Empire, often tends to refer to a people with 'minority', 'marginal' or otherwise secondary status imposed upon them.

Having distanced himself from claims to being native-American, Durham's controversial and parallel bid to self-identify as Cherokee, despite weak or uncertain sources of legitimation for that claim, becomes, in the context of the debates his

DOI: 10.4324/9781003230632-5

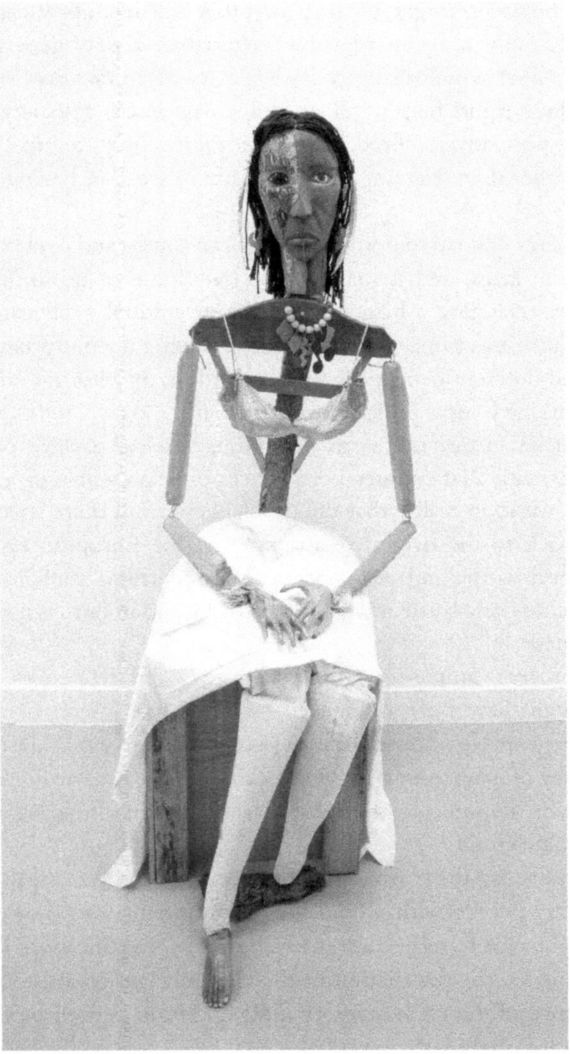

FIGURE 3.1 Example of Jimmie Durham's 'spoof museology'. Jimmie Durham, *La Malinche*, 1988–1991, Guava, pine branches, oak, snakeskin, polyester bra soaked in acrylic resin and painted gold, watercolour, cactus leaf, canvas, cotton cloth, metal, rope, feathers, plastic jewellery, glass eye, 177 cm × 60 cm × 89 cm. Photographed by Christine Clinckx.

work has provoked, a claim to identity that is not necessarily grounded in history, but rather in more subjective or personal criteria (e.g. the ways in which he was raised, a particular family mythology – or 'romance' as Freud put it – of the kind to which many of us are subject) and certain other tentative and perhaps unprovable connections.

The same, however, might be said for other self-identification claims which are increasingly familiar in an age now negotiating a new generation of rights and freedoms, all of which bring renewed levels of controversy and complexity. Nonetheless these rights help us all, as individuals and as a society, to forge progressively and speculatively ahead, as we feel increasingly free to shape identities for ourselves rather than selecting them as 'ready to wear' or having them imposed upon us.

We have already alluded to postmodernism as a source and context for Durham's emergence as an artist, and it may just be that some of postmodernism's most disruptive ideas, including a heightened sense of cultural relativism and a derailment of a modern, linear image of history, are colliding uncomfortably today, either with a new and different generation of related ideas, or with the fullest legacies of postmodernism's own most profound implications.

As many current critical historians – including Ariella Azoulay – point out, when we get to grips with 21st century perspectives on representation, identity, racism, and inequality, we soon realise that the problems we find there have centuries-old roots, dating back to the origins of Empire and the European project of global expansion, expropriation and colonisation: the modernism, capitalism and Empire with which we do daily battle today (in the world, and in our own minds) all seem to be rooted there.

Hence, Durham's simple-seeming assemblages and references to museology (works that might have been influenced by artists like Joseph Cornel or Marcel Broodthaers) are capable of distributing a potent message while always subtly using humour as a way of maintaining strength, of finding a way to avoid falling into rage and frustration in response to the most terrible and insulting legacies of history, progress, and modernism.[4]

Nevertheless, today these works by Durham have proven capable of enraging some of the very people with whom they were intended to show solidarity, and for whom they strived to release alternative forms of identification. The solution to this is not, I suspect, the destruction of the allegedly 'guilty' artist and their work, but an acceptance of the contemporary artist's position as even more peculiar and particular than we might have expected.

That peculiarity involves positioning as a cultural commentator free to address cultures to which the artist may or may not officially belong, while yet resigned to the fact that the culture to which they do, ultimately or most convincingly seem to belong, and from which the artist speaks, is the culture of contemporary art, into whose 'tribe' they have been inexorably and undeniably inducted by a lifetime (in Durham's case, as the recipient of a prestigious lifetime achievement award) embroiled in contemporary art's own rituals, rites, icons, tales, language, dress, and other codes.

All of this qualifies the artist and awards them the power to cultivate and create much lauded 'debate', which is one of the highest and most often proclaimed values to which contemporary art and artists of Durham's generation have come to aspire. Here, the debate raised might attend, among other things, to the profound issue of 'belonging' *per se*, rather than a vindictive argument over claiming to belong to this or to that tribe or culture.

Postmodernism's enhanced relativism has encouraged a greater pluralisation and admixture of references, as well as a greater blurring of distinctions between cultures, including that supposed between 'high' and 'low' (popular) culture. As a result of this enhanced and expanded relativism and pluralisation the style and method of my own research tends to take lessons from the artist's studio as much as from the library (actual or virtual). Thus, while researching Durham for my *Uses of History in Contemporary Art* seminar I serendipitously came across a useful connection in an unexpected place.

While re-reading J.D. Salinger's classic novella *The Catcher in the Rye* I found a passage that seemed to quite precisely illustrate what I interpret as Durham's fundamental intentions.[5] In Salinger's classic novella, the anti-heroic protagonist tries to meet up with his younger sister and is told she might be at the museum. 'Which museum?' he asks, 'the one where the pictures are or the one where the Indians are'. This then leads into an evocative paragraph (a small section of which follows here) recalling visits to the museum as a schoolchild when the class were introduced to Native American or First Nations culture by way of a series of inanimate displays – and their *in*animation is something the writer stresses as an aspect of misrepresentation.

> Then you'd pass by this long, long Indian war canoe, about as long as three goddam Cadillacs in a row, with about twenty Indians in it, some of them paddling, some of them just standing around looking tough, and they all had war paint all over their faces. There was one very spooky guy in the back of the canoe, with a mask on. He was the witch doctor. He gave me the creeps, but I liked him anyway. Another thing, if you touched one of the paddles or anything while you were passing, one of the guards would say to you, "Don't touch anything, children," but he always said it in a nice voice, not like a goddam cop or anything. Then you'd pass by this big glass case, with Indians inside it rubbing sticks together to make a fire, and a squaw weaving a blanket. The squaw that was weaving the blanket was sort of bending over, and you could see her bosom and all. We all used to sneak a good look at it, even the girls, because they were only little kids and they didn't have any more bosom than we did. Then, just before you went inside the auditorium, right near the doors, you passed this Eskimo. He was sitting over a hole in this icy lake, and he was fishing through it. He had about two fish right next to the hole, that he'd already caught. Boy, that museum was full of glass cases[6].

These contrived tableaux – he recalls – showed indigenous peoples frozen forever by their representation within the museological and pedagogical apparatus, as things, as fixed, dead, taxonomised and more or less taxidermised, and thus safely othered, reduced to a manageable image, historicised as past, over and gone.

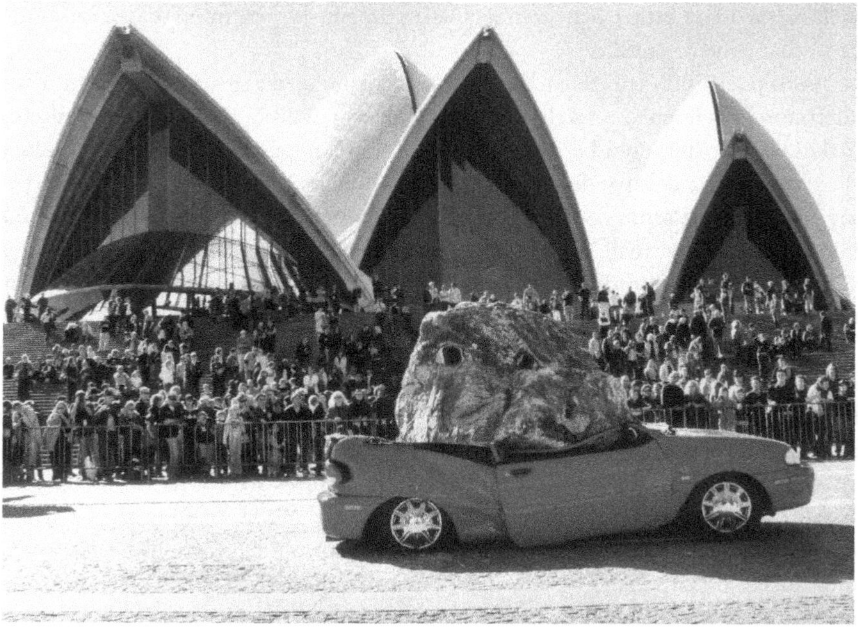

FIGURE 3.2 Jimmie Durham, *Still Life with Stone and Car*, 2004. Car, rock, paint. Installation view, Sydney Opera House, from the 2004 Biennale of Sydney. Photographed by Jenni Carter.

The protagonist's memories are rattled off by Salinger in the casual style adopted by the novelist to suit his adolescent narrator's roguish youthful manner, but this offhand manner – a little like Durham's approach to manufacturing artefacts – only adds poignancy and gravitas to the terrible implications of the museum displays (ultimately the physical and cultural genocide of a people), as well as the way in which, year after year, children of a most impressionable and formative age were, and perhaps still are, indoctrinated into or perhaps now inoculated against a certain pedagogical dogma that can still frame and infuse museum visits.

Probing Durham's work further, I came across repeated images of cars in a variety of settings, assaulted and pinned down by the impact of large rocks. I traced these to a centrepiece work, *Still Life with Car and Rock,* used by Durham to open the 2004 Sydney Biennale. Images of this event show the artist conducting affairs with the Sydney Opera House as a backdrop and a large crowd in attendance. The centre of attention is a bright red, typically suburban hatchback car. Overhead a crane suspends a large rock, and on the rock we see a simply painted face. The expectation might be that the rock will be suddenly released and will crush the car in a shocking instant, typical, we might say, of modernism's propensity for spectacular shocks. However, given that today we can only see the final outcome of the artist's act, in the form of a crushed car with huge stone on top, we might also be left to speculate (unless of course we were witnesses to the event) whether, perhaps, on this occasion the artist might have in fact teased his audience by lowering the rock repeatedly onto the car, perhaps more slowly than expected. In this way (with a sense of inexorable slowness) the work might be seen to also evoke a more ancient force of geological erosion and change, in accordance with ahistorical, in-human, geological or glacial time, as opposed to a more human and modern sense of time and change.

The slow, inexorable time thus communicated by a gradually crushing rock would also perhaps have been more akin to aboriginal Australian belief in the paradigm of *The Dreaming* than to the pressurised, utilised, and minutely quantified time of modernism's own paradigm. The rock that crushes the car, and thus appears to prove the stronger (despite being, technologically more rudimentary), has a simple face painted on to it, perhaps designed to direct us to think of it in an animistic way, i.e., awarding spirit and consciousness to this apparently dumb thing.

Incidentally, any such implied animism could also invoke the way in which modern, suburban car owners might consciously or unconsciously invest a certain 'spirit' into, or award a degree of identity and personality to, their cars – taking pride in their marques, logos, and brands. This might include the fetishisation of a particular bonnet emblem, the way an owner might award a pet name to their vehicle, or perceive a friendly face in the design of the headlights/radiator grill configuration.

Durham's piece thus brings contemporary art audiences into dialogue with pre-historic, geological, trans-human time – including the timeless time of *The Dreaming*. Simultaneously, with his use of a typically contemporary object (a red hatchback car), Durham brings ancient ideas, and ideas of the ancient into proximity with the present, the now, and our everyday sense of time. The result is that Durham might ultimately show us that these apparently very different images of temporality are not in crude opposition but more porous, continuous and reciprocal.

Furthermore, and finally, in engaging with and invoking such ideas of temporality – whether implicitly referring to *The Dreaming* or making a spoof museum – we could say that Durham uses contemporary art, not to reveal the contemporary, nor even to explore history, but rather to remind the contemporary and history of an *a*historical and pre-historical realm that haunts and informs them both.

Notes

1 Jimmie Durham sadly passed away during the completion of this book.
2 See www.sprovieri.com/artists/jimmie-durham.
3 Azoulay, A.A. (2019).
4 Benjamin, W. (1968) p. 102.
5 I can't recall why, but probably due to my interest in adolescent experience and formative moments in memoirs.

Salinger, J.D. (1975) pp. 124–128.

N.B. such a fortuitous and valuable event in the process of 'research' is a reminder always to keep an open mind about how, when, and where, as artists and as creative researchers, we might find and make connections and referents. Unexpected or apparently

incongruous connections can in fact be the most interesting, innovative and valuable of all. Indeed, insisting upon building a 'bridge' that connects two apparently distant or incongruous referents can often prove to be the most creative and rewarding use of our thought.
6 Salinger, J.D. (1975) pp. 124–128.

Bibliography

Azoulay, A.A. (2019) *Potential History – Unlearning Imperialism*. London: Verso.
Benjamin, W. (1968) *Illuminations*. New York: Schocken Books.
Salinger, J.D. (1975) *The Catcher in the Rye*. London: Penguin.

4

PROGRESSIVE TRADITION

Ariella Azoulay and Chloé Zhao (postmodernisms and *Earthrise*)

In the movie *Songs My Brothers Taught Me* (2015), directed by Chloé Zhao, we see the abject injustices suffered by descendants of once abundant Native American Indian or First Nation peoples.[1] And yet hope is sparingly sewn through the fabric of the film, most notably in the words of an artistic member of the community who makes clothes and blankets, including ceremonial dress.

He is helped in his work by the youngest character in the film and tells her that it has been predicted that her generation will mark a new and auspicious beginning for their people. The young girl is seen participating in traditional ritual dances and celebrations.

Given the extreme bleakness of much of the rest of the movie, where alcohol eats out the hearts, minds, and frail economies of the residents of an abject and impoverished reservation, this hope, inextricably derived from and reliant upon tradition, is all the more significant.

Writing here, in and for a modern world and a modern audience, we might tend to think of tradition as anathema to modernism as a cultural paradigm. And we might tend to think that being modern depends upon a shedding or eschewing of tradition.

Pre-, un-, or less-modern people might live or have lived in the same way and in the same places as their parents, grandparents, great-great grandparents, and older ancestors, with traditions handed down from generation to generation. We tend to think of modern people as more dynamic, subject to intergenerational change and conflict, typically leaving their hometown or village as soon as they are able, to seek a new, more modern life, often in a bigger town or city, then living at many addresses as a ramification of social and market forces.

The modern function of the museum serves to preserve aspects of tradition that have been surpassed or abandoned by modernism. As such, tradition becomes

DOI: 10.4324/9781003230632-6

a passive, taxonomised, museological object of interest to a modern audience, yet de-fanged and rinsed of its previous relevance and living agency.

However, modernism has its own problems in keeping pace with technological, cultural, and social change; hence, we all know the term 'postmodern'. Though less fashionable today than it was in the 1980s, when it emerged as a shocking alternative cultural paradigm and perspective, postmodernism remains a disruptive, anti-foundational concept as long as modernism is regarded as, in some way, foundational to our cultural identity. Today, as a new generation takes on the kind of project espoused by Azoulay in challenging the legacy of empire as a product or sibling of modernism, we might want to claim that they are 'finishing the job' started by the 1980s postmodernists.

If we look around us today in search of current dialogues between modernism and tradition, we might note that, in so-called 'leading nations', economic shifts currently mean that more young people are forced to carry on living with their parents for longer than a previous (more modern) generation might have done. This is one small but significant example of the ways in which modernism no longer appears to progress, proudly oblivious to and disrespectful of tradition.

In Ariella Azoulay's book *Potential History, Unlearning Imperialism*, we find the author promoting a radical, confrontational, highly active use and interpretation of tradition.[2] For Azoulay's thesis, modernism always represents empire, or those European empires and their legacies which today take the form of the 'leading nations' or most powerful modern states, all of which began to emerge in the 15th century while 'discovering' the 'new worlds' of the Americas, Australia, etc.

What Azoulay collectively refers to as 'empire', with all its colonising, trading and enslaving, brought European perspectives, languages, religions, diseases, and economics to all-but annihilate numerous ancient and indigenous tribes, peoples, civilisations, cultures, and traditions. As such, Azoulay regards attention to tradition as inevitably disruptive to a genocidal and oppressive interpretation of modernism that we can see emerging not just in 19th century Paris (the putative birthplace of modern art and culture) but all the way back in 15th century 'empire'.[3]

Another way of reconsidering the relationship between modernity and tradition might be to note that postmodernism critiques anti-traditional modernism as having become a tradition of its own. For a certain period of time modernism eschews tradition as anathema to its anti-traditional purposes, and yet a time comes when modernism unexpectedly encounters or produces forces of change greater than itself ('changes to change' we might say, in a postmodern way), and a new that is so unexpectedly new because it no longer prioritises … the new.

Modernism exceeded itself – frothed-up and spilled over the bounds of the container it had created for itself. This event ushers in a time and history in which modernism is no longer contra to, or dominant over tradition, but reduced to just one of several, equal and different traditions, isms, narratives, or cultural paradigms. Hence, and forthwith, we can speak of the modern, postmodern, re-postmodern, pre-modern, altermodern, neo-modern, etc., while wandering among, and wondering where we might belong within these various scenarios.

What brings about this 'change to change' and 'new new' is variously theorised. See, for example, Nicolas Bourriaud's 'Altermodern' essay for his Tate Triennale exhibition in 2009 in which economic and technological factors, for Bourriaud, play a significant part.[4] Modernism as a cultural paradigm may accelerate, to the degree that it exceeds or overtakes itself. It may be that a newly global perspective, inducing a new level of relativism between all perspectives (post-perspectivalism), all paradigms, all isms, emerges from a world that newly connects more numerous points of view.

In the post-World War II era, television and other forms of mass telecommunications, along with worldwide Americanisation, consumerism, mass tourism, leisure, and aviation, all contribute to this. However, it is also tempting to attribute this change of consciousness to a single photograph, an image that is, upon its appearance, seemingly 'above all' images. Seen by billions around the world, each of whom is thereby, in a way, looking at themselves looking at themselves (sic), it is the first image of the earth photographed from beyond its own moon.

Earthrise, an image made in December 1968 during the Apollo 8 mission, stands in for a world that was, at that time, soon to become surveilled constantly by hosts of satellite-born cameras.[5] Perhaps this single image was sufficient

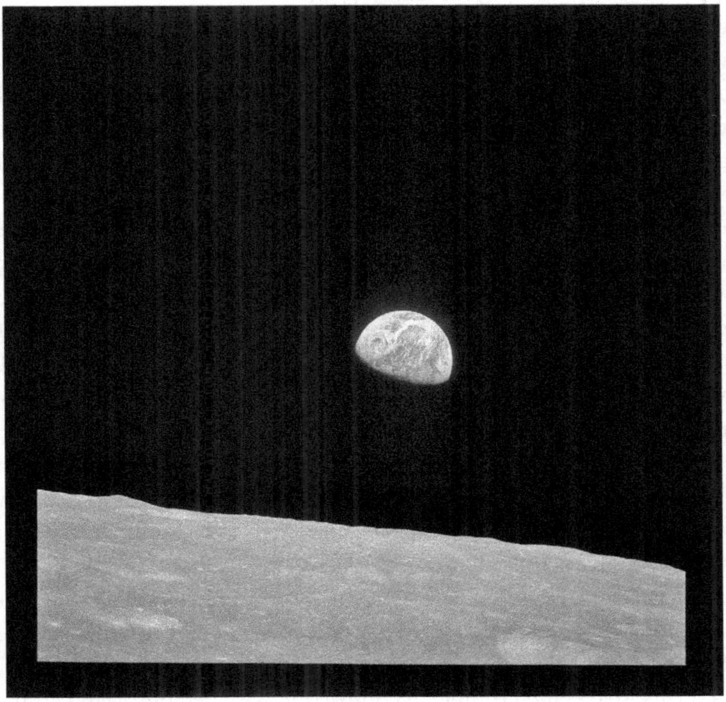

FIGURE 4.1 *Earthrise* second of three photographs taken by Bill Anders at the start of his fourth orbit around the Moon in December 1968. The Apollo 8 images are in the public domain. Courtesy of NASA/WMAP Science Team.

to induce a Copernican revolution, a new sense of global awareness, shifting any remaining and pervading sense of a particular geographical perspective (e.g. a Eurocentric, anthropocentric, or terra-centric point of view). This image might have been enough to challenge or displace a habitually extensive view of the world as a singular, spatial object, a place or a thing to be owned, claimed, discovered, known, and recorded, as opposed to the world as an event, a ball of intensities or behaviours, a 'Body Without Organs' of the kind invoked by Gilles Deleuze and Felix Guattari.

Despite the 'fact' that we have 'known' for hundreds of years that our planet is a spinning, orbiting sphere, *seeing* this image, it seems, is *believing* that same fact, and thus belief might sometimes trump knowledge. The indexical evidence of a photographic image, showing the earth back to itself as a detached, mobile, spherical object in space, one object among similar billions and now seen from beyond another object (the moon), might just have relativised all positionality and perspectivalism on the earth, with profound effects upon the narrative of modern progress that made the photograph possible.

'Seeing is believing' goes the maxim, and while believing may not itself be material, and may not always be rational, it carries great weight. And so, once our beliefs are changed by what we newly or differently see, we must think again, and start over, with a new or different cultural paradigm.

The new relativism possibly induced by our self-imposed encounter with this emphatically 'global' image, *Earthrise*, means that a Eurocentric modernism or any 'modern-centricism' can henceforth be regarded as just one more narrative, leading only to the kinds of ends to which narratives can lead. Modernism as a cultural paradigm, and narrative, led us for sure, but only to the limits of itself, thus leaving all that is other (alter) to modernism to be also and subsequently pursued.

Modernism thus leads beyond its own capacity and beyond its intended purpose, a purpose that, on reflection, started from an earthbound perspective and thus always had something to do with extensity, travel, trade, exploitation, control, and territorialisation, i.e., inseparable from a colonial and Enlightenment model of expansion that aspires to totality; total knowledge of a total object – the world; total ownership of the contents of the world, as in the modern museum, encyclopaedia, or empire. But once the world is seen from elsewhere, and thus believed (rather than merely known) to be something not total and extensive but intensive and eventual, the modern narrative no longer fits, it is over, and leaves us either without a narrative or in need of a post-, re-post-, non-, neo-, or altermodern narrative, or some otherwise, successfully nominated and accepted cultural paradigm.

So, modernism as a cultural paradigm turns out to be just one more myth, one more story, one more tradition. With a newly tangible and irrefutable sense of a scientifically expanded space, modern perceptions and constructions of time and progress shrink, shake, and crumble in comparison with geological and cosmic time. *Earthrise* marks a Copernican revolution and initiates a paradigm shift in which modernism (as a cultural paradigm) and tradition enter a new and different, no longer conflictual, though possibly parallel, relationship.

Today, when an artist like Jimmy Durham (perhaps dubiously or, as some suggest, insensitively) evokes native American-Indian traditions or ancestry using spoof museological strategies and apparatuses, we can see how potent and disruptive this evocation of tradition can be to the modern institution of the museum. Even the relatively light-touch literary approach of J.D. Salinger in his novella *The Catcher in the Rye*, when describing juvenile indoctrination by means of the museum, leads us on to the image of the protagonist as a modern, disaffected, anti-heroic teenager now able to see through the museum's crude reconstructions, of others' traditions, and of tradition as other – now able to see instead the museum itself.[6]

Salinger's protagonist's critical descriptions reveal that he sees museums (or 'the museum') as a modern tradition, thus lacking any privileged perspective or authority, any legitimacy or superiority over and above that which it professes to represent objectively, in the form of artefacts, dioramas, and accompanying pedagogical texts.

Similarly, the artist Folkert de Jong (see chapter 2 in this book) uses his barbaric representations of 17th century Dutch settlers to lead us to a small monument on the Southern tip of the island of Manhattan, marking the moment when the island itself was effectively expropriated or exchanged in return for fripperies. That monument marks a historical occasion on which modernity usurped and abused indigenous traditions, and yet de Jong invites his audience to revive and re-stimulate that abused tradition, to evaluate its own relative integrity and potential for endurance in comparison with a modernity now forced to reconsider and re-evaluate itself, no longer as a triumphant, profiteering victor over tradition, but as a shameful usurper of others' traditions.

Meanwhile, Azoulay's thesis compels us to look for (affirmed) tradition within ourselves; to look beyond and beneath our own modernisms and modernities – perhaps starting (she implies) with our own families, our own names, the places where we were born, in order to thereby access and utilise the potency and protection of our own traditions, to connect with ourselves *as* traditional and as thus rescued from and other to the harsh, dehumanising, and disempowering demands of modernism as a cultural paradigm.

Azoulay therefore refers convincingly to the ways in which modern families are divided and disempowered by the impact of empire as modernity. In the quote that follows, she describes a way in which modern children become ashamed of their parents, and modern parents become ashamed of their children.

> The pattern of destruction is quite the same everywhere. '"Nature," not human agency, was posited as the mediating force for vanquishing […] cultures.' Blanca Tovias writes in relation to the annihilation of the Blackfoot culture in Canada in the late 19th century. That children are ashamed of their parents is human nature not imperial interest, we are told, and each generation has its own right to revolt against its parents. Again, not against imperial violence but against its parents. 'My brother is ashamed of his father,' writes Bouteldja, and adds, to make clear how intrusive the imperial enterprise is,

> '... my father is ashamed of his son ...' There is nothing 'traditional' about tradition: it is not an adjective or adverb that can be appended to people or objects. Tradition is a worldly formation that resists imperialism's offer of emancipation through our withdrawal from this world. Tradition is the most persistent struggle against imperialism, sustained through intergenerational transmission and preservation of some worldly knowledge of being in the world.[7]

Azoulay suggests that by looking for and relocating tradition within ourselves we might contribute to an eschewing of (otherwise hard-wired) empire and modernism as a cultural paradigm. Refusal of these overarching powers might enable us to reconnect with a tradition that is finally freed of the museum's vitrines and pedagogical captions; freed of the entire modern, historical, and historicising apparatus that uses the idea of modernity and modernism, and their attendant history, to effectively segregate, suffocate, and taxidermise potent and powerful traditions – traditions that are otherwise alive, well, and dynamic in their own living, breathing way.

Notes

1 Zhao, C. (dir.) (2015). www.imdb.com/title/tt3566788/.
2 Azoulay, A.A. (2019).
3 Azoulay repeatedly takes the year 1492 as crucial in marking this cultural transformation. Azoulay, A.A. (2019).
4 Bourriaud, N. (2009) pp. 11–24.
5 See www.nasa.gov/multimedia/imagegallery/image_feature_1249.html.
6 Salinger, J.D. (1975) pp. 124–128.
7 Azoulay, A.A. (2019) pp. 320–321.

Bibliography

Azoulay, A.A. (2019) *Potential History – Unlearning Imperialism*. London: Verso.
Bourriaud, N. (2009) *Altermodern – The Third Tate Triennial*. London: Tate.
Salinger, J.D. (1975) *The Catcher in the Rye*. London: Penguin.
Zhao, C. (dir.) (2015) *Songs My Brothers Taught Me*. Significant Productions.

5

SIGRID HOLMWOOD

History performed as a radical gesture

Attending the Artists Studio Company (ASC) gallery and residency space in South London, 2014, I was told that the next show to be held there would be by the artist Sigrid Holmwood.[1] I recalled having been struck by her vivid paintings at a recent themed group show at Saatchi's Gallery, however, at that time I knew little more about her and her process. On further enquiry at ASC I was informed that the artist was preparing for her show by planting certain flowers, herbs, or vegetables in some earth in the yard adjoining the residency space. I subsequently learned that the artist would use these plants, when they had grown, to assist in making her own paint colours.[2]

Calling up some images of the artist revealed her wearing apparently medieval costume and sometimes behaving in videos a little like a medieval mythological witch figure. Not only did she make her own clothes and pigments (according to medieval traditions) but also her own paintbrushes, which sometimes approximated the size of a broomstick – a comparison inferred by some of her poses sat astride the brush.

Holmwood seemed to bait and satirise a misogynist, medieval, and still structurally prevalent fear of women's patriarchally repressed power. Not only has she posed as a witch-like figure travelling on a flying paintbrush but also sometimes wears a phallic nose extension. Applied to a woman's face this device supplants, with the image of the flaccid phallus, any patriarchally dominant foregrounding of the female face as a site of beauty. However, what makes all of this – including Holmwood's paintings – most powerful, most unique, and most discomforting is Holmwood's strange relationship to the past, to history and to tradition.

Why, we might ask, would a 21st-century painter, showing in state-of-the-art contemporary spaces, invoke the past so avidly? Looking at Holmwood's paintings from that period, a strange mix was discernible wherein unusually bright colours, which might be readily associated with the vibrant palette of the modern,

DOI: 10.4324/9781003230632-7

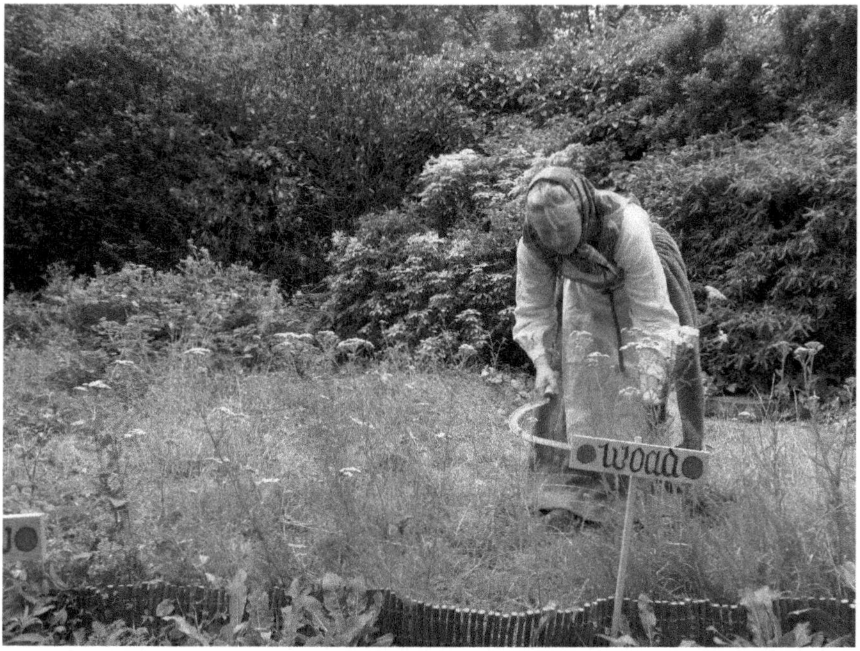

FIGURE 5.1 Sigrid Holmwood, *Peasant Portrait* (the artist at work in costume). Photographed by Gonzaga Gómez-Cortázar Romero.

consumerist, and highly techonologised world, are used to depict rural, ancient, perhaps 'timeless' ways of country life. Many of the paintings also refer to farming and farm animals.

So how do these works constitute and position themselves within contemporary art? The answer perhaps lies in Holmwood's strange juxtaposition of contemporaneity and history, a clash that asks us to question or explain any lazily or habitually assumed binary difference between the two. Is there a clear divide between history and the contemporary? Presumably there is no tangible or actual split, and yet, in many habitual ways we create one, if only perhaps to orientate ourselves, to take pride in our modernity or emote over the lost past.

Holmwood might take a lesson from Walter Benjamin who, writing on fairy tales, suggested that modern people, despite their apparently mature modernity, can continue to learn lessons from such stories, e.g. by adopting and maintaining 'cunning and high spirits' when negotiating with the difficult and dark forces in our lives and in our society.[3] Similarly, Holmwood appears to be tackling serious subjects (the long, deep-rooted history of misogyny, and our anxious relationship with the pre-modern and rural past) wrapped in the striking, amusing, and disturbing image of a woman dressed and behaving anachronistically, going against the contemporary grain, turning back the clock, and making successful contemporary art with a mix of modern and medieval means.[4] And all this is done with a mix of playfulness and

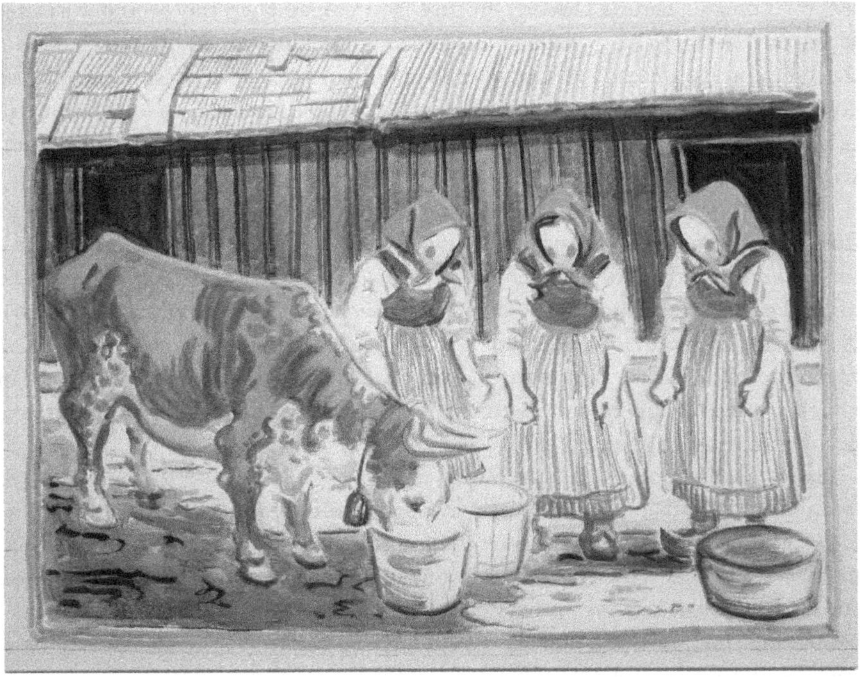

FIGURE 5.2 Sigrid Holmwood, *Three Women and a Cow (Tre Kvinnor Med Kossa)*, 2013. Mushroom pigment made from blood red webcaps (cortinarius sanguineus), chalk, chrome yellow, indigo, and red lead bound in egg on hand-woven linen, 106 cm × 137 cm.

implicit strategy that fits Benjamin's criteria of 'cunning and high spirits' and might place the artist, or us, in a position of confidence and power.

Holmwood and her work could also remind us of the way in which modernity has increasingly emphasised urban and modern, or suburban and postmodern culture, leaving rural culture to be relatively abandoned as something inextricably associated with, or condemned to the past.[5] And this even though the factory-farmed rural landscape, producing chemically treated, genetically modified crops, might be just as 'modern' as the sky-scraping heart of a major city or the carports and lawns of suburbia.

Technologised farming has in fact rendered the countryside a modern environment, leaving areas of wild nature to be – we might say 'unnaturally' – preserved, like something fetishised, commodified, kept in a museum, or even 'rewilded' (a slightly oxymoronic buzzword that insists on the necessity to contrive and cultivate 'wildness' by means of human techniques, and perhaps ultimately for human purposes and perspectives).[6]

In the final pages of Kazuo Ishiguro's emotive novel *Never Let Me Go* (which explores the degree to which 'genetically modified', cloned human beings might still be 'human', 'natural', loving, creative, and empathetic), the central character looks out over flat East Anglian fields, through wire fences on which gather the consumerist detritus of discarded bags and wrappers.[7] The scene might be considered a postmodern parody of Romantic aesthetics wherein a lone figure can often be found gazing thoughtful or inspired into the magnificence of a natural wilderness.

The history of 19th-century Paris, and the birth of modern art (derived in part from the decline of Romanticism), visually and repeatedly maps the story of a modern break and divide between the rural and the urban, as well as the emergence of the liminal suburban realm – sometimes associated with American postmodern culture but originally documented by the French Impressionists. Nevertheless, as late as the 1920s Walter Benjamin, on a visit to Moscow, was still noting the way in which, even the heart of a modern, revolutionary city could suddenly and unexpectedly give on to relatively rural scenes.[8]

Sigrid Holmwood might suggest, by and through her work, that any clear or clean distinction that we habitually make between the rural and the modern, history and the contemporary is always itself unnatural, artificial, and probably related to the increasingly efficient and convenient industrialisation, supermarketisation and distribution of our over-processed, over-packaged animal and plant-based diets. Meanwhile, her practice could also remind us that the average contemporary artist complies relatively thoughtlessly with certain modern presumptions, when, e.g., dressing to work at the studio, or obtaining art materials from a store, rather than carefully, idiosyncratically, and anachronistically (but ultimately more ethically and sustainably) making their own costume, materials, and equipment.

Holmwood's work could be mistakenly read as an extreme example of a certain retro-lust pervading the culture of her generation, according to which contemporary artists might purposefully delimit their processes, sometimes using anachronistic technologies, to divert themselves and their works from the all-too pervasive and generic influence of the commonly shared hyper-modern digital technology.[9] Hence, many an artist might today insist upon using apparently outmoded or outdated processes and equipment – old cameras, film processing, etc. (Tacita Dean, seen in Chapter 6 of this book, is a key example).[10]

In wider popular culture, retro styling has strongly influenced design during the same digitally dominant period, in such a way that, e.g., visiting a trendy urban cafe in 2021 might feel like a trip to an uncertain image of an unreliable past. Meanwhile, vinyl record sales, small organic food suppliers, and microbreweries all boom, and TV series like Charlie Brooker's *Black Mirror* have sometimes balanced digital device-dominated lifestyles with the appearance of vintage cars, as if by way of historical compensation for a too-modern present.[11]

But Holmwood's work does not fit this 'retro' model, she seems unique in her uncompromising approach, throwing herself, her body, her performance, her identity, her costume, and her entire creative process into a direct dialogue with the past in the form of a high-stakes experiment or gamble, as if to test the surrounding context and see what this radical anachronism might produce or provoke.

When Charles Baudelaire made his influential call, in his 1846 salon essay, for artists to paint and write about modern life, modern fashions, and modern manners, he simultaneously troubled and primed his own present, enabling those best suited to represent it to see it anew.[12] To see the present as if for the first time ('we have only to open our eyes' he writes) is also to see it as historical, in that the present is always continuous with and contingent upon the past. The modern artist's responsibility would henceforth be (according to Baudelaire, and later Benjamin too) to capture the present as historic, in a fleeting moment, out of, or from a state of flux and change.[13]

If, in the 21st century, we were to encounter Holmwood in costume, away from the studio or gallery, on a high street perhaps, we might assume that she is performing in some way, raising money for a charitable event, perhaps on her way to or from a re-enactment society, or carnival. Simply being out of time and standing out in this way has the power to draw attention, not only to the artist and the previously un-noted presence of the past (which is in fact always all around us) but also to the special uniformity and norms, the costumes (everyday dress) and gestures of the present. Holmwood's strategy has the power therefore to draw attention to all that we accept un-historically and un-thinkingly *as* the present, the modern, the contemporary, and we might say 'the normal' – which is what a progressive society should always strive to perceive, acknowledge, challenge, and, if possible, move beyond.

Sigrid Holmwood, whether in the art world or out in the wider world – and not just with her costumes and props, but with her strangely gaudily painted rural scenes – brings attention to the historical nature of the present by means of contrast, by making herself an exception, a living, active piece of history, in a present that all-too-often finds it difficult to see, understand, or evaluate itself.

Notes

1 See https://ascstudios.co.uk/event/asc-gallery-sigrid-holmwood-a-peasant-painters-garden/.
2 See www.sigridholmwood.co.uk/.
3 Benjamin, W. (1968) p. 102.
4 See also sections on Hew Locke in the *Dark Horses and Hollow Men: Hew Locke and the Monument – Part 2* (Chapter 20 of this book), while for notions of dress, artist John Akomfrah's interest in costume dramas is also relevant here (see Chapter 10 of this book).
5 See Chapter 20 of this book, (*Dark Horses and Hollow Men: Hew Locke and the Monument – Part 2*), re the urban/suburban divide and its relationship with present and past.
6 Note Alfred Hitchcock's famous scene in the movie *North by North West* (1959), in which a crop-spraying aircraft buzzes a Cary Grant made vulnerable by the absence of any form of natural shelter.
7 Ishiguro, K. (2005) pp. 281–282.
8 Benjamin, W. (2000) pp. 202–204.
9 To borrow the title of a Tate Britain exhibition curated and written about by Brian Dillon, and the book of the same name, see www.tate.org.uk/whats-on/tate-britain/exhibition/ruin-lust. Dillon, B. (2014).

10 See www.frithstreetgallery.com/artists/tacita-dean.
11 *Black Mirror*, TV show written by Charlie Brooker, produced by Annabel Jones for Zeppotron (2011–2013) and House of Tomorrow (2014–2019) and distributed by Endemol Shine UK.
12 Baudelaire, C. (1992) pp. 47–107.
13 Baudelaire, C. (1992).

Bibliography

Baudelaire, C. (1992) *Selected Writings on Art & Literature*. London: Penguin.
Benjamin, W. (1968) *Illuminations*. New York: Schocken Books.
Benjamin, W. (2000) *One Way Street*. London: Verso.
Dillon, B. (2014) *Ruin Lust: Artists' Fascination with Ruins, from Turner to the Present Day*. London: Tate Publishing.
Ishiguro, K. (2005) *Never Let Me Go*. London: Faber and Faber.

6

TACITA DEAN

Seeing and believing (altermodern and veracity)

Tacita Dean first came to my attention at some time in the late 1990s.[1] She showed film works that appealed to something 'historical' then awakening inside me. She seemed to find a lot of support and encouragement for what she was doing, as if touching a latent historical nerve in the contemporary art world, one that wasn't being addressed by the media savvy Young British Artists (YBAs) whose work seemed all about inventing a 'NOW' that competed for sensational headlines.

The enigmatic and mercurial historian and creative writer W.G. Sebald was being lauded at that time in and around academia and the arts intelligentsia. For me, reading Sebald had been something of a mind-changing experience. Dean was an artist who seemed to appreciate his work and who allowed his special approach to history influence her enigmatic image making and elusive narratives.

In 2009, when Nicolas Bourriaud was given the opportunity to curate the London Triennale at Tate Britain, he chose the uses of history in contemporary art as one of his themes and collected a number of artists whom he felt shared this interest – Dean was among them.[2] The inclusion of 'historical' works seems to have led Bourriaud into a reappraisal of the postmodernism that had hitherto framed the arts, not just as a style but as a cultural paradigm with potentially earth-shaking implications. It was in Bourriaud's introductory essay for the Triennale that he introduced and unpacked his term 'altermodern' which, despite not being as influential as Bourriaud might have hoped, still seems useful to maintain, consider, revise, or revisit.

Bourriaud opposed altermodern to postmodern, claiming postmodernism was not only unfashionable but also thoroughly dead and redundant. Altermodern, he suggested, could be a more viable and representative paradigm. One of the best-known attributes of postmodernism was its disconnection from linear, progressive, and teleological history, leaving postmodern society to occupy a directionless and meaningless (in the most liberating and positive sense) loop.

DOI: 10.4324/9781003230632-8

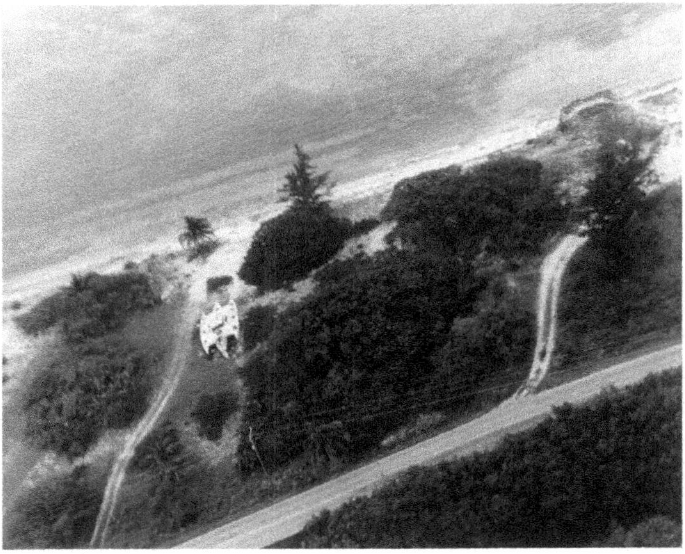

FIGURE 6.1 Tacita Dean, *Aerial View of Teignmouth Electron, Cayman Brac 16th of September 1998.* Courtesy of the artist and TATE Images.

Bourriaud's altermodern however, saw this as overly negative and passive and sought to re-inject some sense of modern agency into worldwide (no longer Eurocentric, modern-centric, or indeed 'centric', but rather other – hence 'alter') culture, emphasising particularly those cultures that had barely benefited from modernism as a cultural paradigm despite being comprehensively exploited by it. Modernism, after all, might not be universally over and done but seen to be arriving at and departing from different nations and cultures at different speeds, different times, and in different ways. Thus, it would be unjust for the so-called 'leading nations' to announce the universal death of modernism at a time when poorer nations were only just starting to enjoy its benefits.

Thus, for Bourriaud, altermodernism meant a re-starting of then dormant history and a reawakening of a kind of modernism, albeit a history and modernism for and of others (alter), particularly others who had not yet enjoyed modernism's benefits. Modernism, to Bourriaud, was never a *fait accompli*, never a thing, but rather an event, something that different nations and cultures aspired to and came to in different ways and by different routes. Bourriaud's curation would therefore example how altermodernism might provide, promote, and share a new sense of a new, or rather 'other' modernism and a reawakening of history for alternative, other, different, and emerging peoples.

Altermodernism is thus an attractive and reasonably convincing thesis, even though it doesn't seem to have taken hold and become part of everyday discourse in the way that modernism and postmodernism clearly and comprehensively did.

Then again, it could be argued that we have evolved into a post-paradigmatic 'paradigm', a post-ismism (*sic*) in which we no longer seek, trust, or need a universal paradigm or ism to contain and guide us, but have rather come to enjoy, or learn to live with a volatile and formless cultural terrain within which various isms and paradigms temporarily flare up as events, present themselves, suggest a temporary solution, reveal a possibility or hypothesis, before fading back into a chaotic default, remaining available, as archived, if and when they might be needed. Altermodern might be considered to be just one of these isms.

One notable sentence or claim in Bourriaud's essay for the Triennale catalogue suggested that history should be seen and used quasi-geographically, not as a way of organising time but as itself a space or place that we enter, explore, leave, and return to. He went as far as to call history 'the last continent to be explored', a phrase that sounds promising, but also (though surely unintentionally), somewhat neo-colonial.[3]

Tacita Dean is one of the artists that Bourriaud chose to represent what he saw as a pervasive surge of reference to history in contemporary art. Dean's film works often have a haunting, historical quality, in that they are either explicitly aware of the aging technologies she uses to make them or have a slightly Romanticist approach to cultivating feeling in response to change, mystery, and loss.

The artist also drew my attention with a 1998 sound piece titled *Trying to Find the Spiral Jetty*.[4] Here Dean recorded herself and a colleague following directions to find and to see Robert Smithson's 1970 land artwork *Spiral Jetty*, then rumoured to have recently re-emerged from the surface of The Great Salt Lake in Utah for which it was created.[5] I still have a recording of Dean's *Trying to Find the Spiral Jetty* on an official cassette tape. I can't clearly recall how I came by it, but this work begins to open a few layers of history within this example of Dean's work.

First, there is the cassette tape itself, something of which millennial, 'digital native' students now tend to be enamoured, despite such cassettes seeming to belong firmly to the pre-digital era. Interestingly, Kazuo Ishiguro (see Chapter 15 of this book) used the device of a fetishised cassette tape in his eerie novel *Never Let Me Go*. There, adolescent organ-donor clones occupy a strangely melancholic mix of a parallel past and a parallel future, generally regarded by readers as chilling, and which we will hopefully never have to occupy ourselves.[6] Like Dean and Sebald, Ishiguro seems to enjoy producing indefinite timescapes in which to set unnerving narratives.

In addition to Dean's Smithson tape, we might consider the history of the Smithson piece itself, the Spiral Jetty, as it rises and fades into and out of visibility like some malleable monument or unreliable memory. In conversation with the artist, Dean pointed out that she had travelled to the site on several occasions and noted this work of land art becoming increasingly 'commodified' as it was made more convenient for greater numbers of visitors. The site is augmented now with a tarmacked parking area, 'helpful' notice boards and signposts, etc., all of which could be said to compromise its previous mystique, derived from relative inaccessibility.

We might also take the opportunity here to note the way in which Smithson, influenced by George Kubler, approached art in relation to an art history seen within geological time. Rather than the relatively short, Eurocentric and anthropocentric history we glean from most popular art histories and from the self-serving logic of modern art's own narrative, seeing and making art in relation to geological time invites us to consider and evaluate art in an *a*historical, transhistorical, and pre-historical context.[7]

This, in turn, might lead us to consider certain affinities between the artists we have mentioned here – Dean, Smithson, Sebald, and Ishiguro – and allow us to draw out a certain sublime pathos for and of which Dean has always seemed to have a special feel and sense. Many of her works have featured loss, obsolescence, and ways in which time creates emotional responses within us; responses that become our only means of representing something otherwise tantalising and ineffable.

One example is Dean's work on the wayward sailor Donald Crowhurst and his ill-fated journey on his yacht *Teignmouth Electron*.[8] A photographic work by Dean, named after Crowhurst's boat, depicts, in a single black and white image, the abandoned hull of the boat lying in the sandy yard of a Cayman Islands beach house. This relatively simple image provides a portal through which we are able to trace the strange and sad life of Crowhurst, a would-be round-the-world yachtsman, and one of several male figures on whom Dean's critical practice has focused. Crowhurst made false claims about his progress in the round-the-world race and eventually seems to have committed suicide at sea, presumably as a result of shame, guilt, and mental illness.

Perhaps what is most interesting for us here is that Dean's black and white image is undeniably historical. It contains a pathos and a narrative that is concealed but not difficult to unpack from within it. It draws us first up into the air of the modern aerial photograph, then down into the details of Crowhurst's sublime misadventure, folly, and tragedy. As such, we can use this image in the way that Walter Benjamin or W.G. Sebald might have advocated that we use any historical resource, i.e., as a springboard not only for 'accurate' historical research but also for wider and more imaginative ramifications sparked by the encounter with whatever image or artefact takes our interest. Thus, there might be more, and might always be more here for us to use, e.g., in the sense that Crowhurst and his story have a peculiar contribution to make to a history of veracity, and, we might say, to the veracity of history.

'Veracity', a memorable word used by Dean in our telephone interview, is not a word that I tend to use myself, and perhaps this is why I have retained it from among all the words we exchanged in our broader conversation. However, it seemed important to Dean and therefore became interesting to me, and so I want to explore it a little more here as a concept relevant to our wider project.

Crowhurst's tale revolves around the importance of truth-telling and the corrosive effects of not avoiding truth. Meanwhile, Dean seems interested in the relative 'veracity' of the analogue photographic and cinematic image as compared with the seeming non-existence of any such veracity for Dean in digital technology. The artist seems to see the digital realm as fundamentally mendacious and unreliable, in that it is not grounded in materiality and therefore actuality.

Considering this, Crowhurst, despite his own undeniable materiality and actuality, might then become a comparably unreliable male figure, equally ungrounded by a lack of veracity. He becomes, after all, swathed in lies and self-delusion. Yet we might, nevertheless feel some form of empathy with, and perhaps pity for him. His story is moving, sad, disturbing – an all-too human tale of aspiration and failure.

At certain times in our lives, we all learn the hard lesson of 'biting off more than we can chew' – as the English say. We all might occasionally feel embarrassment about failings that we clumsily try to hide only to make things worse. And we all might sometimes see our ambitions, aspirations, and self-image fall apart when confronted with the relative force of more powerful and resilient realities or personalities. Such empathic traces of pathos, and of a persona's self-recognition, can also be found in Dean's aforementioned work or works responding to Smithson's *Spiral Jetty*.[9] Smithson also died prematurely, and as a result, we might say, of unrestrained ambitions, while researching a site in a light aircraft (thus invoking for us an echo of the aerial view we see in Dean's *Teignmouth Electron* image).

'Seeing', goes the ancient proverb, 'is believing', and in Dean's *Trying to Find the Spiral Jetty* sound piece, a journey made as if to gain evidence of something real (the appearance and existence of the jetty) ends in yet another example of defeat, becoming another folly. Veracity, it seems, must sometimes lie beyond our reach, a more rare and elusive value than that which we might have hoped and believed it to be. At the same time, there is a possibility that believing in what we *cannot* see (as Jesus says to Thomas [John 20 29]) can be more powerful and profound than entrusting truth solely or primarily to vision.

History, sometimes, often, and perhaps always lies, yet it also relies, crucially, on some form of veracity. Without truth of some kind, a truth at least claimed, what we seek as, or want to be history, may be only a tale, a fable, story or 'chronicle' (a pre-modern form that interested Walter Benjamin). History differs from these other forms, institutions, and traditions in that it claims a veracity that sets it apart from fable, tale, story, and chronicle by its very claim to veracity. In doing so it also relies upon and has recourse to evidence.

History *is* evidence we might say, evidence of the past and of past events that have led us to where and what we now are. Benjamin, writing on photography as an emerging modern form of (or perhaps replacement for) art, commented that photography was more valuable and effective as 'historical evidence' than as 'art' in any previously established aesthetic terms. In this way, photography as evidence, and as historical evidence, is, for Benjamin, more relevant and valuable to a modern society that had left quasi-religious 'cult' values (Benjamin's term) behind and supplanted them with new political, cultural, and historical values.

The proverb 'seeing is believing' may then be relevant and justifiably invoked here, as Tacita Dean searches for Smithson's *Jetty*, which comes in and out of visibility, or as Crowhurst, invisible to other sailors and officials involved in a race, seeks

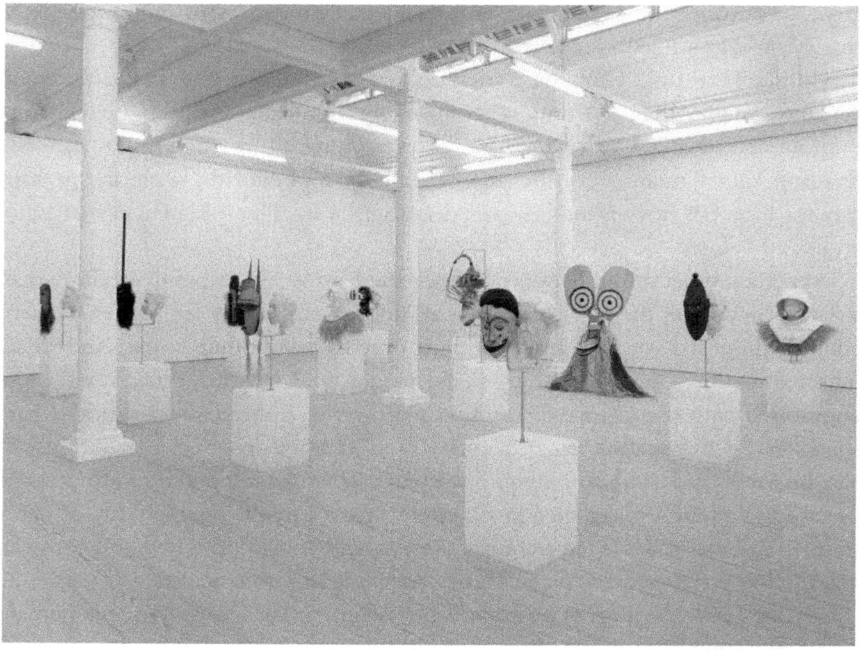

FIGURE 6.2 Tavares Strachan, installation view: *In Plain Sight*, 2020, Marian Goodman Gallery, London. Courtesy of the artist and Marian Goodman Gallery Copyright: Tavares Strachan. Photographed by Lewis Ronald.

to create a mythic map of his own success and progress by using falsified written and radio reports.

History –as a modern, Enlightenment project – is, or seeks at some fundamental level to be true, and in this way may have a different relationship with art than 'the contemporary' which, in turn, has no such need for, or aspiration to, historical veracity. Postmodernism, as a cultural paradigm that distances itself from history also distances itself from certain modern affiliations with truth. However, contemporary, and possibly 'altermodern', artists nevertheless continue to engage with history, perhaps motivated by a need to maintain some important or productive link between the contemporary, history and truth.

N.B. Contemporary artist Tavares Strachan, whose 2020 London exhibition was titled *In Plain Sight* also plays with ideas of visibility and historical truth, using masks to create a dialogue around numerous black historical figures who have been 'disappeared' from the historical record, their achievements effectively hidden.[10]

Notes

1 See www.frithstreetgallery.com/artists/tacita-dean.
2 See www.tate.org.uk/whats-on/tate-britain/exhibition/altermodern.

3 Bourriaud, N. (2009) pp. 11–24.
4 See www.frithstreetgallery.com/audiovisual/tacita-dean-trying-to-find-spiral-jetty-1998.
5 See www.frithstreetgallery.com/audiovisual/tacita-dean-trying-to-find-spiral-jetty-1998.
6 Ishiguro, K. (2005).
7 Kubler, G. (1962).
8 Dean's work on Crowhurst is represented here in book form, see www.frithstreetgallery.com/publications/tacita-dean-teignmouth-electron.
However, the work also resonates with, and is extended by, the artist's video work titled *JG*, see www.frithstreetgallery.com/exhibitions/tacita-dean which also implicates Smithson's *Spiral Jetty*.
9 'Works' – as footnote 8 above, Dean also made a related moving image work titled *JG* which draws yet another male protagonist, the writer JG Ballard, into the plot.
10 See www.mariangoodman.com/exhibitions/416-tavares-strachan-in-plain-sight/.

Bibliography

Barson, T., Campany, D. *et al* (2006) *Making History: Art and Documentary in Britain from 1929 to Now*. London: Tate

Bourriaud, N. (2009) *Altermodern – The Third Tate Triennial*. London: Tate.

Ishiguro, K. (2005) *Never Let Me Go*. London: Faber and Faber.

Kubler, G. (1962) *The Shape of Time – Remarks on the History of Time*. London: Yale University Press.

7

ROBERT SMITHSON AND GEORGE KUBLER

A bus ride in geological time

Robert Smithson's 1967 artwork *A Tour of the Monuments of Passaic, New Jersey* is ironic, or parodic in that it refers obliquely and slightly humorously to other kinds of tour, or guide, and to other kinds of monuments.[1] The most obvious historical reference is the 18th-century Enlightenment's Grand Tour phenomenon, according to which privileged Northern European ladies and gentlemen would complete their aesthetic and historical education by visiting Italy and the Mediterranean, there to take in, at first hand, notable sites – many recently excavated – of classical antiquity, as well as examples of the artistic achievements of the Italian Renaissance and anything else of art and cultural interest.

Much of today's expansive tourism industry remains influenced by, or is a legacy of, this model. Coaches, cruise liners, and airplanes (prior to the global Corona virus pandemic) carry streams of passengers and make brief stops designed for the taking of hurried photographs of world-famous objects and places. Smithson's text and photographs obliquely refer to such activities and do so in the name of contemporary art.

In his text, Smithson sets off on the bus for Passaic in a way reminiscent of the 'Country Life' episode documented in Chapter 1 of this book, and he is, similarly, accompanied by print media – in Smithson's case a newspaper and a paperback Sci-Fi novel. These are both objects of modern media that illustrate a fast-moving society digesting a rapid turnover of information. Newspapers exhale their sensational contents daily, almost immediately becoming real or virtual trash.

Paperback Sci-Fi novels may be inspired, well-wrought works of art, but can also quickly become pulp due to the ways in which publishers are forced by an aggressive marketplace to secure rapid returns on their initial investment and thus offload cumbersome and unprofitable remainders. It is this fast-moving consumer society that Smithson occupies and that provides the social context for the things,

DOI: 10.4324/9781003230632-9

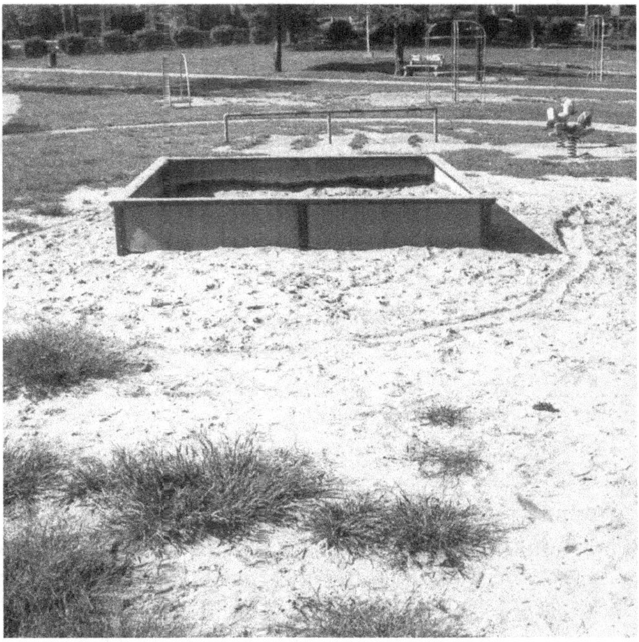

FIGURE 7.1 Robert Smithson, The Monuments of Passaic (The Sand-Box Monument, also called The Desert), 1967 Detail of Monuments of Passaic, 1967; Six photographs and cut Photostat map; Total size: 42 x 288 cm Collection of the Museum of Contemporary Art, Norway Originally published in Robert Smithson, "The Monuments of Passaic," Artforum 6, no. 4 (December, 1967). Photograph: Robert Smithson © Holt-Smithson Foundation/ARS, NY and DACS, London 2022

sites, spaces, and places he deems 'monuments' (thus seeing them primarily historically) when he arrives in Passaic.

We know that the original Grand Tourists, while excited about the growing sense of modernity emerging through the European Enlightenment, revered the past and turned to it for their own benchmarks of beauty and models of artistic achievement. The past – and not the now, the modern, the contemporary, or the future – was, for them, where excellence in art and architecture lies, and this even though so much of the past they admired lies in ruins, having been subjected to the violence of barbarians and the ravages of the elements. In fact, patination, ruination, and fragmentation all became a crucial part of the Grand Tourist's reverence for the past, adding a certain pathos and a heightened sense of value to objects and civilisations that had been destroyed by historical forces, by subsequent, unsympathetic peoples, left to the elements and subjected to the inhuman and inexorable inevitability of change, and ultimately of entropy.

Despite so much destruction, the forms, processes, and values of classical art and architecture were regarded by the Grand Tourists as enduring and even timeless – and here the idea of the 'classic' emerges from, and alongside, reverence for the classical.

While the 'classical' is an art historical term, generally referring to the achievements of Greek and Roman civilisations, 'classic' has today come to mean anything that endures in a similar fashion, even if it is a product of the modern or postmodern era. Hence, we refer to music albums, cars, trainers, or lemon squeezers as 'classic'.

For Smithson, an artist of the late 1960s and thus clearly influenced by modern art, value lies in the modern, the new, in innovation, in concept and novelty, and in a fast-flowing exchange of ideas (a contemporary art *milieu*) that constantly questions what art is and how it might be valued. Nevertheless, while the newspaper he reads on the bus to Passaic points to the art world, to the now, and to the everyday; and while his Sci-Fi paperback imaginatively refers to possible futures, Smithson's focus in this work ultimately remains on the monument, an object and a concept that is arguably pre-, un-, or non-modern. The monument marks and seeks to retain and establish the past, which, in the context of a contemporary art that tends to fixate on the present (the novel, innovation, etc.) can only be deployed or referred to ironically or parodically.

After arriving in Passaic, having shared with the reader, along the way, some of the contents of his mixed-media diet, Smithson describes his surroundings in expressive prose and makes a series of photographs that will run alongside his writing when it is finally presented as an article in a leading art journal. In this way the whole artwork can be seen as perceived and constructed for the very environment and context of modern media.[2]

Throughout Smithson's piece, the artist/writer uses a subjective tone and positionality that allows him to nominate as monuments whatever he chooses to think of as such. Recalling that Passaic is the artist's birthplace, it is worth noting that Smithson inverts the accepted public and collective purpose and function of the monument, turning it into a personalised object. Each nomination is accompanied and confirmed by means of a 'snapshot' (a cheap, poor-quality, popular, and amateur mode of photographic reproduction), and thus we come to note that these personal monuments and their monumentalisation might be regarded as 'events' as much as they might be 'things'.

Marcel Duchamp, who strongly influenced Smithson's generation of artists, famously chose objects to be what he called 'readymades'. He thus transformed them, or their perception, by means of his nomination, using a few words of explanation and a certain personal and intellectual conviction to convince his *milieu*, and eventually posterity, that his choice (a performative 'event') was the only process and criterion required to bring into existence artworks that came to be elevated and revered as some of the most important and indicative of the 20th century.

Along with Duchamp's possible influence, Smithson's assertive subjectivity in nominating monuments might also be inextricably entwined with his use of photography, which must, in its turn, have also strongly influenced Duchamp's nominations (to 'make' a photograph we need only 'take' it). Photography also came to be a means by which the late 1960s generation of conceptual artists came to record hypothetical and conceptual works that might otherwise leave no visible or material record. The photographic medium looms large throughout Smithson's guided tour.

It could be argued that photography encourages an artist (or anyone capable of taking a photograph) to see the world with a more personalised, indeed a monocular vision, peering at and 'capturing' as it were, pieces and places of the world with and within a personal framing and recording device ('my camera', 'my picture'). Making photographs leads each of us inevitably into history and historicisation by creating a personal archive, museum and collection in a way that could also be regarded as a 'nomination of monuments' or at least a personalised selection of supposedly significant events. Events and their images become 'our' photographs and thus 'micro-canonic'. Each image is chosen according to an acquisitive, subjective, individual rationale that might be commonplace but might also be more difficult to explain to others or justify objectively according to any commonly agreed set of aesthetic or cultural values.

In this way, photography also becomes a surprisingly (given its mechanical basis) intimate and expressive medium, one capable of sharing with a wider audience the private experiences and feelings, tastes, desires, visions, tendencies, and convictions of an individual.

Nevertheless, the quick, cheap, and black and white snapshots rendered by Smithson's camera, for all their poor and relatively ephemeral quality, also point us back to a broader sense of history, to a sense of living subjectively in and through a more objective, bigger, grander history. Photography, ever since its invention, we might say, has encouraged all who use it (which sometimes seems to be everyone) to see, live, and think historically.

A newspaper, a Sci-Fi-paperback, snapshots, references to the Grand Tour and to monuments, all of these find Smithson travelling in and through time, history, and modernity. He makes sense of all this complexity, and of this possible confusion, by means of the subjective documentation of his daytrip, i.e., by writing his own story, composing words and pictures into a work that will itself prove enduring, and might in fact be just as interesting and valuable today as it was when first forged 50 years ago. His article/artwork is not only a guide to certain personally nominated monuments; it is, and always was, also a 'monument' to the event it describes.

Meanwhile, as a progressive contemporary artist working in the late 1960s, Smithson might have taken pains to avoid falling into the error of making works that appear merely 'typical' of his times or his *milieu*. The reason he is travelling alone is possibly because, like many modern artists, and of course the Romantics before them, he is in search of a personal, and if possible original, insight or discovery. Rather than confirm any set of given values, as might a classicist or academic artist, the modern artist's role is perceived as being to question existing values, innovating, if possible, by creating new values and by transgressing or developing established values.

It might be interesting then to note that Smithson was not only influenced by the now, the futural, the contemporary, and by history and the history of art in terms of the Grand Tour, he was also influenced by the writing of George Kubler who advocated the unusual method of approaching art history from the perspective of geological time rather than cultural history and human time.[3] Hence, many of Smithson's 'monuments' (and the works of Smithson's wider *oeuvre*) refer to sand, water, mud, stones, rocks, shale, lakes, land, etc., base materials that underlie, precede, and will eventually succeed all modern and human structures and phenomena, along with all the acts and judgements that he describes on his trip.

Inhuman and ahistorical 'entropy' also came to inform and influence Smithson's work and vocabulary. This concept is illustrated by his description, in the *Passaic* article, of a sand box containing two separated colours of sand. By running in circles through the sands they can gradually be mixed, but it would be impossible to un-mix them by simply reversing the running process (though Smithson notes that reversing a movie of the act would at least create this illusion). Thus, a certain entropic bias in the way of the universe is supposedly proven.

This image leaves us with a sense of human inadequacy, and modern inadequacy, akin to that perhaps felt by Grand Tourists confronted with the mighty scale of the ancient past's achievements. It might leave us with a sense of folly and foolishness, and perhaps some trace of sublime Romanticism, when faced with entropic forces so much greater than ourselves. Entropy is also, perhaps inadvertently implicated in the way that Smithson's *Spiral Jetty* came to appear and disappear, to be available and then not available to human sight, subject to meteorological and climatic conditions, beyond the powers of the artist, of man, to control it.

The Romantic poet Percy Bysshe Shelley wrote of *Ozymandias*, an imagined ruin of a colossal monument lying derelict in the desert, a tribute, not to the great man and culture it was intended to champion but rather now to the superior forces of time and the elements that have destroyed and forgotten them and that will also come to destroy and forget all men – the poet, the viewer, the reader and 'man' *per se*.[4] Smithson might be said to complement, compound, or allude to Shelley's sentiment in his own work, but invites the modern media of photography and of printed pages to nevertheless offer some hope of retaining and continuing to celebrate all that he monumentalised on that now well-known day-trip in 1967.

We have recently come to name and consider our own epoch the 'Anthropocene', and as we try to come to terms with the indisputable fact and inconvenient truth that our relationship with our planet is becoming less and less accommodating, less welcoming, and less homely, as a result of, or as a response to its crude abuse and exploitation, Smithson's and Kubler's approach to art, to history and to time might seem more relevant than ever.[5]

Today, any references we might make to monuments and monumentality, come up against increasingly fast-moving and rapidly changing modern life, and simultaneously against the glacially slowly, inexorably changing geological forces and materials that underlie and potentially undermine those activities that we think of as art, and any story we might think of as history. Both a sand dune and the Sphynx can be regarded as differentiated objects or as differentiated events, and both are in a state of relative becoming, entropy and preservation. This might encourage us to consider art, and the activities of contemporary artists increasingly in terms of the production of, and engagement with, events rather than objects, things, and images, while coming to see differentiation in terms not of extensity but of intensity – speed, behaviour, activity, acceleration, and hesitation.

Notes

1 See https://holtsmithsonfoundation.org/monuments-passaic.

2 We might also note here that Walter Benjamin constantly experimented with the possibilities of print and radio journalism as vehicles for thought.

3 Kubler, G. (1962).

4 See www.poetryfoundation.org/poems/46565/ozymandias.

5 See www.theguardian.com/books/2016/apr/01/generation-anthropocene-altered-planet-for-ever.

The work of Joseph Beuys might also be interesting to compare, in its dialogue with inhuman and ahistoric materials and processes.

Bibliography

Flam, J. (ed.) (1996) *Robert Smithson: The Collected Writings*. Berkeley: University of California Press.

Kubler, G. (1962) *The Shape of Time – Remarks on the History of Time*. London: Yale University Press.

8

CHARLES BAUDELAIRE'S 1846 SALON ESSAY

Modern life and modern art as history

At the age of 31, and as a mature student, I finally completed a previously abandoned undergraduate art degree. I had started it at the age of 20 before becoming disoriented when, shortly after I left home to study, my father passed away. Then I neurotically fell out of the course, and it took me ten years of difficult searching and doubting before I finally returned to graduate.

When I returned to study, I found the college environment inspiring and almost overwhelming in terms of the wealth of new ideas in which I became immersed. One of the things that entranced me were the lecture series' that, rather than just teaching me art history, revealed a previously unknown relationship between art, history, and life.

These lectures and their lecturers introduced me to something that changed me then and which still lies here at the heart of this book, its aims and motivations. My lecturers, themselves inspired by the writing and thought of art historian T.J. Clark among others, showed me that, just as 19th-century Paris had gone through turmoil and confronted cultural, political, social, aesthetic, and technological change, so late 20th-century London, in which I was living, was apt to do something similar.[1]

I might have read some history before, and I might have attended some art history lectures, but there was something about the way this group and generation of teachers taught me that was very effective in using art to connect my mind to what I have repeatedly, and perhaps slightly clumsily, referred to here as a 'historical consciousness'. They seemed to show me that this 'historical consciousness' can form a way of life, a philosophy, a society, or a way of understanding and perceiving.

It is true that those same lecturers were introducing me simultaneously to difficult theories of postmodernism, but there was no rift or conflict between those theories (along with their exemplars in artists and writers drawn from the 1970s and

DOI: 10.4324/9781003230632-10

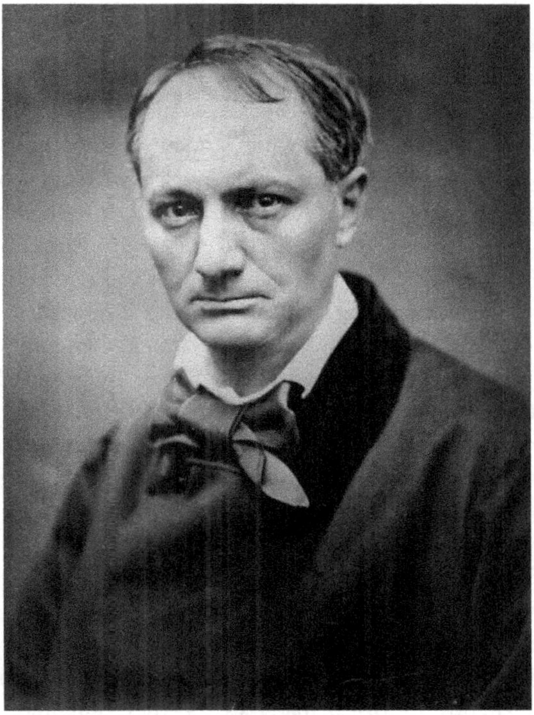

FIGURE 8.1 French poet Charles Pierre Baudelaire (1821–1867). Photographed by Etienne Carjat/Getty Images.

1980s) and the information the lecturers also provided about 19th-century Paris. It seemed to me that these bodies of knowledge necessarily meshed. Each needed the another, in the following ways.

To learn that modernism might be 'dead' or might have 'failed', and that we might thus have entered a postmodern era or cultural paradigm was greatly enhanced by learning, in some detail, about the *milieu* in and from within which modernism itself was forged. I felt as though I had the privilege of being able to see both the start and the conclusion, the 'book ends' as it were, of a profoundly significant cultural epoch and its accompanying paradigm, incorporating modernism and modern art, while also reaching back into pre-modernity and addressing what postmodernism might mean.

The ways in which the ideas and protagonists were introduced also imprinted me (apparently indelibly) with a sense of responsibility to respond by looking historically and creatively at my own experience, by analysing my own times, thoughts, ideas, life, culture, art, and writing through a similarly historical lens. I still think of this 'responsibility' as crucial to what I mean when I use the phrase 'historical consciousness', and I believe I have allowed my life and career, particularly on certain formative occasions, to be guided by just this sense of responsibility.

Studying postmodern theories was literally disorienting. I took it extremely seriously and it made me ill for a while.[2] Especially challenging was the way in which it radically questioned the real, as in Jean Baudrillard's theory of simulation and simulacra, and in the way that other theories evaporated any simplistically linear or teleological sense of history.[3] Meanwhile, studying 19th-century Paris might, to some extent, have balanced and oriented me by clarifying just where modern art, modernism, and modernity came from, and of what they were constituted.

My long-term passion for writing, and art writing in particular, began to take hold at this point. Baudelaire, the 19th-century poet and critic, and his special role and achievement in championing and encouraging a new form of modern art, became a kind of 'hero' for me.[4] Meanwhile, a strange, sometimes baffling, unfinished, but always captivating book written by Walter Benjamin about Baudelaire introduced me to new kinds, complexities, levels and textures of thought, research, reading and writing that somehow linked me both to Baudelaire and to those disorienting postmodern theories.[5] This could be explained by the way that I later interpreted Benjamin's thought as 'proto-postmodern'. I continue to think of that enigmatic book, titled *Charles Baudelaire: A Lyric Poet in the Era of High Capitalism*, as some kind of model or benchmark for my own approach to mixing creative and academic writing.[6]

While Baudelaire's own historical consciousness might have given him the audacity to confidently call for an art of and for his times, Benjamin seemed adept in looking at apparently historical materials (be they buildings, objects in shop windows, photographs, movies, or quotes from other authors) and reconsidering the habitual ways in which we might think of them as 'historical'. Again, perhaps in this way Benjamin could be considered 'proto-postmodern' and linked to postmodern theories of post-history or non-linear history.

Whether I aligned myself with Baudrillard, Benjamin, or Baudelaire (or Barthes for that matter), or found myself trying to understand how they might all fit and work productively together, their combination provided a dynamic stimulus to finding a personal way of expressing the familiar sense we have of connecting change to meaning, whether as commentators on collective culture or as spokespersons for our own immediate experience.[7]

The phrase, 'connecting change to meaning' (above) might even be an attempted definition of history. We give value to the process of change, whether in terms of our own lifetimes or in terms of the part we play in longer swathes of history. What I discovered on my degree course, and what I later pursued as a question in my PhD, and am still pursuing and sharing here and now in writing this book, is the question of what part art and writing might play in that evaluation, that process of translating and representing historical consciousness.[8]

In a few paragraphs of an edited version of Baudelaire's Salon of 1846, I have repeatedly found, while working with students who come for the first time to this classic text, not only a summary of what modern art is, could, and should be, but also the proffering of a certain kind of 'license'. This license, I believe, endures today and still has the potential to inspire artists in the 21st century, if only as proof of our underlying role and purpose, and as proof of the importance of the relationship between art and history, which – almost paradoxically – provided the crucial chemistry from which modern art was born. Here is a taste of the extract from Baudelaire:

> But to come to the main and essential question, which is to examine whether we have a specific kind of beauty, inherent in new forms of passion (elsewhere translated as 'new emotions'), I have noticed that the majority of artists who tackle modern subjects have contented themselves with public and official subjects, our victories and our political heroism. Even so, they do it with an ill grace, and only because they are at the beck and call of the government that pays them. But there are private subjects that are much more heroic than these. Scenes of high life and of the thousands of uprooted lives that haunt the underworld of a great city, criminals and prostitutes, the *Gazette des Tribunaux* and the *Moniteur* are there to show us that we have only to open our eyes to see and know the heroism of our day.[9]

In the salon essay's title we also find the phrase 'Heroism of Modern Life', and there Baudelaire has already thrown down a gauntlet while starting to play ironic, modern (or perhaps even proto-postmodern) games. Heroes are associated with classicism and the past, and so – we could assume – might not belong in modern life or modern art at all. One way of progressing to a thoroughly modern art might be to purge established culture and dispense with all references to classicism and the past, but this might be a totalitarian solution of the type we see in later modern and modernising regimes Then again, a kind of totalitarian fervour, e.g., for the supremacy of reason, did pervade elements of the French revolution (and we might ironically add, did so to an *irrational* degree).

Baudelaire however sees a way to progress and modernise, not by dispensing with or erasing history but by re-purposing it, finding its modern equivalents (e.g. who are our modern 'heroes'), or by finding ironic ways of referencing history so as to show that while we may be no longer part of a past time we are consequently able to look at and use past times from a new and different perspective.[10]

If we fast forward from this subtitle ('On the Heroism of Modern Life') to nearer the end of our edited selection from Baudelaire's salon essay, we find Baudelaire seeking illustrations of modern beauty and providing modern alternatives for the art historical nude, that staple of academic, classical, pre-modern art practice. Again, Baudelaire advocates, we need not crudely dispense altogether with this traditional genre but can inventively find its modern equivalents, perhaps parodying, satirising, or in other ways modernising the nude along the way.

In this salon essay Baudelaire therefore provided a raft of suggestions or implications regarding the possible contents of a modern art, including events derived from everyday media in the form of newspaper stories. There the daily recording of relatively minor events comes to constitute and collate a modern history that in turn cultivates a modern historical awareness of the relative import (or heroism) of seemingly 'small' or unimportant people and events. Furthermore, rather than distancing himself from the previous Romantic generation of artists, poets and critics, Baudelaire asks his audience not simply to be more sober, less Romantic or emotional but – in one of the most intriguing of his suggestions – calls for new passions (which can also be translated as 'new emotions') that need to be felt, recognised, named, and represented by the artists and cultural commentators of modern life and times. Is there then a history of passions or emotions? If so, what might today's newest, most modern, postmodern, or perhaps altermodern passions or emotions be? To me this remains a fascinating question.

Baudelaire stresses that we do not need to go or look elsewhere in time or space to find sources of creative inspiration, but rather (simply) 'open our eyes' to what is playing out before us, open up to that which we have not yet seen for what it is; not yet seen as worthy of our attentions or the attentions of art and of history. And it is perhaps this assertion more than any other in the influential critic and poet's writings that proves most influential and enduring. Being or becoming a modern artist (and we can also say 'contemporary' artist here) doesn't require anything more or less than a consciousness changed and inextricably entangled with a new way of seeing and a way to see things anew – *any* things or events, be they old or new.

Baudelaire practices what he preaches when, e.g., describing modern life as a 'pageant' (in a translation by Jonathan Mayne). Even this choice of word, usually associated with tradition (the apparent antithesis of modernity, and, like 'hero' associated with classicism) sees everyone and everything modern as a great contrivance and performance, a carnival; sees modern life, great and small, as newly 'marvellous'.

Baudelaire gives a further example, of a modern consciousness being no less a historical consciousness in the anecdote of the founding of a medal to mark a political event. He points out that, in order to appropriately mark a modern event, we need an artist capable of doing so in a modern manner, as the alternative would be incongruous and ineffectual. Thus, both form and content are scrutinised and analysed in search of the potential of their renewed relationship in the context of modern art.

For Baudelaire, there is modern beauty, modern heroism, modern nudes ('in the hospital … in the bath'); there are modern events, themes, and subjects. There are even new passions and new emotions, and all of these are discernible to someone who has acquired a new way of looking by means of a new awareness of the historical nature of their modern consciousness. A modern person is a person who lives in and as history, caught up in modernity's 'pageant' and driven along by history's mysterious forces, which leave us enthralled.

Allusions to the past, far from providing a nostalgic escape from modernity, only confirm the historical nature of our present, in which we – as Baudelaire says, apparently paradoxically – 'celebrate some funeral'. To celebrate a funeral is to occupy a new and initially awkward historical condition. It is, perhaps, to mark and enjoy a newly heightened awareness of change, and to applaud the meaning we can glean from change itself – from passing. The modern motto that we hear emitting from within the thoughts of Baudelaire, and those 19th-century artists influenced by him to create modern novels, poems, and paintings, might then be: 'The past is dead, long live the past!'

Notes

1 Particularly, Clark, T.J. (1985).
2 Foster, H. (ed.) (1987).
3 Baudrillard, J. (1983).
4 Baudelaire, C. (1992) pp. 104–107.
5 Benjamin, W. (1983).
6 Benjamin, W. (1983).
7 This group of relevant thinkers and theorists whose names coincidentally all begin with the letter 'B' eventually shaped my long-running seminar titled 'The B-Team'.
8 See https://okpaul.com/phd-a-hesitation-of-things/.
9 Baudelaire, C. (1992) pp. 104–107.
10 Here it is hard to resist citing one of my favourite recordings, by Aaron Neville, titled *Hercules*. The lyrics document the toughness of life in the 1970s Afro-American ghetto and proclaim that the only way to negotiate and survive these challenging socio-economic conditions is to take on the persona of a 'Hercules', a classical hero of great strength and fortitude. Neville, A. (written by Allen Toussaint) (1973).

Bibliography

Baudelaire, C. (1992) *Selected Writings on Art & Literature*. London: Penguin.
Baudrillard, J. (1983) *Simulations*. New York: Semiotext(e).
Benjamin, W. (1983) *Charles Baudelaire – A Lyric Poet in the Era of High Capitalism*. London: Verso.
Clark, T.J. (1985) *The Painting of Modern Life – Paris in the Art of Manet and His Followers*. London: Thames & Hudson.
Foster, H. (ed.) (1987) *Postmodern Culture*. London: Pluto Press.
Mayne, J. (1964) *The Painter of Modern Life and Other Essays*. London: Phaidon.
Neville, A. (written by Alan Toussaint) (1973) *Hercules* (music recording). Warner-Tamerlane Publishing Corporation.

9

CAO FEI, YU HONG, TIE NING, AND JIA ZHANGKE

Memory, return, and afterimage

It seems a long time ago now that I first saw Cao Fei's video artwork *Whose Utopia?* (2006).[1] It may have been while it was installed for a season at London's Tate Modern gallery. However, I have a feeling that when I encountered it there, I had already seen it in some other context.

Memory is like that – elusive, mercurial and fickle. Sometimes we experience a strange sense of the familiarity of events. Sometimes we don't even know if we are remembering at all. We call '*déjà vu*' or 'uncanny' those experiences that seem strangely familiar, and 'strangely' because we might consciously, rationally know that we are experiencing something for the first time, while feeling inexplicably that it is not the first time at all.

The Romantic philosopher F.W. Nietzsche seemed to think that, as modern people, without resource to God and the corresponding teleology of the Bible, one way that we can explain our sublime relationship with time and experience (and therefore justify the value of our lives in a temporal realm where everything passes) is if all events, including ourselves, ultimately return, and are thus always in a constant and eternal state of returning.

There is then, in this Nietzschean way too, a 'strange familiarity' to life, to living, to everything.[2] We may not necessarily be going anywhere, or leading to anything, other than that which already is, in a beautiful but purposeless and meaningless circularity. So, what might this mean for history?

For Nietzsche, being or existence is rather becoming and *per*sistence. To return is to become what you already are, and to return to what already is. To return is thus to *per*sist rather than to exist. Thus, the seemingly unopposable dynamism of time is a constant condition of, not loss or gain but of return, a positive value that we can embrace and affirm. It may then be return, and not attainment or destiny, that produces, for Nietzsche, the fundamental and ultimate sense of meaning and

DOI: 10.4324/9781003230632-11

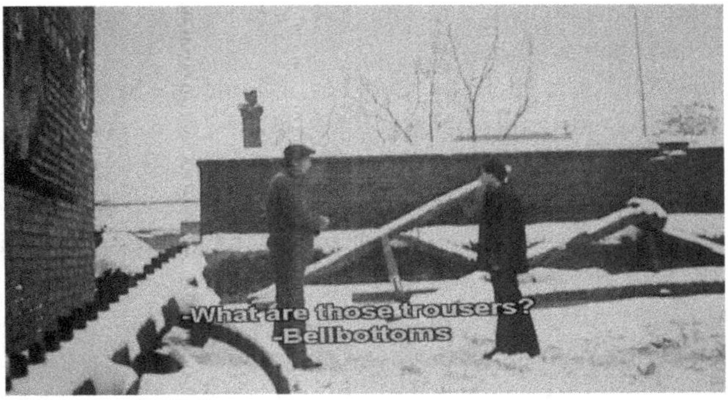

FIGURE 9.1 *Platform*, 2000, movie directed by Jia Zhang-ke. Distributed by Artificial Eye. Screenshot (at 12 minutes and 15 seconds).

purpose (what he elsewhere calls the 'Will To Power' perhaps) that is invested in and which motivates our lives.

While some of our other faculties and resources might be more reliable, we can enjoy memory in a particularly sensual or 'aesthetic' way, perhaps because memory 're-minds'. It reminds us of our subtle humanity, of the vulnerable uncertainties that make us who and what we are; it reminds us of what survives and persists, and what falls away into what we call the past And this cannot yet be comfortably accounted for by our own logic and reason or by more collective and objective science.

Whose Utopia?, the video by Cao Fei referred to above, features workers in a light bulb factory in China. Their jobs appear dull, their labour 'alienated', but Cao Fei imagines them managing to keep their dreams and fantasies alive (and necessarily so) as a means by which to survive their otherwise inauspicious, restrictive, or barely tolerable conditions; by which to survive both psychologically and, we might say, spiritually. Using little more than their imaginations, their dreams, they can at least partially escape from something that might otherwise be impossible.

They need dreams to keep their spirits intact, but the factory is also and already a kind of highly contrived dreamspace. Factory managers (as well as supermarket managers) are aware that the industrial and repetitive nature of the spaces and activities they oversee cannot function without the intervention, mediation, or salve provided by piped popular music, usually of a 'classic' and fondly remembered kind. The factory worker and supermarket shopper therefore both enter into a realm of sensual memory, a history of emotions, every time they enter the store or factory to carry out their otherwise all-too banal but necessary task.

The future may be another place to which we might like to escape, and here Cao Fei's title, and her searching question *Whose Utopia?* is pertinent. Individuals have their dreams, while societies and nations have others. How can we reconcile these? This is perhaps one of the biggest of all modern, political questions, the answer to which might draw us, not just into dreams, utopias, and futures but also into history, into a way of living a meaningful narrative that makes some acceptable sense of time and change.

In *Blueprints* (2020), a show by Cao Fei at London's Serpentine Gallery, an elaborately installed video, titled *Nova* (2019), invited us to enter the history of a theatre or cinema whose role and purpose has been adapted to changing times and influenced by changes in technology and culture.[3] Apart from partially reproducing the old theatre or cinema, both as an installation in the gallery and as a movie set for the filming of *Nova*, the video's narrative extrapolates certain characters and events into a Sci-Fi fantasy future. This might look dystopian, but the video at least ends with a happy scene of reunion set in a heavenly realm. What the artist means by this, what the artist themselves believes about utopias, Sci-Fi predictions, etc., remains unclear, and yet the audience is sent away on a kind of 'high' or positive note by the upbeat finale, their own dreams perhaps injected with renewed vigour.

In 2019, a group show of Chinese contemporary artists was curated for London's Lisson Gallery. Here artists juggled with the idea of the now and the notion of the contemporary, while also referring to various ways to use history. The show's title was *Afterimage: Dangdai Yishu* – notably half-Chinese and half-English.[4] The first half of the title, *Afterimage,* implies residue, endurance, and delay; the second half, *Dangdai Yishu*, translates into English as 'Contemporary Art'. When a curator (partially) names a contemporary art show '*Contemporary Art'*, they may be simply stating a fact, and yet, the juxtaposition of the term with *Afterimage* surely points to something more complex. The show's press release presents an unusually long meditation on just what contemporary art might really mean, both for art in general and particularly for this curator and the artists and works chosen for the show.[5]

One interpretation we might take from the (translated) title *After Image: Contemporary Art* is that contemporary art, or perhaps art in China now – through the eyes of this curator and this exhibition at least – is an 'afterimage'. This seems to suggest that it is never immediate and present (and not therefore what we normally think of as 'contemporary') but something that has occurred previously and is only now seen for the first time in and at a moment subsequent to its original occurrence.

Could this apply to all images? Are all images perhaps 'afterimages'? If I look at something brightly illuminated and then quickly close my eyes, or if an image is quickly flashed into my eyes causing me to close them (always a little too late), then that image persists in negative form within the ensuing darkness as an 'afterimage'. This 'afterimage' can only be seen 'after' its initial event, when a material memory lingers imprinted on the light-sensitive receptors of the body.

Victor Wang, the curator of the Lisson show, may then want us to think of its collected Chinese contemporary art works in this way, not as images but as afterimages, and/or to think of contemporary art in general as such an 'afterimage', 'dis-immediated' as it were, and thereby made retroactive. It is as if, no matter how contemporary the art and the artist may be, Wang wants us to see within their work that which is past.

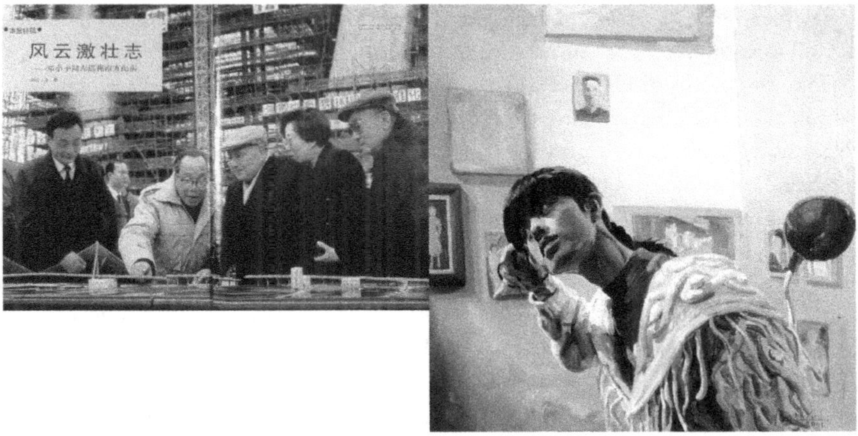

FIGURE 9.2 Yu Hong 26岁故事片《冬春的日子》剧照, Twenty-six years old. A photo showing a scene in the film *The Days* 1992, 2001 Acrylic on canvas, newspaper. Print: 68 cm × 100 cm. Print: 26 3/4 in. × 39 1/4 in. Painting: 100 cm × 100 cm. Painting: 39 1/4 in. ×39 1/4 in. (HONG010001). ©Yu Hong; Courtesy of Lisson Gallery.

Yu Hong, one of the artists in the *Afterimage* show, does explicitly refer to the past, as if to practise she must necessarily look back. So perhaps this too is a kind of afterimage, a way of living in the present with our attention necessarily turned to the past. Yu Hong uses a simple but effective strategy of juxtaposing, directly and literally, reproductions from magazines that illustrate 'big', 'important', national stories and events, alongside painted scenes of contemporaneous events from the artist's personal or private life.

The audience of Yu Hong's work is invited to regard, compare, and seek a dialogue between paired images, one drawn from her personal history and another drawn from national history. Thus, we might be moved to consider our own lives and the relative importance of personal events, couched or folded within or alongside the relative importance of national or international events. Yu Hong's strategy is unassuming and yet it has far-reaching and powerful implications, addressing something that concerns us all. She invites us to compare the mix of *gravitas* and frippery regularly received from official mass media, with the relative seriousness and modesty of supposedly 'smaller' events in our own lives, our own history.

Something comparable happens in the movie *Platform* (2000) directed by Jia Zhangke.[6] Here we see a small theatre company making transitions into a new era, as China, in the late 1970s, through the early 1990s, processes its communist ideology and cultural revolution and enters a new phase which, in the movie, is opening to a broader range of international influences and cultural expressions. The lifestyles we witness in the movie seem quite dull, impoverished, inauspicious, and repressed, but are now subtly enlivened by the occasional intervention of pop songs, flared jeans, cigarette smoking, and experiments with hairstyles and make-up, as well as speculations about new kinds of intimate relationships.

Like the works of Cao Fei or Yu Hong above, *Platform* positions its protagonists within their own material lives and life stories, yet guided and influenced by their relationship with greater powers – in this case national, international, social, cultural, and technological changes that collectively we might tend to call 'history'.

Whether a personal life or a national narrative should be referred to as a story or as history is debateable. The larger, or 'more historical' a figure becomes, the more story-like their lives correspondingly become. The history of a nation is always a necessarily simplified complexity that seems to render it more story than history. An exceptional individual life may come to be referred to as inextricable from 'great' historical events, as in, e.g., the deified or quasi-hagiographic lives of Stalin, Marx, Mao, Van Gogh, or Michelangelo. At the same time, every life is 'exceptional', at least in that it is unique and worthy of representation and evaluation, if only to the person who lives that life.

It is in this way that the so-called 'history from below', 'microhistories', and 'the history of everyday life' have become important elements of a progressive culture where history is deployed and cultivated as an expansive, creative, critical, dynamic, and democratising force. Meanwhile, conservative and reactionary societies tend to be narrowly selective and exclusive in their approach to, and use of history, overblowing and mythologising the importance of the nation, along with a particular ideology and its leading exponents, while strategically selecting national figures and events and utilising the most orthodox monumental traditions to represent them as influential figures.

We have already brought together here several examples drawn from China and can continue to do so by now also referring to a short story written by Tie Ning entitled *O Xiangxue*.[7] This small but memorable work once again situates people's individual lives and stories amid apparently bigger events and a fast-changing world. It is set in a remote rural, mountain village where modern growth, progress, and technology bring a railway line and its trains, carrying new kinds of people and even a new sense of time. A train stops at the village at precisely the same time once a day, but only for one minute. Correspondingly, one of the new exotic and desirable objects that the villagers are able to admire through the train's windows is a rich passenger's miniature watch. New people, new faces, new objects, new exchanges, desires, and aspirations all come via the train to excite the village and its inhabitants, most notably the adolescent girls who are the story's focus, and who represent change and the future.

This charming but no less historically charged short story draws all these elements into play, creating a small (perhaps we could say 'life-size') but profound and moving psychological drama for the central figure, a girl named Xiangxue. As we saw in other examples above, it is once again the mysterious and inexorable force of history, and seemingly history's very own narrative, that transforms the 'small' individual history or story of Xiangxue's life.

Xiangxue's exacerbated desires lead her to be literally swept up and away by the train, but only for her to immediately return to her village by means of the unfaltering modern railway line. On her lone journey through the night, she sees the natural, traditional environment in which she has grown up as all anew, through new eyes, with a changed consciousness.

We might note that every individual story, and the individual acts that make each story (as well as each life, and the individual acts that make each life), can, must, and do, in their turn, influence and change history, albeit (and even if) in tiny, but countless, incremental ways. Ultimately, we are all 'historical figures' worthy of remembrance.

Perhaps there is something Romanticist about this kind of historical consciousness, a Romanticist residue, as embraced by Nietzsche in many ways, including his vision of 'eternal return', but also discernible in any contemporary art that equates and reconciles, in a noble, meaningful way, the lone, vulnerable individual with the greatest, widest, highest, infinite, eternal, and sublime forces of time, and of 'the times'; of history, of the world, and ultimately of the universe.

Supposedly small, even tiny events loom large in our lives, becoming formative, significant, life-changing, and in our very own private or intimate way, historical. Similarly, the contemporary artist might like or prefer to be associated with the now, and perhaps only with the now, and yet every artist's relationship with the past and future, with the self and the nation, the world, and the universe, is also inescapable and deserves to be acknowledged, never denied.

Notes

1 See www.caofei.com/works.aspx?id=10&year=2006&wtid=3.
See www.tate.org.uk/art/artworks/cao-whose-utopia-t12754.
2 Nietzsche, F.W. (Walter Kaufmann, ed.) (1968) pp. 544–550. Or Nietzsche, F.W. (Bernard Williams, ed.) (2001) pp. 194–195.
3 See www.caofei.com/exhibitions.aspx?id=140&year=2020; www.caofei.com/works.aspx?id=82&year=2019&wtid=3.
4 See www.lissongallery.com/exhibitions/afterimage-dangdai-yishu.
5 Osborne, P. (2013). Peter Osborne and Hito Steyerl were also in conversation regarding the launch of this book at ICA London on 21 March 2014.
6 Also referred to as '*Zhantai*'. See www.imdb.com/title/tt0258885/.
7 Balcom, J. (ed.) (2013).

Bibliography

Balcom, J. (ed.) (2013) *Short Stories in Chinese.* New York: Penguin Books.
Nietzsche, F.W. (Walter Kaufmann, ed.) (1968) *The Will to Power.* New York: Vintage.
Nietzsche, F.W. (Bernard Williams, ed.) (2001) *The Gay Science.* UK: Cambridge University Press.
Osborne, P. (2013) *Anywhere or Not at All – Philosophy of Contemporary Art.* London: Verso.

10

JOHN AKOMFRAH

Hauntological history and costume drama

John Akomfrah made his name and reputation with Black Audio Film Collective, and with historical and archival works like the well-known *Handsworth Songs* (1986). In his work *The Call of Mist – Redux* (2012) he reminds us of our project here, associating supposedly 'big' collective or objective history with far more intimate, personal history.

The work is informed by the passing of the artist's mother, to whom it is dedicated. Such an event looms enormously large in any individual life, but Akomfrah contextualises it against the apparent timelessness of a sublime Scottish landscape, invoking geological time. The loss of a mother is a sublime experience in that it leaves us reeling without adequate form, meaning, purpose or scale, and so, in a way, both this loss and this landscape become transhistorical or *a*historical.

Massive material monuments mark and effect historical change, but so does the rich archive of photographic and moving images with which John Akomfrah has long been concerned. He has been contributing to this archive throughout his career, whether in creating his own additions to it or when editing footage from the archive and sharing excerpts, as he did in his *Hauntologies* show at Carroll/Fletcher gallery in London (October–November 2012).

I came away from that show predictably still 'haunted' by an array of moving and by still images of moving events. Since that time the Carroll/Fletcher gallery has closed, and all attempts to access its archive and even its previous homepage meet only with online culs-de-sac and morbid 404 Error messages. This reminds me, however, to trust and value the resource of my memories, which can be both inaccurate and enhancing in relation to the truth or actuality of past events.

I was aware for many years of the artist John Akomfrah, but a moment came when it seemed to me that my own work and interests aligned more closely with his.[1] That was when I grew interested in using the idea of romance and Romanticism to investigate the relationship between the contemporary and the past, and to use

DOI: 10.4324/9781003230632-12

romance and Romanticism as a challenge to our relatively dry-eyed, cerebral, modernist relationship with art and culture. At *Hauntologies,* I discerned what I thought of as a Romanticist (a term that is always somehow unfashionable and from which the artist might well want to distance himself) tendency in Akomfrah's work.[2] I saw this in, for example, the aforementioned, re-edited work *The Call of Mist – Redux* (2012).[3]

I recall and have now re-viewed a scene from the video, in which a lone figure arrives in mountainous scenery by means of a Sport Utility Vehicle (SUV). The scene is rendered in saturated, high contrast tones of black, white, and gray (sometimes further tinted with browns, purples, and greens, but always a basically monochromatic image). I also recall now that the figure in the video is transporting an urn, presumably symbolising the artist's mother's ashes to be scattered or simply carried through this remote timeless wilderness on a last beautiful journey to witness places and things she might have loved or might not otherwise have visited. Either way, it's surely a way of saying goodbye, of thinning the line between life and death, between being together and being apart, between being here and being no longer here.

Offering up our own fathomless encounter with life's measure to the immeasurable scale and age of the landscape, seems to provide the possibility of a kind of reconciliation, and again invokes a Romantic's aesthetic way of gleaning spiritual value from the remote margins of an increasingly secular society.

In the same exhibition, some more modest video works collectively titled *Psyche* (2012) and shown on small, wall-mounted video monitors, illustrated excerpts from the artist's dialogue with the history of film, as well as with what the artist referred to at the time (perhaps in the booklet that accompanied the show), as his interest in 'costume drama'.[4]

I subsequently saw other Akomfrah works at Lisson gallery (the artist's home gallery) in which a dialogue with the past did indeed depend, partly at least, on references to dress, costume, and on reconstructed performances of people now lost to us, differenced by time and death as inhabitants of that 'other country', 'the past', where, as novelist L.P. Hartley famously put it, 'they do things differently'.

Dress and fashion, like popular music, design, and architecture, occupy sites of history that are never closed to or distanced from us by institutional walls and doors. Their presence, their legacy is something we live in and within every day. Nevertheless, 'costume drama' as a focus of interest for a contemporary artist, might still come as something of a surprise, if only because of its associations with mainstream blockbuster movies, Sunday-evening TV and a potentially nostalgic, conservative, or reactionary passion for things past.

Notions of dress have turned up in several places during the preparation of this book, and here I also recall that curator Karen Alexander, in an online discussion of *Black Chronicles*, a major exhibition crated by and initially held at the Institute of International Visual Arts (iniva), London, 2014, stressed the importance of dress, of clothes, of style and fashion (which is and has, of course, a whole rich history of its own) in adorning that show's previously uncelebrated and almost forgotten figures, who continue to speak to us today as it were emboldened by their photographed costume and associated body language. In *Black Chronicles* this is captured by photography's own, special historicising process, which attempts to capture and transmit forever what happened once upon a time in a long-ago fleeting moment.[5]

Is it possible then for an artist like Akomfrah – whose career has shown him to be conscientiously engaged with the past, in a most progressive and responsible manner – to extract from 'costume drama' some form of credible and convincing image that might then serve as a vehicle for the themes and concerns that motivate him, his practice, and his audience? I wanted to telephone interview John Akomfrah for this book (along with Tacita Dean, Pablo Bronstein, and Sigrid Holmwood), but his schedule disallowed it, and so I am inclined here to rely upon memories and extant knowledge to see what kind of relevant writing, ideas, and history this produces.

As ever, there are gaps in my personal knowledge, and quirky twists in my personal logic regarding what I am writing. But only as much perhaps as there are gaps in *all* knowledge, twists in *all* logic, and unjust hierarchies of knowledge that presume to distinguish the known or scientifically proven fact from vaguely remembered hearsay, that may nevertheless be of importance to a particular person for a particular reason at a particular time. All that is known, as with all that is past, is a tracery of lingering events; events of knowledge, events of the known and unknown; of the barely or thoroughly known; the once known and subsequently forgotten.

From the knowledge I already possess, and can draw upon here and now, I can at least assert that the word 'hauntology' was coined by the radical philosopher of deconstruction Jacques Derrida, when he wrote a book, late in his career, alluding to Marx and Marxism.[6] Marxism is a thread that occasionally appears within this book, if only because Marxism is inextricably caught up with a modern and historical view of the world and influenced my own formation. Marxism might therefore not survive, thrive, or fit so well into a postmodern, *a*historical or transhistorical time, culture, or society, but it has certainly had a powerful influence on my generation and my personal development (albeit, not so much in an intellectual, academic, or dogmatic way, but more because of my working-class upbringing and consequent life experience, while gradually climbing and/or falling in some awkward form of class migration).

Jacques Derrida seems to have thought and written his way through and beyond his own generation's existing notions of the relationship between language, experience, writing, and speaking, thus bursting the bubble of a generation's established system of understanding. He delivered us (as many philosophers or anti-philosophers of his generation, often inspired by Nietzsche, hoped to do) not to a more fundamental but rather to an anti-foundational method or forum for challenging questions. He achieved this, not so much via the trajectory of a progressive modern innovation as by reminding us to turn inside-out the language in which we already think, ask, and answer questions. His contributions came necessarily wrapped in neologisms, e.g. *hauntology, grammatology, différance,* etc., but it seems inappropriate to thus evaluate these as 'new' when they are designed to encourage us to constantly un-work and rework that which is given.

After Derrida, we seem newly inclined to concede to living and working with and within uncertainties, intangibilities and inaccessibilities that modernism and Enlightenment might have sought to eradicate by means of progress, logic, reason, and particular forms of organisation. Today, we might justifiably feel that to truly and sincerely, adamantly and determinedly seek what we are seeking, we have to live and work with the un-given of what we '*have not*' as much as with the given of what we have, i.e., work with what we *cannot* as much as with what we can, with what we *do not know* as much as with what we *do* know.

Hence, though I cannot speak to John Akomfrah at this time, and though I cannot revisit the show via the Carroll/Fletcher gallery site because it is defunct, leading me to a fatal-looking 404 Error message, still I am able to consult all of this in a way, and even if, given a Derridean understanding that encourages me to blur clear distinctions between presence and absence, it might be their absence that I consult.

I did manage to interview Sigrid Holmwood (see Chapter 5 of this book) and she talked about the way, in her recent doctoral research, she pursued materials as much as ideas, and that, through pursuing materials (reminding me of journalists saying 'follow the money') she accessed fascinating depths and details of worldwide historical research, some of which she shared over the phone. Holmwood also pointed out that she thought this materialist approach was 'very Marxist'.

Derrida's book, *Specters of Marx*, in which the neologism 'hauntology' appears (itself an apparition perhaps), takes a theme of ghostliness, referencing both the first scene of Shakespeare's *Hamlet* and the first spectral line of Marx and Engels' *Communist Manifesto*, to explain the author's, and society's, relationship with and vision of Marx and Marxism today (the subtitle of Derrida's book, by the way, is *The State of the Debt, the Work of Mourning and the New International*).

Ironically, the outcome of this investigation may be that Marxism is no longer regarded as reliably material or materialis-able, but in the late 20th century bordering on the 21st century, when Derrida is writing, could almost be said to be re-spiritualised, transforming its relationship with people, politics, history, socialism, communism, and class.

When Marx wrote his modern theories of political emancipation in the 19th century it was acknowledged that he was emulating Hegel, whose own theories emphasised *im*material values and utilised images of spirit and mind; albeit with Marx re-rendering those Hegelian values, images and devices in materialist terms. Marx nevertheless seems to have taken and retained Hegel's Christian-influenced model of a society that moves historically towards the pinnacle and resolution of its possibilities. Marx however made this idea and ideal newly concrete and material; made it all about real people, real money, real resources and processes, working towards the outcome of a real worldly emancipation.

Hence, I, and John Akomfrah, along with Sigrid Holmwood and Jacques Derrida, all grew up in a society where there was, and still is, I hope, some underlying, often barely visible but nevertheless present sense of pursuing a transformative project of emancipation, wherein all those who have contributed to modernism, however visibly or obliquely, but who are not, and have not been adequately recognised and rewarded, shall and should eventually see their own ideal of justice and reward delivered.

But all of this is perhaps less certain now than when Marx inscribed his project into modernism and onto the late 19th and early 20th century – the era of his great initial influence. Marx's ideas rank among the most influential and formative of his time. His ideas grew to be realised or made manifest in various interpretations, e.g., by worldwide labour movements, the Chinese communist state, the Soviet Union, various Socialist, Social Democratic, and Marxist states, including Cuba, and many others that went through a Marxist phase (including several African states) as part of a liberative, decolonising, post-Imperial trajectory.

Derrida's *Specters of Marx* however, was published in 1993, after the fall of the Berlin wall and the collapse of the Soviet Union, events that many opponents to Marxism saw, and wanted to see, as an end, failure and limit of Marxism's ideological aspirations worldwide. Yet Derrida as a philosopher knows that ideas never die – that ideas matter, whether or not they refer to immateriality. Even if we hide, purge, or forget ideas, they are likely to re-emerge, trouble, and haunt us.

Furthermore, any idea in materialised form has always and already compromised its ideal state (that being something that is constantly disputed and locally interpreted) so that the Marxism of China, of post-colonial African nations, of Cuba, of East Germany, or of the Soviet Union will surely always differ from Marx's original ideas, ideals, and intentions, and also differ from each other. In fact, Marx is said to have stated, in response to a particular manifestation of his ideas, that if that was Marxism, then he himself was not a Marxist.

Thus, ironically, given Marx's rejection of Hegelian spirituality, Derrida – writing as a late 20th century, inspired, verbose and we might say florid philosopher – seems to suggest that what is of greatest value in Marxism may nevertheless survive today in ghostly form. For Derrida, the ghostly form of *hauntology* (supplanting the fundamental understanding of an *ontological* basis to the word and its comprehension) conveniently fits his wider philosophical project, wherein trace, liminality, and deferral (all concepts easily associated with ghosts) help to form a critique of presence – presence which, along with ontology, has perhaps ruled the roost of our understanding for too long and can now concede to the equal value of absence, or of a liminal state between presence and absence that dispenses with their crude and habitual distinction and binary opposition.

Perhaps Derrida's deconstructive method, his neologisms and wordplay are ultimately more effective than any Marxist revolution or other form of reification of Marx's ideas. If so, then Derrida might claim to have surpassed, superseded, and exceeded Marx, in sophistication, finesse, currency, complexity, effectiveness, and appropriateness. After all, hauntologising the previously ontologised world is not a promise that we must wait for to be fulfilled, nor an ideal that we must fight for in the streets. It might just supplant the kind of transformative emancipation long promised but never fully delivered by 18th-, 19th-, and 20th-century revolutions.[7]

As a way of returning now to John Akomfrah, and of also drawing from his contemporary Tacita Dean (see Chapter 6 of this book), it is worth noting that an alternative understanding of *hauntology* might arise from its association with the virtual and digital realm.

New technologies have changed the very nature and understanding of materiality in my lifetime, with potentially significant implications for ontology, for Marxism's innate materialism, and his purposeful distancing from Hegel's 'spiritual' model. The digital arena invites us to interact with *virtual* (quasi-spiritual perhaps) images, texts, games, scenarios, etc. Meanwhile, all kinds of previously actual and material operations are converted to the more convenient virtual realm, which is itself a non-material, more ethereal, and perhaps ghostly realm.

Artists John Akomfrah and Tacita Dean are aware of the ways in which such technological changes are affecting the production of images in our time. Dean campaigns to keep alive (or provide an 'afterlife' for) the manufacture of 20th-century celluloid movie film, which she uses as a material in her work. For her, the digital does not and cannot replace or supplant the idiosyncratic qualities of film. For Akomfrah, a history of photographic and moving-image technologies is available to an artist whose work has always been bound up with archives of the mechanised and/or otherwise technologised and reproducible image.

As we have seen here and elsewhere in this book, different eras of technology produce different qualities of images; and images of different people are thus brought into and made visible to history. In this way technologies, archives, and the notion of haunting seem to have a special interrelationship.

To conclude I just want to return to the question I would have liked to have asked John Akomfrah, i.e., concerning his interest in 'costume drama'. As we have said, the phrase 'costume drama' brings to mind art and culture of a moribund or conservative kind, and yet the costume drama is indeed a form or style, a particular 'way', with which a wide audience is familiar and comfortable, of telling a story and attempting to immerse us in history (and here, not for the first time, nor for the last in this book, a dialogue, not yet fully articulated, grows between history and the idea of dress).

We might then also venture the possibility that history is (if not to itself then at least to us, us as an audience, a perspective, a gaze) itself a 'costume drama' – something visible, dramatic, dressed-up, and acting away for the endless fascination of the contemporary.

After all, that which is lost and irredeemable, that which is out of sight and out of reach, takes on a strange presence through our concern, fetishistically 'dressed' as it were by our need to see and know and have it as more tangible and accessible. Perhaps history is that dressing, that dressing-up and fleshing-out of all that is inaccessible.

Notes

1 https://iniva.org/library/digital-archive/people/b/black-audio-film-collective/.
2 https://artreview.com/december-2012-john-akomfrah/.
3 www.lissongallery.com/artists/John%20Akomfrah/artworks/the-call-of-mist-redux?image_id=7570.
4 www.lissongallery.com/artists/John%20Akomfrah/artworks/the-call-of-mist-redux?image_id=7570.
5 https://vimeo.com/209666646.
6 Derrida, J. (1994).
7 We could also consider here the *Rêve Général* movement whose revolutionary aims were based on a word play.

Bibliography

Derrida, J. (1994) *Specters of Marx – The State of the Debt, the Work of Mourning, and the New International.* New York: Routledge.

11

PABLO BRONSTEIN

Critiquing neo-Georgian aesthetics in a lingering postmodern paradigm

In a photograph from a magazine of the artist Pablo Bronstein in his home/studio, you can see that it is not the average artist's studio or typical white-cube-like space. It seems to be nestled into what looks like the ground floor or basement room of, what we might be led to believe by the artist's work, an 18th-century town house (in fact it turns out to be the artist's home in Kent, on the English coast).

Perhaps Bronstein prefers such an environment within which to make his contemporary art that has always seemed to be 'of' the past; always making overt references to architecture and design drawn from previous centuries. Bronstein's work, which I first encountered in a 2011 show at London's ICA, could be said to confront the audience with a certain power invested in the architecture and design of a pre-modernist era.[1] This is a form of architectural and design power (Bronstein sometimes refers to it as 'pomp') that modernism relinquished in order to promote a language and power of its own.

Should we then call Bronstein a pre- or postmodernist? Postmodernism is such an unfashionable term that today it is starting to sound provocative again. However, Bronstein's work never lets us know whether he likes or loathes the materials and references with which he plays. The artist and some commentators on his work seem to stress certain ironic and absurd qualities. The works might be jokes that you may or may not 'get'. While you are trying to work this out, you can of course admire the craft that goes into their creation. This includes an acquired, well-honed illustrative drawing style and the purposeful fashioning of images and objects that necessarily live in a kind of limbo, somewhere between present and past.

Reading the artist's illustrated book *Pseudo Georgian London*, as I did, rapidly, and from end to beginning, might be a good way into understanding his position and the style of his thinking. The drawings there celebrate failures, monstrosities, and awkward attempts by architects, usually to conjure value from a low budget and a distorted idea of the achievements of the Georgian epoch. The book's understated,

DOI: 10.4324/9781003230632-13

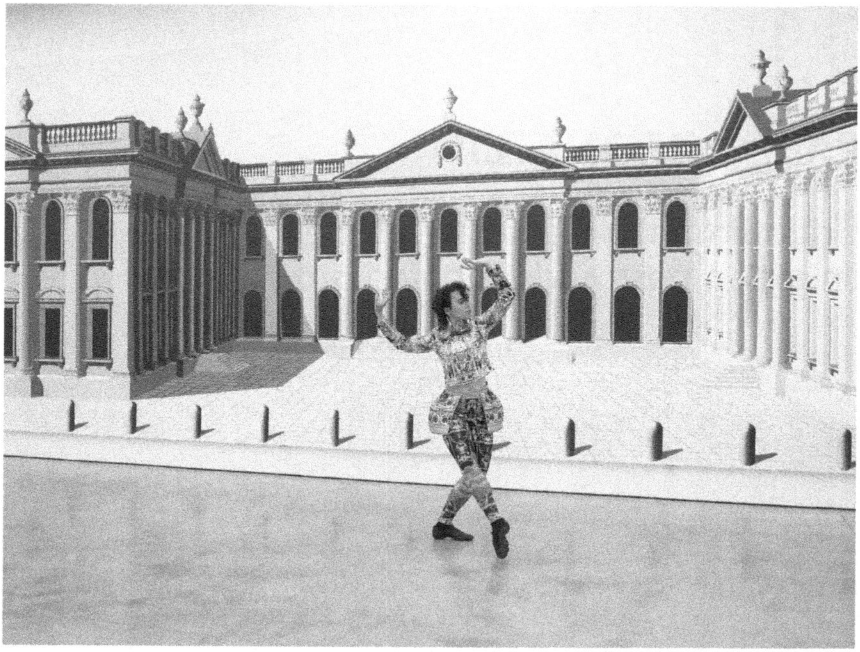

FIGURE 11.1 Pablo Bronstein: installation view, *Sketches for Regency Living*, ICA, London, 2011. Courtesy of the artist, Herald St, London and ICA, London. Photographed by Steve White.

slightly tragic humour gets under the reader's skin the more we read. And finally reaching the epigraph 'For my hard-working parents' might be the moment to laugh out loud at this parody of the values and language of British Conservatives, for whom we might ultimately have to lay the blame for the car-crash of social aspiration and aesthetic vulgarity that is ultimately illustrated here, in witty word and scratchy image.

There is a three-way tension, or pull, of a kind, in the juxtaposition of (on one hand) Bronstein's idiosyncratic, instantly recognisable contemporary art practice, and (on another) the contemporary exhibition spaces in which he exhibits, and (on yet another), the rich historical language of architecture and design with which he persistently confronts us.

History waits to be read, mis-read, re-read, to be inscribed and re-inscribed on the city's streets as a living museum. Those streets, and even (on London's annual 'Open House' days) some of its most interesting buildings, are free to enter.[2] Just as when we listen to pop music and its own popular history on the radio, we do not need to be wealthy, nor obtain a reader's ticket to tend to architecture's archive. Its language, stories, and voices surround, contextualise, and shape us. One of the few remaining benefits of living, in the 21st century, as an artist or an art student, in an almost impossibly expensive historic city, is that no matter how little we might have left in our pocket or bank account, we are still allowed and able to peruse the city and read its story, interwoven with our own, in the brick and stone, glass and steel, concrete and tarmac of its buildings and roads.

Sadly however, my own home city of London, like many others I hear (and I fear), is fast losing its history – if that is really possible. London is 'losing history' at least in respect of the fact that many idiosyncratic areas (though never the richest, we might add) long identified with special cultures, services, communities, qualities, buildings, materials, etc. (e.g. the musical instrument district, the electronic equipment district, the rag trade district, costermongers' district, soho etc.) are being rapidly demolished, transformed, and replaced with generic contemporary architecture that houses generic brands and all-too-familiar stores. Soon, it seems, there will be no reason to visit London in particular, because what it will have to offer will be largely identical to every other major city.

Nevertheless, it seems that, where we look for history in the city, we can yet still find ourselves, either as an individual that the city has formed or as a society and community that has, in turn, played some part in forming the city. Walking in our city (a city we have increasingly come to call our own as it has increasingly devoured and captured us), we might locate, note, and recall certain inspired urban moments that arise in a special, *flaneur*-like 'downtime' wherein we, the city, and history momentarily become one (W.G. Sebald, the peerlessly imaginative writer of modern history, does this to great effect in his book *Austerlitz*).[3]

Anyone who has lived in London for a decade or more will have become familiar with its palimpsests of epochal architectural styles. As a Londoner killing time one introspective afternoon, I recall making a long-postponed personal pilgrimage up Ludgate Hill, conscientiously negotiating its relatively steep slope, passing its mix of modern shops and ancient churches, on up to the top of the hill and the impressive West-facing entrance to St Paul's Cathedral. I then forged Eastward, noting the unique idiosyncratic qualities of the Barbican to the North, and eventually encountering *30 St Mary Axe* (the so-called 'gherkin') amid other masterpieces of Hi-Tech architecture perversely crammed into the bustling 'square mile' of the City of London.

On my way I believe I might have noted one or two roads (the name 'Watling Street' comes to mind) with apparently unnecessary curves and bends. These always seem to betray a pre-modernist logic of a kind that did not follow and favour the demands of the motor car, nor prioritise the modern, capitalist grid system that, in its most extreme form, defines and defiles younger cities like New York or Los Angeles.

A curious London wanderer might have also noticed that, following the Georgians (with whom Pablo Bronstein seems enduringly preoccupied), the Victorians and their Edwardian successors seem to have in-filled residential areas of the city with relatively parsimonious dwellings apparently provided for the not particularly affluent but reasonably solid and stable, modest lower middle class, indicative perhaps of certain socio-economic shifts taking place in the Victorian age. These appear to have superseded, as an expression of cultural 'regime change', the more elegant and assertive Georgian architecture of tall narrow houses with high ceilings and long windows built on wide roads and around luminous squares, all backed-up with generous mews.

In conversation with Pablo Bronstein, I mentioned that I wasn't aware of any buildings in which the Georgian poor (those not directly servicing these houses) might have lived, but the artist suggested his own extensive research revealed that these enduringly elegant houses were not in fact 'single occupancy' but often contained more than one family sharing their tall structures, basements, attics, and elevated spaces.

Thus, while each era's architects might express the culture and socio-economic system of which they are a part, how those buildings and that city are actually used, in posterity and even in their own lifetime, is largely out of their control. And here, perhaps, is where a certain irony, parody, and caricature can all step into the gap between an architect's delimited ideal and the greater, unpredictable complexity of real and lived experience – a zone of uncertainty and potential absurdity that Bronstein has marked out for his mysteriously contemporary but undeniably historical practice.

In addition to being a strange mix of wit, tribute, and critique, Pablo Bronstein's art may yet also entertain subjective and psychological elements, as his historical-looking work, encountered in contemporary art spaces, cannot help but insist that the past (central to Freud's modern science of a subject's mind) undeniably, if unconsciously, forms and informs us. The past lies all around us and within us, sometimes hidden or repressed, but just as often overt, providing our very environment, dwarfing us, making us feel anachronistic before ultimately outliving us, either as resilient object or as intangible memory.

Architecture is a tangible form of history, an art through which we necessarily move. While Schlegel famously referred to it as 'frozen music' Walter Benjamin was interested in the way in which we are influenced by architecture while barely aware of it, experiencing it in a special state of distraction (one of his own persistent themes) and absorbing it through osmotic and habitual 'tactile appropriation'.

> Buildings are appropriated in a two-fold manner: by use and by perception – or rather, by touch and sight. Such appropriation cannot be understood in terms of the attentive concentration of a tourist before a famous building … Tactile appropriation is accomplished not so much by attention as by habit.[4]

When I had an opportunity to speak with Pablo Bronstein by telephone, the first thing I noted was that he no longer lives in the city but (as mentioned in our introduction above) in a small town on the English coast – though he surely remains capable – given his extensive knowledge of and research into the history of architecture – of observing details and layers of historical architectural evolution even in his newfound, relatively modest setting.

Many small English seaside towns, bereft now of their 18th- and 19th- century popularity, and missing their traditional mix of labour and leisure economies, have become popular as sites for young families' second homes, boltholes for stressed Londoners, post-Covid 'work from homes', artist's affordable residences, and online cottage industries. Pictures of similar towns to that in which Bronstein lives show that they either disallow or do not attract much in the way of modernising development (notwithstanding the occasional dramatic intervention by a sea-side museum or gallery). As such, they are able to retain and share those charms that only the past can grant, gifting residents and visitors a sense of occupying an alternative, parallel, perhaps gentler, slower, less voracious and more reconciled time and place. Here we can live – for an hour, a day, a year or two, or even the rest of our lives, to some extent at least, within the past.

Small coastal towns also offer the quiet backdrop and constant reminder of the limits of humanly habitable space (and thus the limits of architecture), giving on as they do to the sea, an ever-present example of sublime and inexorable change marked by eternally susurrating recessions and returns. But even here, the technical evolution of semi-residential oil platforms, and those wind turbines that tend today to cancel out the enigma of the horizon, provides hints of the potential for future maritime colonisation, habitation, and architecture.

To look long at architecture is inevitably to encounter history, but to look long at the sea, as into valleys from a mountain peak, is to look out from a place within history into timelessness, to look out of humanity into something unfathomable, into the beyond of history that beguiled the Romantics as they, in and for their own time, acknowledged, and attempted to provide an alternative and salve for, the relentless and inexorable onset of industrialisation and urbanisation.

Bricks and mortar are a relatively enduring response to fickle elements from which we need protection. Buildings can be fashioned in an infinite number of ways, from Georgian square to Hi-Tech tower or humble fisherman's shack. Nevertheless, Bronstein's professional and creative gaze seems satisfactorily fixed upon the Georgian period in particular (though he has also addressed postmodernism as an architectural style and also considered it as a cultural paradigm, not only as mere style). When I spoke to the artist we seemed to agree that, while postmodernism as a style can soon and easily be rendered unfashionable, and can even experience rebirth, postmodernism as a cultural paradigm is something far more profound (we could say anti-foundational), disruptive, and not so easily denied or superseded.

Along with other artists referred to in this book, Pablo Bronstein's work has much to offer to seminars and workshops, artworks and writings related to history in contemporary art and culture. I see now that his gift may lie in perversely perpetuating a postmodern-seeming strategy that retains credibility and shows that there are still knotty and awkward postmodern propositions to be thought through, more postmodern work to be done, in an era when postmodernism as a style is unfashionable. The built-in resilience and endurance of Bronstein's work may be down to the fact that, as we have said, he acknowledges the truer and greater profundity of interpreting postmodernism as a cultural paradigm rather than as a mere style.

If so, we might connect our thoughts and words here on Bronstein, to some of our other protagonists, e.g., our repeated references to Ariella Azoulay (see Chapter 4 and elsewhere in this book), but also to the possibly proto-postmodern ideas of Walter Benjamin and F.W. Nietzsche that also recur. All these thinkers seem interested in a wholesale critique of the modern paradigm in which they find themselves, as well as a thorough critique of any presumptions regarding the purpose and forms we tend to award to history.[5]

Meanwhile, we could compare Bronstein's approach to Gilles Deleuze's own peculiar method of delving into the history of philosophy and re-purposing what is found there, as, e.g., when he develops his theory of the 'neobaroque' from his affirmation of Leibniz.[6]

While Bronstein may be producing subtle and witty commentaries on architectural power, or creating entertaining parodies and *faux*-historical objects, the fact that he emphatically and persistently deploys the affirmative anachronism of a neo-Georgian aesthetic in a 21st-century arena seems to demonstrate that he is aware of the need for a contemporary artist to probe, question, and to use and re-use history, if only to find a way to see the present more clearly, more truly, and to contribute to it more constructively.

Notes

1 See https://archive.ica.art/whats-on/pablo-bronstein-sketches-regency-living.
This is perhaps an appropriate place to mention another architectural intervention at the ICA buildings, by the artist Cameron Rowland titled *3 & 4 Will. IV c. 73* at the Institute of Contemporary Art, London, 29 January to 19 April, 2020. See http://thisistomorrow.info/articles/cameron-rowland-3-4-will.-iv-c.73

from which:

> … in the upstairs galleries ... comparisons are made between the practice of branding slaves as chattel and the current programme of tagging and monitoring used by the U.S. parole service

and:

The caption for 'Encumbrance' (2020) outlines the history of 12 Carlton House (the site of the ICA) and its transfer under George IV from a royal household to rental accommodation that continues to provide revenue to the Crown Estate. Rowland stresses that in general the Crown Estate provides 75% of its revenue to the Treasury and 25% to the monarch. The artist then rolls into this exposition references to the trading of mahogany (synonymous with the slave trade) and five mahogany features within the interior of the ICA – four doors and a handrail. By assigning these features to a mortgage investment that is exempt from the historic contract, Rowland is able to disrupt the flow of profit to the Crown Estate, effectively and selectively diminishing the value of the property.

2 See https://open-city.org.uk/how-to-take-part-in-open-house-festival.
3 Sebald, W.G. (2001).
4 Benjamin, W. (1968) pp. 239–240.
5 *Theses on a Philosophy of History* in Benjamin, W. (1968), Nietzsche, F.W. (1980).
6 Deleuze, G. (2001).

Bibliography

Benjamin, W. (1968) *Illuminations*. New York: Schocken Books.
Bronstein, P. (2017) *Pseudo-Georgian London*. London: KoenigBooks.
Deleuze, G. (2001) *The Fold, Leibniz and the Baroque*. London: The Athlone Press.
Nietzsche, F.W. (1980) *On the Advantages and Disadvantages of History for Life*. Indianapolis: Hackett.
Sebald, W.G. (2001) *Austerlitz* London: Hamish Hamilton.

12

WALTER BENJAMIN'S *THESES*

History's mental gymnasium

Anyone coming to Walter Benjamin's *Theses on the Philosophy of History* hoping to acquire a solution to the puzzles they present, regarding history, is likely to be disappointed, but might nevertheless be enthralled and intrigued by Benjamin's collection of riddles for us to solve.[1]

Benjamin's term 'theses' might well be used ironically here as, instead of a carefully worked through, continuous argument, arriving at some kind of theoretical conclusion, Benjamin uses an aphoristic form equally reminiscent of Zen Koans or excerpts from the *I Ching*, or those fragmentary quotes, ideas, observations, and statements gathered together as Benjamin's *Arcades Project*.[2] All of these lack the structural and narrative context of a 'thesis', we might argue, and instead require the reader to pick them apart, interpret, compare, and juxtapose them anew every time they are re-read.

In these short formations, the words remain the same of course but re-reading them reveals that both the reader and the world in which the words are read, have always and necessarily changed. And so, this text, one of the last pieces Benjamin completed before his premature death, was perhaps a most appropriate format for Benjamin, who had experimented with form throughout his career, as a writer and thinker, contemplator of and commentator on, history.

The aphoristic form draws us into an urgent and immediate event of interpretation (we are not able to wait until later in an essay, chapter, book, or page, for clarification); and leads us into an event of meaning-production which remains 'live' and eventual in that it is never established. In this way it might be considered ultra- or trans-modern, in that it cannot become 'a thing of the past' (it is neither 'thing' nor 'past') but needs to be acknowledged as crucially and primarily eventual.

Given the above, it might be unwise to attempt a reading of the *Theses* as something accumulative, homogeneous, identifiable, or consistent. Rather, the reader is advised to extract just one of the small theses, focus on it for a given period of

DOI: 10.4324/9781003230632-14

time, chew it over, handle it like an object that we might or might not choose to purchase, discuss it, make what we can of it for the time being, then put it back in its original place while noting that, while we may have done little or nothing to change its status, it, and our process of considering it have nevertheless changed something – and if not the world to any great degree, then at least ourselves to *some* degree.

We might then (here risking the mixing of multiple analogies and metaphors) consider the theses a 'mental gymnasium', a text that we go to in order not to know it or be done with it, but to make ourselves fit to read, to think, to interpret texts in general, and those relating to history in particular.

Benjamin drew influence not only from Marxism but also from his Jewish upbringing which may have exposed him to a hermeneutic tradition involving the repeated scrutinising of scriptures while considering and endlessly reconsidering their possible interpretation. As a result, such texts never become presumptuously definitive but remain respectfully just out of any particular reader's reach. We might think of Benjamin's *Theses on the Philosophy of History* written in this spirit, i.e., as knotty texts that ultimately point us, not to their clarified solution but rather to the irresolvable enigmas of history, teleology, and the persistent presence of the past.

This dialogue transports us to a possibly transcendent and metaphysical realm thrown up by modernism as a cultural paradigm and by its cultural divorce from God, a separation that leaves modern people dependent upon their relationship with time (no less exalted and enigmatic than God), and also with reason for their sense of orientation and purpose.

Importantly for our project here, Benjamin uses his Koan-like aphorisms to bend, re-shape or shatter many given assumptions about the shape of time or the forms we give to history. This implicates – for his time and generation as well as for our own – those hopes and beliefs (including movements, isms, and ideologies) whose promises and realities are founded on such assumptions – e.g., 'How can we place our faith in any leader who promises to lead us "from A to B" if we question that very direction, that misuse of our alphabet, that implied linearity, proximity, distance, difference and directionality, as well as that assumption of cause and effect?'

Marxism may be habitually regarded as a modern, rational, materialist political system, and yet Benjamin, who is perhaps as Jewish as he is Marxist (and perhaps as Dadaist and Surrealist as either), subtly implies that Marxism carries with it many 'messianic' and teleological traits, unwittingly imported from the kinds of religious belief that Marxism purports to eschew in its prioritisation of reason and materiality. Furthermore, without these religious hangovers, Marxism doesn't work as a viable system. It starts out by nobly 'getting real', describing our actual and factual material conditions in capitalism, but then makes the quasi-religious, un-materialist, unrealistic, and perhaps un- or irrational promise to deliver us to some better time and place, enabled by a better political, social, and economic system.

It might be that a large part of the current uncertainty of left-wing thinking stems from honest confrontation with this fundamental weakness in the foundations of left-leaning modern thought. Meanwhile, right-wing politics exploits this philosophical weakness shedding doubt upon any promise of betterment – a stance memorably framed by the US Republican Party's one-time presidential candidate Sarah Palin when describing Barack Obama's agenda disparagingly, as 'that hopey, changey thing' (though of course Obama's idea succeeded and Palin's failed, at least for a time).

We may not be able to confidently provide a pre-, post-, or alter-modern replacement for Marxism here, but we can however, as noted above, use Benjamin's *theses* as a 'mental gymnasium' that might sharpen, test, challenge, and refresh our habitual thinking in such a way that it could make for ourselves a viable, current, and convincing way of thinking and working historico-politically.

Notes

1 Benjamin, W. (1968) pp. 253–264.
2 Benjamin, W. (1999).

Bibliography

Benjamin, W. (1968) *Illuminations*. New York: Schocken Books.
Benjamin, W. (1999) *The Arcades Project*. Cambridge, MA: Belknap.

13

EXPLORING THE OUTMODED

A fragment of Benjamin's Surrealism

In Walter Benjamin's essay on *Surrealism* we come across a rich paragraph concerning what he called 'the outmoded'.[1] Here Benjamin interprets the work of Surrealism and its leader Andre Breton as drawing out what he calls 'revolutionary energies' from 'the outmoded':

> Nothing could reveal more about Surrealism than their canon. Where shall I begin? He (Breton) can boast an extraordinary discovery. He was the first to perceive the revolutionary energies that appear in the 'outmoded', in the first iron constructions, the first factory buildings, the earliest photos, the objects that have begun to be extinct, grand pianos, the dresses of five years ago, fashionable restaurants when the vogue has begun to ebb from them. The relation of these things to revolution—no one can have a more exact concept of it than these authors. No one before these visionaries and augurs perceived how destitution—not only social but architectonic, the poverty of interiors, enslaved and enslaving objects—can be suddenly transformed into revolutionary nihilism. Leaving aside Aragon's *Passage de l'Opera*, Breton and Nadja are the lovers who convert everything that we have experienced on mournful railway journeys (railways are beginning to age), on Godforsaken Sunday afternoons in the proletarian quarters of the great cities, in the first glance through the rain-blurred window of a new apartment, into revolutionary experience, if not action.
>
> They bring the immense forces of 'atmosphere' concealed in these things to the point of explosion. What form do you suppose a life would take that was determined at a decisive moment precisely by the street song last on everyone's lips?[2]

DOI: 10.4324/9781003230632-15

We may be aware that Surrealism was often referred to by its leader Andre Breton as 'the Surrealist revolution', and it is worth considering that this revolution would, did, or does take place by means quite different from that of other modern – e.g., Haitian, French, American, or Russian – revolutions. The Surrealist revolution requires a transformation of mind and is a psychoanalytic event inspired by Freud rather than an idealist revolution inspired by Rousseau or a materialist revolution proposed by Marx.

For Breton, seen by us here through Benjamin's eyes, it is not only modern people but modernism itself that has a mind, spirit, and unconscious. So, while modernism prides itself on its primary motivation and justification as progress, that progress (as Benjamin alludes to in his *Theses on the Philosophy of History*) is not necessarily one-way, linear, or fully conscious of itself and its consequences.[3]

One material sign or piece of evidence for this might be the way in which modern productivity and mass production creates the unanticipated fallout of what is here called 'the outmoded'. The modern phenomenon of the flea market is one of the best ways to understand this (though Benjamin will provide more examples, as we will see). In his novella *Mad Love* (*L'Amour Fou*) Breton describes a visit to a flea market with the artist Giacometti.[4] They both choose objects from the eclectic and illogical disorganisation with which the flea market confronts its customers. We might say there is something Freudian about all these outmoded and discarded objects; things that once had a value in being modern and new, valued as tools, gifts, clothes, or even the debatable value of those things to which the English give the nonsensical names Nik Naks or Bric-A-Brac.

Once, all these things had a specific context, e.g., a pair of shoes belonged in a box in a shoe shop, then on a particular pair of feet, and perhaps on a shoe rack in someone's hall. Now, at the flea market, they have lost that context and are thrown, perhaps even losing their partner in the process, into random relationships and juxtapositions, gradually becoming increasingly worthless and meaningless as they descend to the status of unwanted and un-sellable goods.

However, it is worth recalling here that a classic definition of Surrealism's own peculiar notion of beauty is: '... as beautiful as the chance encounter of a sewing machine and an umbrella on an operating table', a verbal assemblage whose material equivalent might only be encountered in the modern flea market.[5] Note, however, that this is a new beauty, a modern, 20th-century beauty, based not necessarily on sight or aesthetic proportion but on the value of incongruity, complexity, heterogeneity, and juxtaposition – all typical, we might say, of modern, urban life.

Things become discarded because they are outmoded, broken, or pushed, by fashion, out of fashion (N.B. fashion may be another important modern or historical spirit, and something to which Benjamin occasionally refers in his *oeuvre*).[6]. For Benjamin, interpreting Breton, there are also forms of the outmoded that are not simply things or objects. In the paragraph from his essay that we are here and now starting to close-read, Benjamin creates a broader list of outmoded phenomena, which includes:

> the first iron constructions, the first factory buildings, the earliest photos, the objects that have begun to be extinct, grand pianos, the dresses of five years ago, fashionable restaurants when the vogue has begun to ebb from them.

and he suggests that all of these are invested with 'revolutionary energy'.

Benjamin also uses the term 'revolutionary nihilism' and this suggests that, once an object, event, hemline, or building loses its newness, it also loses its place in the modern order of things and thus becomes disruptive, because, in losing its cultural and historical place it has lost its meaning and thus brings into question not only its own value but also the value of the place it once held. Set loose from its place in the modern order of things it then becomes available for the projection of other, uncontrollable or unpredictable meanings and uses. This potential disruption might then be one way in which the Surrealist revolution operates or intends to succeed, i.e., by upsetting the logic and reason of modernism and putting in its place a different, less conscious, more unconscious interpretation of the purpose and content of modern life.

Modernism separates things from their meanings or makes the relationship between things and meanings more malleable, mercurial, and even (as exploited by photography) more momentary. Both Surrealism and Dada, variations of avant-gardism, claim this phenomenon as an arena within which a modern art can play and experiment.

We are of course always implicitly referring to Freud here, advocating the value of unconscious relations and the interpretation of sleeping and waking dreams, wherein seemingly incongruous things and events are juxtaposed, requiring some way of making sense of them, of interpreting or re-interpreting them, or demanding that we accept that there are things about ourselves and our modern lives of which we will never make sense.

In the paragraph to which we are attending, Benjamin goes on to expand a list of evocative examples of the outmoded, this time related to the mysterious concept of 'atmosphere'. Simultaneously we are implicitly asked whether atmosphere has a place in a rational, scientifically understood modern world. We might seem to know what we mean by 'atmosphere' and yet it might be equally difficult to scientifically define.

Benjamin's list of atmospheric and outmoded modern events (or events in some way related to the outmoded) runs as follows:

> mournful railway journeys (railways are beginning to age) … Godforsaken Sunday afternoons in the proletarian quarters of the great cities … the first glance through the rain-blurred window of a new apartment.

We might still recognise some of these experiences today. Sundays, for example, still seem to have a distinct and special atmosphere, even though our modern, or postmodern, Marx- and Nietzsche-influenced culture is supposedly no longer 'religious' but, on the contrary, made modern precisely by its secular rejection of the superstitions and irrationalities associated with religion.

The 'proletarian quarters of the great cities' (again invoking Marx), in being 'Godforsaken' particularly on 'Sunday afternoons', also seem convincingly replete with aforementioned 'revolutionary nihilism'. Perhaps this is because it is there (in the proletarian quarters), and it is then (on Sunday afternoons) that a modern human being, or more specifically a member of the modern working class, is momentarily, and on a weekly recurring basis, faced with a lack of structure, meaning, teleology, and historical purpose, and in such a way that they might be inclined to question and perhaps even challenge their lifestyle and the society that produces it.

However, Monday morning's re-imposition of structure, involving the obedient rush to work, the dutiful donning of livery (a kind of branding), and the return to all kinds of cultured and performative ways leading into a given hierarchical structure of rank and class (involving fear of the boss, fear of redundancy, of bailiffs, of one's 'betters'); the entering back into a given hierarchical structure of discipline and of subservience to other men and machines, into precise schedules, clock-punched time, etc.; all of this comes ineluctably back around again each Monday morning, just soon enough to quash and repress any revolutionary potential that the freewheeling, irreligious and potentially meaningless or nihilistic weekend might have nurtured.[7]

To continue close-reading Benjamin's list: train journeys might seem to be archetypally modern, arriving in the early 19th century with associations of speed, leisure, futurism, cosmopolitanism, internationalism, and democracy, but here we are reminded (as if everything has a Freudian flipside) that trains are aging, and their journeys can also be 'mournful'. It is, after all, another unexpected consequence of or fallout from modernity that, where speed is promised, delay and diversion are often delivered as many a commuter made late by delayed trains or trapped by jammed traffic in a potentially high-performing vehicle will attest. (We might recall here that the innovative French film maker Jean Luc Godard featured a black-humoured, almost painfully parodic seven-minute camera pan along a tragic traffic-jam in his otherwise optimistically titled 1967 movie *Weekend*).[8]

As for Benjamin's: ' … first glance through the rain-blurred window of a new apartment …' we might think here of the peripatetic author himself as typical of the modern city-dweller, or at least the modern city-dweller whose lifestyle is bound up with a noble but unprofitable occupation in the arts, and who is consequently and repeatedly forced to find new, temporary, affordable lodgings in the expensive and crowded city.

We know that Benjamin moved, travelled, and fled often in his career, and that he wrote a meditation titled *Unpacking My Library*, presumably influenced by his nomadic way of life.[9] Hence, any ideal image of or aspiration to a more grounded literary figure or sedentary professorial academic can be seen in Benjamin's career to be constantly disrupted by capitalism and modern politics, by combined forces and changes which (we must say thankfully) led to Benjamin's life-long experiments with journalistic and aphoristic forms of writing, and the collecting of fragments of his own and other people's writings.

Meanwhile, the 'rain-blurred' window and the 'glance through' it is a seemingly dramatic and Romanticist device, though again one probably inspired by all-too-real events. It invokes not only a romantic nomadism but also the modern subjectivity or sovereignty that both Breton and Freud could identify as a source of modern alienation and an engine of modern liberation.

Benjamin eventually completes this fertile and rewarding paragraph on the outmoded with a peculiar question, one that it is nevertheless tempting for us to want to answer or respond to (and which I have sometimes set as an essay question for seminars on which this book is based). The question is as follows:

> What form do you suppose a life would take that was determined at a decisive moment precisely by the street song last on everyone's lips?

The 'street song last on everyone's lips' presumably refers to what we now call pop music. English playwright Dennis Potter once made a series of innovative TV Dramas titled *Pennies From Heaven* (1978), *The Singing Detective* (1986), and *Karaoke* (1996), the first two of which showed characters living in 1920s, 1930s, or 1940s Britain so obsessed with the popular music of their day that it repeatedly and audibly intervenes in their lives and shapes their communications, decisions, and identities.[10] Potter's device was not new, being traceable through the long history of the musical, and perhaps back to the ancient use of the repetitive and collective

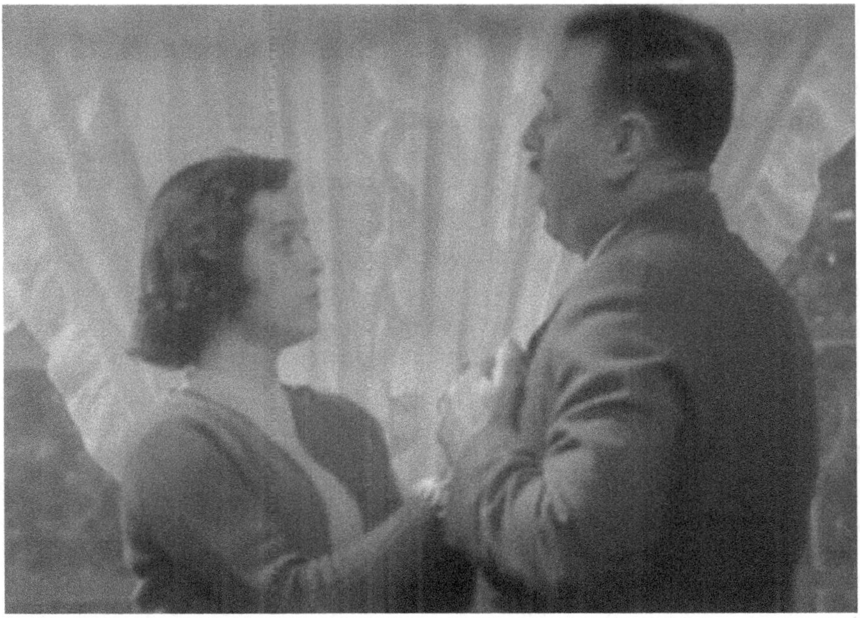

FIGURE 13.1 Dennis Potter, *Pennies from Heaven,* 1975. Directed by Peirs Haggard and produced by Kenneth Trodd. Screenshot (at 17 minutes and 30 seconds).

chorus in classical drama. But Potter laid a contemporary critical slant upon it – as does Benjamin – and delivered it, with a slightly discomforting air rarely deployed by artists of the time using this particular medium, into 1980s sitting rooms via the influential technology of television.

Benjamin may be interested, within his arcane question, in the way that popular songs (like the restaurants or dresses mentioned above) soon go out of fashion after being exhausted by their rapid mass dissemination via radio, gramophone, sheet music, and performance. The pop song is indeed a typically modern phenomenon even if it does have folk roots and bears traces of the long history of 'choruses' alluded to above.

Benjamin's question (which might now, under analysis, be becoming less peculiar) reminds us of a feeling, and one we might all know, of being mentally hijacked by a pop song that will not 'get out of our head' once we have heard it (sometimes referred to disparagingly as an 'earworm'), and/or a pop song that we seem to fall in love and can't wait to hear again and again.[11] With their simplistic, meaningful or meaningless choruses, pop songs may even seem to offer a solution – albeit a temporary one – to the difficult questions underlying our identity and our day-to-day existence, and thus may indeed promise to 'determine a life', as Benjamin suggests.

A Surrealist might therefore be interested in the idea that 'at a decisive moment' (they also championed chance events and unintended acts) one of these songs, and particularly one that has just recently become outmoded (no longer salient as new but nevertheless pervasive and familiar enough to be part of the material make-up of our cultural environment), might be capable of determining the 'form' of a life, i.e., influencing not only a life's direction but also giving that life a vocabulary, a style, and a simplified meaning.

Having been turned in the direction of popular music, and its own relation to the past and to history, we might linger here a little longer to take the opportunity of also considering what the music critic and writer Simon Reynolds termed *Retromania* – the title of his book about pop and its relationship with the past.[12] Though living with apparently futuristic technologies, we can't help noticing a contemporaneous and attendant wave of apparently compensatory or complementary archive culture. Our interest in old or older photographic processes, in typewriters, vinyl records, retro-styled cars and bars, is a sign that our postmodern culture has rejuvenated and re-economised 'the outmoded', bringing it (back) into the play of the market. Nevertheless, like the contents of the legendary Trojan horse, this 'retromania' might contain elements of critique that are disruptive to an economy that still, and necessarily, foregrounds the primary value of the new and novel as central to our values and aspirations.

Perhaps nowhere else is the continued and possibly critical value of the outmoded more alive than in the realm of the DJ (originally 'disk jockey'), a figure upon whom much of Reynold's book relies. Radio listeners and the clientele of nightclubs, music streams, or record shops all today have a vast time-scape of pop musical history available to them, which they enthusiastically explore. In doing so,

they continuously promote what might be called an alternative tradition
the tradition and history of an alternative culture.

The role and identity of the DJ was given a huge boost by the massive late 20th-century success of Hip-Hop (see Chapters 21 and 22 of this book), which is itself at heart an archival culture enabled by and infused with new technologies. Twenty-first century teenagers and twenty-something students and readers – also referred to as 'millennials' and 'digital natives' – are very aware, not only of the music of their own generation but also of at least one or two generations that preceded them. Simultaneously, 50- and 60-year-olds are fascinated by, and supportive of up-and-coming radical bands that younger admirers, ironically, might not be able to afford to financially support in the way of record sales, gig tickets, T-Shirts, and other fan merchandise.

Meanwhile, tuning-in to a radio station today will allow us, often without any financial outlay, to enjoy an almost infinitely eclectic mix of new music from all over the world, as well as music from different decades and other centuries, all in wildly different genres, and traditions, interlacing classics and 'oldies' with vertiginously experimental emerging modes and styles.

One website named *radio.garden* (N.B. this is its full title and web address) allows us to scroll and scour the globe, zooming-in to listen to what is currently being played, seemingly by every worldwide radio station.[13] In these ways, pop music, along with its historians and theorists the DJs, can maintain some grip at least on those 'revolutionary energies' promised by Breton via Benjamin, and that conflate past and present, keeping open, by means of this form of cultural history, some sense at least of an alternative narrative – the counter-narrative of a counter-culture that has grown into the strange phenomenon of a radical and progressive tradition.

All of this provides some way out of the otherwise intimidating, restrictive, and demanding regime of a thoroughly commodified lifestyle that increasingly tries to create our future for us by predicting and pre-empting what we might say, do, write, or buy next. With our future apparently usurped it seems we can nevertheless attempt to 'colonise' the past as a potential space of freedom.

So, to return to Benjamin's slightly arcane question: 'What form do you suppose a life would take that was determined at a decisive moment precisely by the street song last on everyone's lips?', despite much, rightly sceptical doubt about the continued potency and eficacy of popular music as an arena of critique and as an engine of possibility, here we are nevertheless tentatively promoting popular music as a model for contemporary art and artists interested in finding ways to use the past and history in search of a valid means of practising, and of positioning a practice.

Much of our freedom and hope is so often captured and curtailed by a nexus of capitalism, consumerism, and technology. The very words we write are even anticipated and completed for us by forms of predictive text, symbolic of a burgeoning post-human regime. And yet we still have our ears, our voices, and our bodies with which we are able to listen, discern, choose, sing and dance, and then perhaps use the very same networked consumerism and technology (imposed upon us moment by moment) to send our own voices and messages back out into and across the world, even if as mere 'messages in bottles', i.e., even if we cannot plan or predict how they will be heard or whether they will have any significant affect.

Thus, it might just be that a song, a lyric, or for that matter a riff or a beat can still today 'determine the form of a life', particularly – according to Benjamin – if and when they occupy that slightly uncanny hinterland between the new and the forgotten that he refers to as 'the outmoded'.

Notes

1 *Surrealism, The Last Snapshot of the European Intelligentsia,* in: Benjamin, W. (2000), pp. 225–239.
2 Benjamin, W. (2000), p. 229.
3 Benjamin, W. (1968), pp. 253–264.
4 Breton, A. (1988).
5 André Breton discovered the phrase while reading *Les Chants de Maldoror* by poet Comte de Lautréamont.
6 Ekardt, P. (2020).
7 An interesting link is suggested here to artist Cao Fei's video *Whose Utopia?,* discussed in chapter 5 of this book.
8 See www.imdb.com/title/tt0062480/.
9 Benjamin, W. (1968), pp. 59–68.
10 Potter, D. (P. Haggard, Dir.) (2004); Potter, D. (J. Amiel, Dir.) (1986); Potter, D. (R. Rye, Di.) (2010). See www.imdb.com/title/tt0077060/?ref_=fn_al_tt_2; www.imdb.com/title/tt0090521/?ref_=fn_al_tt_2.
11 Benjamin's contemporary and colleague Siegfried Kracauer also featured, in his book *The Salaried Masses,* a female secretary of a 1920s office, nicknamed 'Cricket' because she knew by heart and 'chirped' all the latest hits, all day long, and to such an extreme that Kracauer claimed that, rather than her knowing the songs, the songs knew her. Kracauer, S. (1998) pp. 70–71.
12 A theme also explored in my own artists' self-published books: O'Kane, P. (2017, 2018) *Technologies of Romance Parts I & II.* London: eeodo.
Reynolds, S. (2011).
13 *radio.garden.*

Bibliography

Benjamin, W. (1968) *Illuminations.* New York: Schocken Books.
Benjamin, W. (2000) *One Way Street.* London: Verso.
Breton, A. (1988) *Mad love (L'amour fou).* Lincoln: University of Nebraska Press.
Ekardt, P. (2020) *Benjamin on fashion* [electronic resource]. London: Bloomsbury.
Kracauer, S. (1998) *The Salaried Masses – Duty and Distraction in Weimar Germany.* London: Verso.
O'Kane, P. (2017, 2018) *Technologies of Romance Parts I & II.* London: eeodo.
Potter, D. (P. Haggard, Dir.) (2004) *Pennies from Heaven.* London: BBC.
Potter, D. (J. Amiel, Dir.) (1986) *The Singing Detective.* London: BBC.
Potter, D. (R. Rye, Dir.) (2010) *Karaoke.* UK: Acorn Media.
Reynolds, S. (2011) *Retromania, Pop Culture's Addiction to Its Own Past.* London: Faber & Faber.

14

BEGUILING MEMORIES

Memory palaces, wunderkammers, Proust, and *La Jetée*

The past and history are different things. Memory is distinguishable from that which is remembered. One of the great, canonic artworks of modernity is Marcel Proust's novel, the title of which is usually translated into English as either *Remembrance of Things Past*, or *In Search of Lost Time*.[1] We might ask how and why memory meets modernity in Proust's *magnum opus*, and what is the special relationship between memory and the modern?

Elsewhere in this book we have noted that, while pre-modern societies might well have archived, hoarded, and collected for their own reasons, the museum is a peculiar expression of modern societies. To have a museum is to be modern, and *vice versa*.[2] The most modern (or first to be modern) of societies, set the pace and establish standards regarding museums that other societies, making their own way into modernism, necessarily followed and still follow today.

There, in the 'case' of the museum, a form of remembrance is utilised in order to separate the modern from something other than modern – presumably the pre- or non-modern. Until of course there comes a (possibly postmodern) time in modern societies when they begin to build museums *of the* modern: of modern art, modern design, of modern this or that, and even museums of the future, a museum of Sci-Fi, and of course a 'museum of everything'.[3]

A major public museum recently built in Seoul, South Korea is titled *The National Museum of Korean Contemporary History*, a name that brings two of the key words in our own title ('contemporary' and 'history') into a slightly awkward union.[4] If we are here to write and to read 'History in Contemporary Art and Culture', then what might 'contemporary history' mean? It is worth considering, but fortunately I can report that a visit to the museum in question confirmed a suspicion that it is in fact a museum whose remit is to cover relatively recent, i.e., 20th century and mainly post-World War II Korean history.

DOI: 10.4324/9781003230632-16

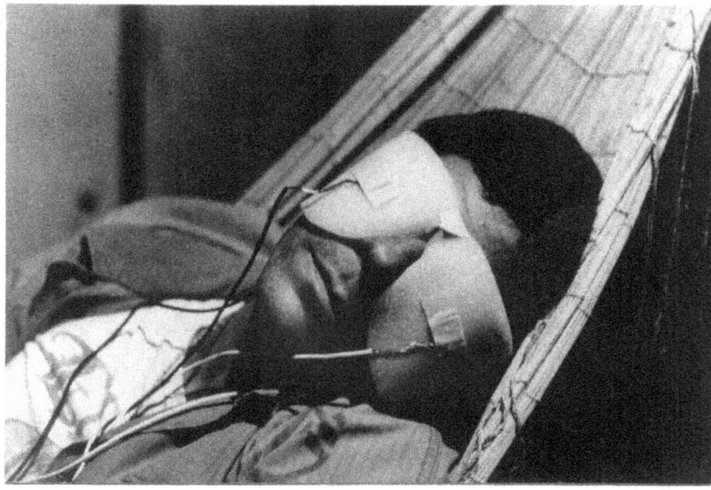

FIGURE 14.1 Chris Marker, still from *La Jetee* (1962) movie. Courtesy of Argos Films.

Proust's great experimental novel of memory may have been influenced by other variously scientific experiments by other modern novelists, like Zola, Flaubert, and Tolstoy. However, Proust saw memory as crucial and central to the making of a modern novel, as a medium in which his writing would be steeped, perhaps because modernism, in seeing itself as progressive, dynamic, and forward-looking, is thereby, albeit inadvertently, delivered into a new, intrinsic, and special relationship with the past and with memory (just as we can see modernism inadvertently producing a proliferation of 'the outmoded' as a corollary to the proliferation of the new).

Roland Barthes, in his influential 1967 essay *The Death of the Author*, pointed out that Proust's novel ends at the moment that it becomes possible for the protagonist to write it:

> Proust himself, despite the apparently psychological character of what are called his analyses, was visibly concerned with the task of inexorably blurring, by an extreme subtilisation, the relation between the writer and his characters; by making of the narrator not he who has seen and felt, nor even he who is writing, but he who is going to write (the young man in the novel- but, in fact, how old is he and who is he? – wants to write but cannot; the novel ends when writing at last becomes possible), Proust gave modern writing its epic.[5]

Thus, a circle is both opened and closed, a bubble is formed in which we find a lifetime, find ourselves, and find the modern novel all newly defined by the relationship with memory, in an attempt to create a newly accurate representation of a modern consciousness as something (and as someone) steeped in memory, resulting in an unprecedented way of writing.[6]

Memory, however, is not history, and it is history that we are primarily concerned with in this book and therefore in this chapter (despite its title). Proust took 13 years to write his *Remembrance*, a period spanning the whole of World War I. It might well be that his aim was to supersede the grand historicism of a Tolstoy or Pasternak, as well as the overtly realist modernism of a Zola, and to replace them with a new and newly scientific model. Nevertheless, memory still focuses on the past, to which history of course is also turned, and so here we have a possible overlap between history and memory, a possible challenge to history from a memory that would supplant history.

And why not, after all the 19th and early 20th centuries that spanned Proust's life and career also celebrated the inventions of photography, cinema, 'talkies', and sound recordings; recording media and devices of unprecedented sophistication that were so popular in their rapid implementation, acceptance, and dissemination that they might be suspected of having had a profound influence, both on the way in which we perceive memory and the way in which we think of history too – and all of this with a combined and corresponding influence on the way human beings ultimately see themselves in terms of memory and history.

We might recall that Charles Baudelaire, in his 1846 salon essay (see Chapter 8 in this book), called for artists to attend to everyday modern subjects, objects, stories, and themes, hailing these as just as heroic and beautiful as subjects, objects, stories, and themes of and from the classical past; of and from the Renaissance; or of and from the then relatively recent Romantic period.[7] For Baudelaire, calling upon a historical consciousness was a sign of an artist's modernity, making the artist and their art modern by heightening consciousness of their own moment and event in history, a moment or event that, in being modern, was not however an exception to, or moratorium from history. And so, the modern invariably and inevitably relies upon and emerges from a historical consciousness or renewed awareness of the part that history plays in making us who and what we are, as individuals, as a society or *milieu*.

While Proust was related to the philosopher Henri Bergson (Bergson married Proust's cousin), both Proust and Bergson later influenced Gilles Deleuze and his writings on time, cinema, and the virtual. *Matter & Memory*, the title of one of Bergson's books, points to his appreciation of the more thoroughgoing part that memory might play in a modern understanding of the world as a whole.[8] However, memory is of course nothing new and Frances Yates in *The Art of Memory* also traces forms and structures by means of which things, events, etc., could be remembered in and for pre-modern times.[9] Perhaps most notably Yates reintroduces us to the model of the memory palace. The memory palace is an imaginary structure by means of which we can spatialise mnemonic devices, a bit like a virtual house or museum in our mind.[10] As such, this model might be compared with the more concrete *wunderkammer*, a typical image of Enlightenment's encyclopaedic ideals according to which it was hoped and intended that a right place could be found for everything by a systematic means that intended everything to become known, labelled, and organised into an effective and comprehensive system of knowledge.[11]

However, while the memory palace would only use an *imaginary* space as a device by means of which to remember, the *wunderkammer* is a real object, embodying, in its divided spaces, the simultaneously real and ideal aspiration to control everything as known, as knowable – as knowledge.

Before ending this chapter, we can briefly invoke here another reputedly classic artwork, long a staple of undergraduate art students' cultural diets. Chris Marker's *La Jetée* (1962) is a 28-minute movie made up almost entirely of black and white still images, plus a few frames of cine film, all overlaid with a monologue and – a little like Proust's novel – ultimately leaving us suspended in a strange circularity or bubble of time as the narrative bounces between past, future, history, story, and memory.[12] There we encounter a tale that features a dramatic attempt to save a life and thus save the world, as well as a brief romantic episode staged in a museum. This scene once again allows us to consider the peculiarity of the museum as a modern means of utilising structured memory to manifest and represent our uncertain or uncomfortable relationship with modernism.[13]

It is also worth mentioning (lest we forget) the reminder given us by Jacques Derrida in his essay *Plato's Pharmacy*, that the birth of writing was accompanied by fear that writing would destroy our ability to remember.[14] Contemporary artists can hopefully take from our short chapter here a way of thinking about and using memory as a special medium, mechanism, or process capable of transforming that which is remembered. Meanwhile, we should also maintain some distance between memory and history while trying to ascertain what they do for each other, how they might work together or merely differentiate themselves.

Whether we think of Proust and Bergson, of the Renaissance-era memory palace, of the Enlightenment *wunderkammer*, of the mix of still and moving photographic images in Chris Marker's film, or even of the act of writing itself, memory can always provide us with a process and a potential for practice, as well as a content that we can examine and explore at leisure (as history), in a culture that is thoroughly and increasingly archived.

Memory, as a medium in which we are consistently steeped, will always subtly shift perceptions from the realm of pure receipts beyond the clutches of knowledge, into a mercurial, uncertain environment that offers infinite possibility and strange transformations caused by a temporary suspension of form and value.

Notes

1 Proust, M. (C.K. Scott Moncrieff, trans.) (2006).
2 I would like here to draw attention to the chapter titled *Giving Form to History* (Chapter 23 of this book, which includes a description and critique of the *Apartheid Museum* in Soweto, South Africa.
3 See https://nationalfilmandscifimuseum.com/; www.musevery.com/#main.
4 See www.much.go.kr/en/mainen.do.
5 Barthes, R. (1977) p. 144.
6 Virginia Woolf was influenced by both Proust and Henri Bergson to attempt something comparable in her experimental novel *Mrs Dalloway*.

7 Baudelaire, C. (1992) pp. 104–107.
8 Bergson, H. (2004).
9 Yates, F. (2008).
10 A model in which Calvino or Borges, and perhaps Proust might well have been interested.
11 Avidly invoked and reborn in the practices of historical artist Mark Dion.
An idea troubled and satirised in Michel Foucault's preface to his book *The Order of Things*, but also earlier in Flaubert's *Bouvard and Pecuchet*.
12 H.G. Wells' Victorian novel *The Time Machine* seems an obvious referent. Wells, H.G. (2005).
Marker, C. (dir.) (2003). See www.imdb.com/title/tt0056119/.
13 H.G. Wells' 19th-century novel *The Time Machine* might also be an influence and/or precursor here.
14 *Plato's Pharmacy* in: Derrida, J. (1981) pp. 63–171.

Bibliography

Barthes, R. (1977) *Image Music Text*. London: Fontana.
Baudelaire, C. (1992) *Selected Writings on Art & Literature*. London: Penguin.
Bergson, H. (2004) *Matter and Memory*. New York: Dover Publications.
Derrida, J. (1981) *Dissemination*. Chicago, IL: University of Chicago Press.
Marker, C. (dir.) (2003) *La Jetée & Sans Soleil*. UK: Nouveaux Pictures.
Proust, M. (C.K. Scott Moncrieff, trans.) (2006) *Remembrance of Things Past*. Ware: Wordsworth Editions.
Wells, H.G. (2005) *The Time Machine*. London: Penguin.
Yates, F. (2008) *The Art of Memory*. London: Pimlico.

15

A MELANCHOLIC PAST-PRESENT TENSE

The novels of Kazuo Ishiguro

The last page of Kazuo Ishiguro's novel *Never Let Me Go* does well to summon up and summarise the purpose of that novel, and perhaps of all modern novels.[1] In Walter Benjamin's essay *The Storyteller* he takes pains to distance the novel from the more ancient tradition of storytelling, and suggests that while a good story has a moral, the modern novel, written by and for a single, lone person, inevitably deals with the meaning of life.[2]

Furthermore, and for related reasons, the novel's ending – sometimes explicitly signalled *FINIS* – differs in clarity and purpose from the way in which a traditional storyteller might bring their own story to an end. The traditional storyteller's story might well invite another story to be told by another teller. The novel, however, is much more a world of its own, enclosed within covers, written by someone in isolated circumstances, and read by the same. And this has a profound influence on its meaning, its purpose, and its ending, which in some way needs to culminate and distil, in a single moment of closure everything that the novel has been for and been about.

Barthes wrote of Proust's epic *Remembrance of Things Past* (see Chapter 14 of this book) that its great achievement lies in the fact that it told the story of someone who, only at the conclusion of the novel, is at last capable of writing the novel that we have just read.[3] Benjamin meanwhile quotes a closing passage from Flaubert's *Sentimental Education* to make his own points.[4] We all know one or two endings to novels that we wouldn't change for the world, and which may even seem to surpass the achievements of the novel as a whole – F. Scott Fitzgerald's concluding line to *The Great Gatsby* comes to mind: 'So we beat on, boats against the current, borne back ceaselessly into the past'.[5]

Like Ishiguro's last page, this last sentence does everything a novel's conclusion should do in allowing a thoughtful moment of reflection before breaking the spell that has been cast (since the novel's opening line) on reader and writer alike by the

DOI: 10.4324/9781003230632-17

event of the novel at hand (Shakespeare's concluding line for *The Tempest* also comes to mind). These examples might also remind us of our inescapable suspension in time, in between life and death, of the vagaries of memory, and of the mysteries of life and death.

Movie director Francois Truffaut achieved something similar to Proust, Fitzgerald and Ishiguro when, closing his early, charming, autobiographical work *400 Blows* (1959) he has the child protagonist run across a wide beach to the edge of the sea and then suddenly freeze with the frame, changing from movie to still as he turns to camera, simultaneously conjuring the word *FIN* to appear.[6] In that moment the director seems to share with us a new existence and corresponding new existentialism born of the new technology of the movie-camera/editing-machine nexus. In moving from moving image to still in conclusion, a movie becomes simultaneously a life and a death, incorporating the childhood that the film has portrayed but also the entirety of the child's life-to-come, however long or short that might be. Thus, a new pathos, one provided again by new technology, pierces our heart (and it may be worth noting here that Chris Marker's *La Jetée* [see Chapter 14 of this book] also trades on a special emotive relationship between the black and white still image and the black and white moving image).

All the examples above tell us something, not just about endings, novels, or movies but about life and experience in general as mysteriously steeped in the vagaries emerging from our relationship with time's passing. Considering Ishiguro's novel as a whole, then others of his novels, and perhaps all that he has written, we gain a sense of a pervasive, melancholic, past-present tense, a narration that is always, in some way reflecting, even while participating in the now, and while seemingly also moving 'forward' into the future of a narrative shrouded in feint gloom.

Today, Ishiguro plays down the Japanese roots that he successfully and consciously explored and exploited at the start of his career, and yet the slightly melancholic and equally matter-of-fact aesthetic he so often produces in his rather un-dramatic narratives is reminiscent of the Japanese aesthetics of *Wabi Sabi* and/or *Mono No Aware*. Interestingly, Ishiguro has claimed that a strong influence on his writing style might have been the Japanese Manga comics sent regularly by his grandparents in his early years in England, and if we watch some Anime movies (a moving-image equivalent, or off-shoot of Manga) we might indeed recognise something Ishiguro-like about the strangely deadpan Romanticism they can often espouse.[7]

Anyone who read Ishiguro's *Never Let Me Go* and then felt disappointed by the way in which the movie version manifested the tale, might have preferred an Anime or Manga version that could perhaps have used drawings to portray the characters slightly less specifically than they are once inhabited by the recognisable and perhaps predictable faces of rising – and consequently ubiquitous – British movie stars.

Anime and Anime have their very own self-consciousness, as particular forms of media, and just as Benjamin draws our attention to the particular relationship that stories, novels, and movies might have to their endings, so Anime and Manga are infused with the influence upon their narratives of the art and the technology of drawing. Drawing and narrative (which might, in a Manga comic, include sophisticated use of variable, interrelated frames to denote different aspects of temporality) combine in a special way that delivers atmosphere – that mysterious concept we know and experience but cannot explain. And this atmosphere itself is, in some way, Romanticist in the sense that it implicates narrativity, charging a space with a sense of eventuality, of presence, of pending events or of some trace of a past event.

Anime tales invariably feature youthful protagonists who reflect the main audience's own adolescent experience, and so it is perhaps inevitable that these tales will negotiate profound conundrums of existence, purpose, and destiny that adolescents are both young enough and old enough to believe they can, either subjectively or objectively, solve. All of this takes place against the backdrop of a quietly repressed fear that life – or the life that 21st-century capitalist democracy expects us to lead – may be more 'flat', predictable, dull, uneventful, repetitive, and meaningless than the audience had previously imagined.

Thinking back to Ishiguro's characters and their way of responding to their environment (whether in *The Remains of the Day*, *Never Let Me Go*, *The Buried Giant*, *The Unconsoled*, *Klara and the Sun,* etc.), we might see our description of Anime, its characters and narratives, as relevant, comparable, or similar.[8]

However, above, we briefly mentioned two aspects of Japanese aesthetics that are also important to embrace and understand, if only as an important extension of, or challenge to certain dominant and long-established European aesthetics. As an aspect of imperial modernism, aesthetic styles, tendencies and values have oozed out from Europe and the USA, over and into every other global culture, technology, economy, and aesthetic. *Wabi Sabi* and *Mono No Aware* differ from modernist aesthetics, and differ also from each other but could be said to converge, to become evident and even prevalent in Ishiguro's novels, at least in the form of a certain pathos and special beauty extruded from aesthetic austerity.

In Ishiguro's *The Remains of the Day*, the butler driving his Ford motor car to England's West Country is able to see English landscape in a stereotypical, simulacral, idyllic and slightly nationalistic way, just as it was all introduced to him by images in a patriotic popular guide book. Meanwhile, in the final page of *Never Let Me Go*, we see that the much represented and Romanticised English landscape can also be appreciated, according to what Charles Baudelaire once called 'new forms of passion' (also translated as 'new emotions'), i.e., appreciated not for its wild drama or quaint prettiness but for its littered and over-cultivated flatness which nevertheless draws forth the aesthetic response of a special kind of pathos in which the subject empathises with the universal entropy that will eventually 'rubbish' everything[9] (Robert Smithson, seen in Chapter 7 of this book, would have been interested in the same).

Ishiguro's books, their characters and narratives, never seem to stop feeling conscious of time-past, time-lost, time as elusive, enigmatic, and ephemeral – hence our necessarily emotive and aesthetic response to time, a response which might, in itself, be regarded as a kind of 'patina'.[10] An aesthetic response to the past seems to be pervasive and irresistible. One national newspaper currently includes within its virtual culture pages 'galleries' of recently discovered photographs from bygone decades. These nostalgic cascades are designed to be avidly clicked though by all who relish a familiar and feint pleasurable pain upon witnessing the strange beauty of a special form of irretrievable loss that was perhaps inaugurated by the invention of photography – that mass melancholia-machine now so ever-present and embedded in our lives as to have become almost immanent.

Marcel Proust saw time's loss as the potential core of a modern aesthetic, the site and substitute perhaps for a reckoning between man and modern godlessness. Proust is of course a writer's writer, one whom every novelist feels a duty to investigate in order to win their own license to write. Kazuo Ishiguro's rather deadpan writing style doesn't show explicit signs of Proust's more decorative influence, and yet, as we have already suggested, Ishiguro imbues his novels with – and we might say steeps them in – an acute awareness of passing time and lost time, lost opportunity and loss *per se*.[11]

When Walter Benjamin wrote of *The Storyteller* and compared this ancient role with that of the modern novelist, he stressed the material influence of the novelist's inescapable dialogue with a given number of bound pages that produce a foreseeable point at which a novel will and must always end. Benjamin seemed to imply that this precipice, the end of a novel beyond which none can go, is akin to a modern, secular death, and thus to the ultimate loss of time. However, in our examples here, from Ishiguro, Proust, Fitzgerald, Trouffaut, etc., it might be seen that artists can attempt to cheat this death by writing or editing in such a way as to produce affects, atmospheres, and plays with tense and temporality that place us – while in the midst and in the company of the book, movie, or other work of art – within a bubble of timelessness, a place where history no-longer determines experience but where art shapes and defines a particular quality of time, or even a short-lived escape from it.

Notes

1 Ishiguro, K. (2005).
2 Benjamin, W. (1968) pp. 83–110.
3 Proust, M. (C.K. Scott Moncrieff, trans.) (2006).
4 Flaubert, G. (1941).
5 Fitzgerald, F.S. (1950) p. 188.
6 See www.imdb.com/title/tt0053198/.
7 Shinkai, M. & Hagiwara, Y. (2018).
8 Ishiguro, K. (2005, 2010, 2013, 2016, 2020).
9 Baudelaire, C. (1992) p. 106.
10 E.g.,

> … the sheen of older things connects us with the past in ways that shiny products of modern technology simply cannot. And since older things tend to be made from natural materials, to deal with them helps us to realise our closest connections with the natural environment.

From: https://plato.stanford.edu/entries/japanese-aesthetics/.

11 In one televised interview Ishiguro also described (slightly elusively and inconclusively) a period of feverish illness at a crucial point in his career, during which he claimed he found Proust's most renowned novel with his foot, caught up within the covers at the end of his sick bed.

Bibliography

Baudelaire, C. (1992) *Selected Writings on Art & Literature*. London: Penguin.

Benjamin, W. (1968) *Illuminations*. New York: Schocken Books.

Fitzgerald, F.S. (1950) *The Great Gatsby*. London: Penguin.

Flaubert, G. (1941) *Sentimental Education*. London: J. M. Dent & Sons.

Ishiguro, K. (2005) *Never Let Me Go*. London: Faber & Faber.

Ishiguro, K. (2010) *The Remains of the Day*. London: Faber & Faber.

Ishiguro, K. (2013) *The Unconsoled*. London: Faber & Faber.

Ishiguro, K. (2016) *The Buried Giant*. London: Faber & Faber.

Ishiguro, K. (2020) *Klara & the Sun*. London: Faber & Faber.

Proust, M. (C.K. Scott Moncrieff, trans.) (2006) *Remembrance of Things Past*. Ware, Hertforsdhire: Wordsworth Editions.

Shinkai, M. (dir.) & Yoshihiro, H. (prod.) (2004) *The Place Promised in Our Early Days – Voices of a Distant Star*. Japan: Anime Limited

16

FOLK TALES AND FAIRY TALES

Calvino, cunning and high spirits, hearts, chains, and liberties

If we open Italo Calvino's collection of *Italian Folk Tales* and perhaps read one tale per day (they are short and spectacular), we might feel ourselves and our world to be imbued with a new sense of possibility.[1] In these stories, anything can happen, at any time, and usually does. However, they are also repetitive, and we soon get used to the motifs of the three sons or three daughters, of the King's daughter, the beautiful princess, the castle, the poor old couple, etc., and the stories also tend to end happily, often with a promising marriage.[2] Thus, at the same time as offering us an escape into a pre-modern world, where science, logic, and reason seem to have been less influential, these stories also remind us of the importance of their structural elements, the bones of a story that stop it from dissipating, make it memorable, and thus available to an oral tradition.

Walter Benjamin's essay on storytelling can be found in the collection of his writings titled *Illuminations*, which also contains his *Theses on the Philosophy of History*.[3] In this collection we can therefore find Benjamin's unique mix of intellect, knowledge, critique and creative imagination brought to bear in various ways on the concept of history, both taking a philosophical approach to history and comparing history with story. At one point *The Storyteller* essay lingers on folk tales and fairy tales and suggests that they form a crucial foundation for all of us.[4] As children, fairy tales (often repetitively told) teach us how to confront difficulties using what Benjamin calls 'cunning and high spirits'. These two attributes might well be useful and attractive to the contemporary artist, and we might see them at work elsewhere in this book, e.g. in the art of Folkert de Jong, Jimmie Durham, Hew Locke, Sigrid Holmwood, or Robert Smithson. Meanwhile, it might also be seen that 'cunning and high spirits' relate to the process and practice of making, telling, and writing stories, as well as to the imaginative form of critique for which Benjamin is revered and renowned.

DOI: 10.4324/9781003230632-18

Benjamin historicises both storytelling and the fairy tale when he suggests that *all* stories emerge from something like fairy tales; tales which are ultimately ways of keeping what he calls 'myth' at bay – and by 'myth' Benjamin appears to mean all of our fear (ancient, primeval or modern) of all of the unknown; all of our fear of all of our ignorance and limitations; all of our fear of the night, of darkness and of shadows, real and metaphorical.[5]

Meanwhile, in his *Theses on the Philosophy of History,* Benjamin uses the form of the aphorism – short, pithy, witty sentences or paragraphs that invite constant re-reading in order to extract their potential contents and value. This formal experimentation, typical of Benjamin's explorative *oeuvre*, then allows his aphorisms to systematically mock and critique many pre-established and presumptuous ideas concerning the form, structure, image and scale of history. Before we write history, or decide who or what belongs in history (Benjamin suggests) we need to think carefully about, and critique our assumptions concerning just what history is, or might be. And if history is not what we assumed it was then how does it differentiate itself from, or arise within modernism to apparently stand above story.

When we critique history as fundamentally, as formally, and as *archly* as Benjamin does here, we expose it to the accusation that it may not differ so much from story after all, and that history may itself be 'myth', a site of fearful ignorance as much as a site of proud knowledge. History (as myth) and its assumptions might even be something from which we need to protect ourselves with the aid of storytelling.

Italo Calvino's collected *Italian Folk Tales*; the stories collected in Germany by the Brothers Grimm; or those found within the Arabic classic *1001 Nights*, all reveal similar combinations of fantasy and repetitive structure.[6] This might be a signal to contemporary artists who need not only 'cunning and high spirits' as a freedom to play, experiment, and speculate, but also an awareness of, and attention to, the kinds of structural elements that are needed to make a credible contemporary work, practice, or career. Calvino, having collected and published the Folk Tales relatively early in his career subsequently developed the kinds of formal experimentation for which he is perhaps more famous and which he shares with the experimental literary group named Oulipo (also influenced by the 'magic realism' of Jorge Luis Borges). In Calvino's Oulipian works, and perhaps most notably in his *If on a Winter's Night a Traveller …* we can see how freedom and imagination (anything can happen and probably does) are productively harnessed to a strong, self-imposed structure.[7]

Here, slipping once again into autobiographical anecdote, the name of a German postmodern rock band, that I encountered in the early 1980s, comes to mind – *Freiwillge Selbstkontolle* translates into English as *Voluntary Self Control.*[8] We might discuss reasons why voluntary self control might be a typically postmodern strategy for an artist, but for the time-being simply note that the influential (perhaps proto-postmodern) German philosopher Friedrich Nietzsche alluded to something similar when he wrote words to the effect of: 'If you can chain down your heart you can give your spirit infinite liberties'.[9] The point here is perhaps that freedom, imagination and play are not enough for the philosopher, not enough for the teller of tales, and not enough for the contemporary artist. We need 'high spirits' but we also need the 'cunning' that might be found in those formal and structural elements that we might also think of as 'strategy'.

To access what Nietzsche calls 'infinite liberties', or maximum freedom, we, paradoxically or contradictorily need to 'chain down our heart'. This can be interpreted as necessarily imposing (if only to protect ourselves from our own passions, desires, and weaknesses) our own structures and parameters on those 'infinite liberties'. The postmodern German rock band, *Voluntary Self Control* concur then with Nietzsche's sentiment while also helping to illustrate Italo Calvino's Oulipean methods (influenced by fairy tales and folk tales) of harnessing our freedom and imagination to strict structures that, rather than confine our works, will make them memorable, repeatable, and knowable.

Peering into the worlds of the Brothers Grimm, into *Italian Folk Tales* or into *1001 Arabian Nights,* invariably invites us to think and create in a non-, post-, pre-, or perhaps altermodern way, and this in turn might help us identify just what 'modern' is or means. One story that modernism (as a cultural paradigm) tells about itself is that it is *not* a story. It prefers to think of itself as history and therefore sanctioned by an objective, overarching, Enlightenment institution. Modern people might believe that we have grown and progressed by setting (mere) stories aside as imaginative entertainments while pursuing the superior agenda of 'real' history. However, Benjamin's enquiries, both into storytelling and into the philosophy of history (separately or in combination), open a deeper, longer, more difficult scenario, one that locates history within the greater, more ancient realm of storytelling; or perhaps locates history outside storytelling as a temporary, modern exception to the more ancient and universal default paradigm of storytelling.

This could have serious consequences for modernism as a cultural paradigm, and these potential consequences are what makes Benjamin's theses so profound, particularly if considered in conjunction with his *Storyteller essay.*

It may even be these very 'serious consequences' that ushered in postmodernism. Modernism now appears to be built or based upon a fiction or myth of its own rather than on the scientifically provable 'knowledge'; knowledge that is its own toolbox and criteria but knowledge that it might like to claim as its firm foundation in asserting superiority over unhistorical story-based cultures of pre- or non-modern others.

This kind of critique of history is already a staple of postmodern thought (making Benjamin yet another proto-postmodernist). It is the kind of idea that made or makes postmodernism a paradigm shift (almost impossible to truly and adequately comprehend and accommodate) rather than a mere change of style.

In 1980s academia, books appeared with titles like *On the Museum's Ruins*, *Has Modernism Failed?,* and *The End of History*, but Benjamin's small, knotty, 1930s *Theses on the Philosophy of History* had already considered such unthinkable thoughts.[10] By means of his unique use of creative imagination, allied to knowledge, study, research, intellect, and of course his artful writing (all of which we might describe as 'cunning and high spirits'), Benjamin opened a wide range of possibilities for us to inherit (thus also giving concrete form to his beguiling assertion, within the theses, that 'our coming was expected on earth'). Today these possibilities ask to be kept open and alive for imagined further and future generations.

Nicolas Bourriaud called history 'the last continent to be explored' for contemporary artists, and indeed, history, story, memory and tradition together provide us with seemingly limitless possibilities, with an arena in which we are able to deploy and to experiment with both the nature and the degree of our freedom.[11] As we have seen above, fairy tale and folk tale do not only provide us with models of freedom but also with lessons in life, ways to survive, and a model of self-imposed structures that will enable us to glean the maximum benefit from our freedoms.

Notes

1 Calvino, I. (1981).
2 Angela Carter, notably in *The Bloody Chamber*, revised such stories from a late 20th-century feminist perspective, parodying, expanding, and transforming them, both to reveal their patriarchal and misogynist base and to rewrite them as feminist parables. Carter, A. (1979).
3 Benjamin, W. (1968) pp. 253–264.
4 Benjamin, W. (1968) pp. 83–110.
5 It might be worth comparing here Benjamin's 'myth' with Jacque Lacan's concept of 'The Real'.
6 Grimm, J. & Grimm, W. (1909); Lyons, M. & Lyons, U. (Trans.) (2010).
7 Calvino, I. (1993).
8 See www.subup.com/fsk/artists.html.
9 Or: 'Bound heart, free spirit – If one binds one's heart firmly and imprisons it one can allow one's spirit many liberties.' Nietzsche, F.W. (1990) p. 93 (No. 87).
10 Referring to: Crimp, D. & Lawler, L. (1993); Gablik, S. (2004); Fukuyama, F. (1992).
11 Meanwhile noting that Ariella Azoulay and others might baulk at the apparent but unintended colonial implications of Bourriaud's implied acquisitiveness. Bourriaud, N. (2009) pp. 11–24.

Bibliography

Benjamin, W. (1968) *Illuminations*. New York: Schocken Books.
Bourriaud, N. (2009) *Altermodern – The Third Tate Triennial*. London: Tate.
Calvino, I. (1981) *Italian Folktales*. New York: Harcourt Brace Jovanovich.
Calvino, I. (1993) *If on a Winter's Night a Traveller*. London: Everyman's Library.
Carter, A. (1979) *The Bloody Chambe*. London: Victor Gollancz.
Crimp, D. & Lawler, L. (1993) *On the Museum's Ruins*. Cambridge, MA: MIT Press.
Fukuyama, F. (1992) *The End of History and the Last Man*. London: Hamish Hamilton.
Gablik, S. (2004) *Has Modernism Failed?* London: Thames & Hudson.
Grimm, J. & Grimm, W. (1909) *The Fairy Tales of the Brothers Grimm*. London: Constable.
Lyons, M. & Lyons, U. (Trans.) (2010) *The Arabian Nights: Tales of 1001 Nights. Volume 1*. London: Penguin.
Nietzsche, F.W. (1990) *Beyond Good and Evil (Maxims and Interludes)*. London: Penguin.

17

HISTORY OR DREAMING

Wade Davis on Jared Diamond

In January 2013 (an earlier historical epoch where and when, I recall, I found time and money enough to regularly buy and read a hard copy of a national daily newspaper) I came across a review of a new book. The reviewer's name was Wade Davis and the book was *The World Until Yesterday: What Can We Learn from Traditional Societies?* by Jared Diamond.[1] Something about Wade Davis' review made me slow down and re-read. I copied some of it out and later shared it with students of my seminar. Several years later, I am still using it as a reference, a way to help me make certain points.

Davis referred to Australian aboriginal culture. He claimed that in all of their many dialects the aboriginal Australians had no word for 'progress'. He also made the claim that the aboriginal Australians had no words and concepts for the temporal and linear procession of past, present, and future – but let us just stay with progress.

Davis claimed that this apparent obliviousness regarding progress pointed to a kind of radical ultra-conservatism, a conservatism of the most desirable kind, at least in that the aboriginal Australians, rather than being motivated by the central and essentially modern idea of progress, were guided by an aspiration to conserve, and leave the land and the planet as it was at the moment of its creation.[2]

It may be unwise, unjust, and incongruous for either myself or Wade Davis to in any way attempt to represent (and inevitably misrepresent) a radically other and different culture and belief system, of which, I suspect, we know and *can* only ever know very little. And yet it is hard to resist taking up and trying, at least, to emulate some aspects of a way of thinking so unlike that which has shaped and guided our own culture. Radically other ways of thinking might proffer and provide us with a glimpse of a radically different perspective on many of our most central and fundamental assumptions about what we call 'history'.

DOI: 10.4324/9781003230632-19

Obliviousness, contempt, or total disregard for the notion of progress brings into question, and into new light, all those uses of history that lie at the heart of the modern culture that contemporary art and artists might presume to represent. Let us imagine a society without the idea of progress at its heart. It might be a society no longer titillated constantly by the new; by rolling, breaking, hourly and daily news; by trending tweets and the season's new look. Furthermore, it might be a society (if we could even call it that) in which human beings no longer see themselves as primary, privileged, technologised, and entitled to use the planet's resources as they wished, but rather see themselves as revering and deferring to the planet's own ways and means, its unique forces, rhythms, demands, and requirements.

A society or community without a word for, or concept of 'progress' might be a society whose interpretation of evident change sees meaningless (in the most affirmative sense) cycles and circles, of birth, death, and rebirth, rather than a dynamic, thrusting teleological and technological line forging into the future and by this means providing meaning and purpose.

Gleaning further disruptive thoughts from Davis' review, if we as a society and as individuals could dispense with the habitual orienting schema of 'past-present-future' – something so apparently fundamental to our perception and understanding that it is practically impossible to imagine existing without it – what kind of understanding and experience would we be left with, or gifted with? It might be a kind of schizophrenic horror and perceptual crisis in which we are unable to escape a constant now; or perhaps a blissful immanence in which we never feel the need to appeal to anything other than that which is (not what was, nor what might be). Either way, our reasoning and the meaning we give to experience would be fundamentally altered – partly by being stripped of narrative, as Martin McQuillan states in his introductory essay to *The Narrative Reader*:

> What if there were no more stories? What if stories, contrary to narrative theory's fundamental article of faith (that narrative, like love, is all around us), were coming, or had already come, to an end? How would we know? What would we do? How would we identify or constitute the 'we' of these questions?[3]

As suggested above, such truly radical (and here 'radical' etymologically alludes to 'roots') ideas seem impossible for modern people to embrace or put into practice, and yet if we take Davis' assertions or claims seriously, we must at least imagine the alterity (the radical difference) of peoples and persons who live, or strive to live, always confronted by the apparently inexorable and innate hegemony of modernism. While possibly 'doing damage to our thought' (as Jacques Derrida has said), trying to accommodate such alterity might at least allow us to *imagine* alternatives to the fundamental assumptions of our modern thinking and to simultaneously reveal to ourselves the idiosyncrasies, shortfalls, and limits of our own structures, representations, and perceptions. We might then at least play with these radically other thoughts – as we are trying to do here – even if we are not able to really embrace, imbibe, or inhabit them.

Something similar happens when confronting a certain element in the work of Walter Benjamin. Writing in his *Theses on the Philosophy of History* Benjamin took a playful approach to the profoundly serious task demanded by his title.[4] One thing that is sure about Benjamin's *Theses on the Philosophy of History* is that they strive to avoid any usual philosophical method, and so, we might say, they pursue the aim of creating theses that cannot themselves be regarded as 'historical', in that they cannot become established or dogmatic, or in that their aphoristic quality creates a volatile and playful arena, productive of further questioning rather than productive of anything resembling a conclusion.

In theorising and critiquing 'the' philosophy of history, Benjamin confronted something crucial and central to modernity, as well as coming face to face – it could be said – with the ultimate focus of his life's work. Like some spirited but ill-equipped anti-hero (Kurosawa's *Samurai* comes to mind), using only the apparently inadequate means of a basketful of short paragraphs, Benjamin confronted, did battle with, and we might even say defeated the famously formative and formidable historical schemas of Marx and of Hegel.

If we read Benjamin's theses carefully, we begin to see that, rather than tell us what history is he deconstructs habitual and ingrained assumptions and perceptions about history's form, motive, agency, dynamism, and purpose. Along the way, Marx and Hegel are jostled and provoked by the suggestion that the systems, schemas, edifices, and legacies they created were built on dubious, presumptuous, perhaps simplistic, wishful and we might say all-too-modern (though not 'altermodern') foundations.

To jump, as we have done here, from Wade Davis' review to Benjamin's theses might seem to create a surprising connection or incongruous juxtaposition, but hopefully it can be seen that both confront us with similar challenges to our habitual evaluations of history and progress. Benjamin, repeatedly – though always subtly – mocked (and here we might recall his admiration for Dada) the assumption that history has a particular purpose, shape, or direction, even though all Communist, Socialist, and Left-leaning hopes must, it seems (and blindly if necessary), believe in and depend upon this.

Benjamin also compares the implicit teleology of history, in both Marx and Hegel, with the kind of theological promise that modern rationalists like Marx might claim to have eschewed in their desire to attain the heights of reason, and to from there see, shape, and determine the politics of modernity.

Therefore, Benjamin in his critique (and if Davis is correct aboriginal Australians too) provides a possible means by and with which to radically undermine and question history and its 'use' in ways that are valuable, for artists especially and more broadly for modern and contemporary society. Such fundamental disruptions are valuable because they are likely to make us think, work, imagine, create, and critique for ourselves these and other fundamental assumptions by which we live, thereby revealing and suggesting new, different, and other assumptions or assertions by means of which we might not yet, but nevertheless might also or otherwise live.

Then again, and if I might conclude this essay with a slightly humbled *coda*, these optimistic statements of my own might yet lead me, or you the reader, to question whether perhaps such enthusiastic affirmations should be tempered, as they may just be further examples of an all-too-ingrained, progressive and modern way of thinking.

Notes

1 See www.theguardian.com/books/2013/jan/09/history-society.
2 Acknowledging that my own cultural distance and differentiation from Aboriginal Culture makes it impossible, or very difficult at least, to understand whether a word like 'planet' is at all applicable here. See also reference to *Earthrise* in Chapter 4 of this book.
3 McQuillan, M. (ed.) (2000) p. 1.
4 Benjamin, W. (1968) pp. 253–264.

Bibliography

Benjamin, W. (1968) *Illuminations*. New York: Schocken Books.
McQuillan, M. (ed.) (2000) *The Narrative Reader*. UK: Routledge.

18

'I DON'T BELIEVE IN THINGS'

Gilles Deleuze, history, and event

Monuments might mark events and might mark people associated with significant events. All of this singles out those people and those events and makes them special. However, what happens to history and to the monument if we come to see *everything* as event, including even ourselves? That is what the radical French philosopher Gilles Deleuze suggests in several interrelated texts that I came across while studying for my masters degree (MA) in Visual Cultures.[1]

Even as an undergraduate I had found myself beginning to explore the idea of an artwork as an event rather than as an object, image, or idea. My work at that time involved the display of large-scale, pre-cut, adhesive messages thrown up on college walls in arresting places. They would appear unexpectedly, sometimes overnight, remain for a while, and disappear again. I noticed, after a few attempts, that though I laboured over the words I wanted to use, as well as the design, font, letter-spacing, and their location, it was in fact the event itself, the event of their installation, appearance, and disappearance that thrilled me most. At the time, I didn't have a vocabulary of 'event' with which to articulate and contextualise what I was doing and thinking, and nor did my tutors or peers. Now, however, I see that I may have been toying with what I have come to call 'the event paradigm'.

The event for me is not really about its content, nor about the one who presumes to create the event (e.g., the artist); rather, the event is pre-subjective and non-human, immanent and non-representational. It is as much about the event's anticipation and recollection of it as it is about its execution and temporary manifestation. The event, it seems to me, was always going to happen and will also always have happened (Nietzsche's concept of 'eternal return' might be helpful here). Furthermore, there is no clear dividing line between the event's anticipation, manifestation, and recollection. I think the event is perhaps also Bergsonian and/or possibly Einsteinian in this way.

DOI: 10.4324/9781003230632-20

Bergson and 20th-century science were important influences on French philosopher of the event Gilles Deleuze, who has shaken philosophy up, partly by mining its past and partly by incorporating 20th-century scientific developments. Abhorring abstraction, Deleuze nevertheless revels in head-spinning re-descriptions of existence and experience, partly in terms of becoming and event. He creates philosophy at what often seems to be a molecular level, where every 'thing' is as temporal as it is spatial; is an event defined not by extensity but by intensity – speeds, hesitations, and other forms of behaviour.

Like many of my peers on my MA programme, my studies were laced with, and motivated by a certain desire to find a personal specialism, as well as the masters students' sense of having one last chance in the role of student to intellectually and academically 'get to the bottom of things'. However, I soon noticed that whenever I used the word 'things' as a preconception it began to attract inverted commas. These commas showed me that 'thing' was no longer a word I could take for granted and was henceforth under suspicion.

More and more often it seemed that 'thing' was not the correct word for what I wanted to express or investigate. I noted that Martin Heidegger had written some authoritative but arcane works on *das ding* (the thing); however, while I found his writing and thinking beguiling, and occasionally inspiring, it was also often impenetrable to me.

Probably all of us use the idea of a 'thing' as a habitual baseline, default, or catch-all term when we can't be more specific. Or we may vaguely refer to any-thing and every-thing as if, in our language our philosophical enquiries and our experiences, the 'thing' was that 'bottom' to which we, as philosophical enquirers, want to get. However, one of the reasons that the 'thing' started to attract inverted commas for me was that some experiences and aspects of living didn't seem to fit the model of 'things', e.g., images might not be things, the virtual realm might not be made up of things, ideas might not be things, and certain other experiences might not be adequately or appropriately described as 'things'.

At that time, myself, my fellow students, and my professors all seemed obsessed with deciphering the legacy and meaning of texts by Gilles Deleuze. It was while reading Deleuze that I came across the idea that we could substitute the thing, and in a way surpass and accommodate the model of the thing, with the model of the event. That is to say, in my desire to get to the bottom of things, I went, with Deleuze, beyond 'things' and reached a new, more useful, 'bottomlessness' where it was the (intensive) event and not the (extensive) thing that provided a paradigm for understanding what I had previously thought of as objects, images, ideas, and many other ingredients of experience.

In one short text Deleuze responded to a question concerning what is a human subject today, e.g., is it a person, an identity, a sophisticated animal, a linguistic being, etc.? Deleuze answered that a subject today is akin to 'a wind, a season, or 5 o'clock'.[2] In another interview, Deleuze simply confessed: '… you see, I don't believe in things'.[3]

I began to gain a picture of Deleuze's universe in which there are no extensive objects but rather a swirl of intensive behaviours (something like a sky populated with moving billowing clouds), not clearly divided into extensive and exclusive things, but differentiated as events.

Remaining unromantically true to 20th-century discoveries in the sciences, Deleuze saw many well-worded philosophical ideas being displaced and rendered outmoded by an image of a universe now composed of energies and behaviours rather than conveniently divided into discreet objects identified by language and taxonomised as knowledge.

Interestingly, if, like Deleuze, we stop believing in things and embrace an event-based paradigm, we might see how (intensive) events can exist, or rather take place, 'one in the other' (a phrase that occurs occasionally in Deleuze's writings and which was once the name of a Deleuze-inspired London art space). (Intensive) events are not exclusive in the way that (extensive) things are. Events territorialise only to then deterritorialise, perhaps offering us hope of re-understanding and renegotiating our all-too territorial, conflicted, and exclusive world. And in this way Deleuze also seems to stress the porosity, interrelatedness, and collaborative nature of such an eventual world.

In addition to being a radical and innovative philosopher, whose works are often portrayed as futural and innovative, Deleuze is a historian. The way he pursues and uses history is by looking back through the history of philosophy and seeing various, perhaps unexplored, under-exploited, misunderstood or under-appreciated ideas that he is able to reappraise and reconnect in new ways. Together these become elements of his own dynamic (never fixed or dogmatic) philosophy.

One of the philosophers Deleuze was interested in was Leibniz, whom he has used to express his own ideas of a contemporary 'neobaroque' paradigm. Deleuze was never a postmodernist but was an influential contributor to the post-structuralist generation of creative French thought emerging in the late 1960s and whose influence became more widespread and influential at a time that coincided with the heyday of postmodernism. In Deleuze's discussions about the possibilities of a neobaroque paradigm he seemed to see, or foresee that certain ideas and models, according to which a 17th-century baroque philosophy might have operated, could be useful to us today in accommodating new and unprecedented levels of complexity (postmodernism, chaos theory, new technologies, globalisation, migration, climate change a breaking down of the established world order etc.), as well as accommodating a new appreciation of motion, process and becoming for which philosophy has thus far not adequately accounted.

If we picture a baroque sculpture or painting, or observe baroque music or dance, we can see dissymmetry, cascades, and swirls as what Deleuze (following Nietzsche) referred to as 'becomings'. Becomings imply not only a constant state of motion, change and event but also a sense of infinity, akin perhaps to a baroque, 17th-century Catholic paradigm. This is a way of picturing how events and a neobaroque model might help us understand the 21st-century world as something more temporal, motile, and fluid than we had previously thought.

In Deleuze's world, materiality is never an immobile 'thing' or 'things' but something always behaving in a certain manner, changing at a certain speed, interacting, contingent, and reciprocally defined by everything else that is also behaving thus. It might therefore be better to describe some 'thing', any 'thing' we experience as an event rather than as a 'thing'.

Even the most apparently static objects – Deleuze might implicate the relative motion and change involved in, e.g., the great pyramid, a glacier, a sand dune or a mountain – are in fact moving and becoming (often, from our own relative perspective, infinitesimally and invisibly slowly) as they flow from one state, one place, and one configuration into another (Robert Smithson and George Kubler – see chapter 7 in this book – might be interested).

Given such an eventual, neobaroque model, all becomes event, including ourselves. What we thought of and described as a 'thing' is merely a misguided or self-interested perception, a *de*ception in fact. It is a temporal delusion, a becoming, and a kind of hesitation between one temporary state and another. A thing is thus a thing only in the eye of a beholder who would like to consider their own perceptions as sovereign but who is in fact themselves equally and contemporaneously motile, perspectival, changing and hesitating, only at a differential pace or rate in a universe where all is becoming (and we might say, with respect to Nietzsche, 'returning'); where none is merely 'being' (the key modern philosophical term perhaps), and where events supplant things as a paradigm.

What might this mean then for our writing and thinking of history? Deleuze's philosophical interventions, outlined above, invite us to think of history in a neobaroque, eventual manner. In one of Deleuze's interviews he claims that one of his favourite phrases (in the book he wrote on Leibniz) is: 'There is going to be a concert tonight'.[4] If we take Deleuze at his word, we can see that this statement is indeed full of energy, potential, and promise, revealing that Deleuze's view of the world is more tensioned and ready to become than a world described more habitually (we might say anthropocentrically, and conveniently) as mere sedentary and extensive 'things'.

If Benjamin, Smithson and Kubler, the aboriginal Australians etc. can all provide us with different ways of thinking of history, then so does Deleuze, revisiting, re-interpreting, and redeploying thoughts and thinkers of the past, as well as rendering the whole of experience eventful or eventual. And the usual way in which we think of, mark, and commemorate certain events or people as exceptional surely collapses and dissolves into this universalisation of eventuality. Now, perhaps it is easier for us to see ourselves as akin to 'a wind, a season, or 5 o'clock'.

These events, that we are too, do not just exist, they *happen*, they *per*sist, they also happen to each other and occur one-in-the-other, i.e., without excluding each other, as 'things' do. This writing, as academic as I can make it, as lucid as I can make it, is also purposefully laced with personal eventualities that concede to the way in which a life in the world can operate alongside, within, outside, and beyond academic form, voice, and method. Thus, any linear, teleological form and purpose that we try to give to history also becomes an interplay of forces and events from which we cannot stand aside, judge, and organise, but in which all of our actions are embroiled and occur, as events within events within events (*sic*) *ad infinitum,* as in the infinite swirling of a baroque painted ceiling.

So where and what is history now? What form can we give it? What form does it take? Who and what is worthy of being marked, elevated, and enlarged to 'larger-than-life' proportions, made supposedly permanent and resilient, cast in bronze, or carved in stone and celebrated with a lapidary caption while our understanding of a universe composed of things, which makes it possible to think of people as things, is toppled by an alternative, eventual or neobaroque paradigm?

Notes

1 *What Is an Event?* In: Deleuze, G. (2001) pp. 76–82; *What Is Baroque?* In: Deleuze, G. (2001) pp. 27–38; Deleuze, G. (1990) pp. 156–163; *A Philosophical Concept* in: Cadava, E. (ed.) (1991) pp. 94–95.
2 *A Philosophical Concept* in: Cadava, E. (ed.) (1991) pp. 94–95.
3 *On Leibniz* in: Deleuze, G. (1990) p. 160.
4 Deleuze, G. (1990) p. 160.

Bibliography

Benjamin, W. (1968) *Illuminations*. New York: Schocken Books.
Cadava, E. (ed.) (1991) *Who Comes after the Subject*? London: Routledge.
Deleuze, G. (1990) *Negotiations*. New York: Columbia University Press.
Deleuze, G. (2001) *The Fold, Leibniz and the Baroque*. London: The Athlone Press.

PART II

Longer essays

19

DARK HORSES AND HOLLOW MEN

Hew Locke and the monument – Part 1

Some years ago, when I was mostly teaching undergraduate sculpture students, I turned the focus of the group in the direction of 'the monument' while asking myself, the students, and, in a way, the monuments themselves, how we should see or use this artistic and social tradition today.

I soon confirmed that when studying monuments, it is good to be based in a major city where you can find monuments all around you. However, the American sculptor Robert Smithson (see Chapter 7 in this book), in a well-known work, found or nominated monuments in a suburban space beyond the city's limits. His article, ironically titled *A Tour of the Monuments of Passaic, New Jersey* begins at a bus station from where a bus-ride takes him out of the city to begin his tour in a place where he is perhaps least likely to find any existing, official or actual monuments.[1]

Interestingly, we don't expect to find monuments of great individuals in the suburbs of our cities, nor do we grow up in suburbs with a sense that historical greatness or memorable feats and events emerge from within the suburbs. But this might be precisely why the artist Thomas Hirschhorn purposefully and perversely located monuments – one to the philosopher Gilles Deleuze (2000), another to dissident Surrealist thinker Georges Bataille (2002) – in seemingly incongruous suburban locations.[2]

The traditional monument, so often an enlarged, martial, bronze male figure, regularly accompanied by an enlarged, martial, bronze horse, with the whole elevated on a high stone plinth, is, as we have said, found in greatest numbers in the city, in the capital city, and in the centre of the capital city. There the monuments seem to have been driven into the cityscape like huge black nails establishing and maintaining for posterity, certain dates, people, and events, all seen from a certain influential perspective as formative of the nation's achievements.

A little empirical research into the subject however (which, for me, initially involved walking the streets of the capital, alone or with students in discussion)

DOI: 10.4324/9781003230632-22

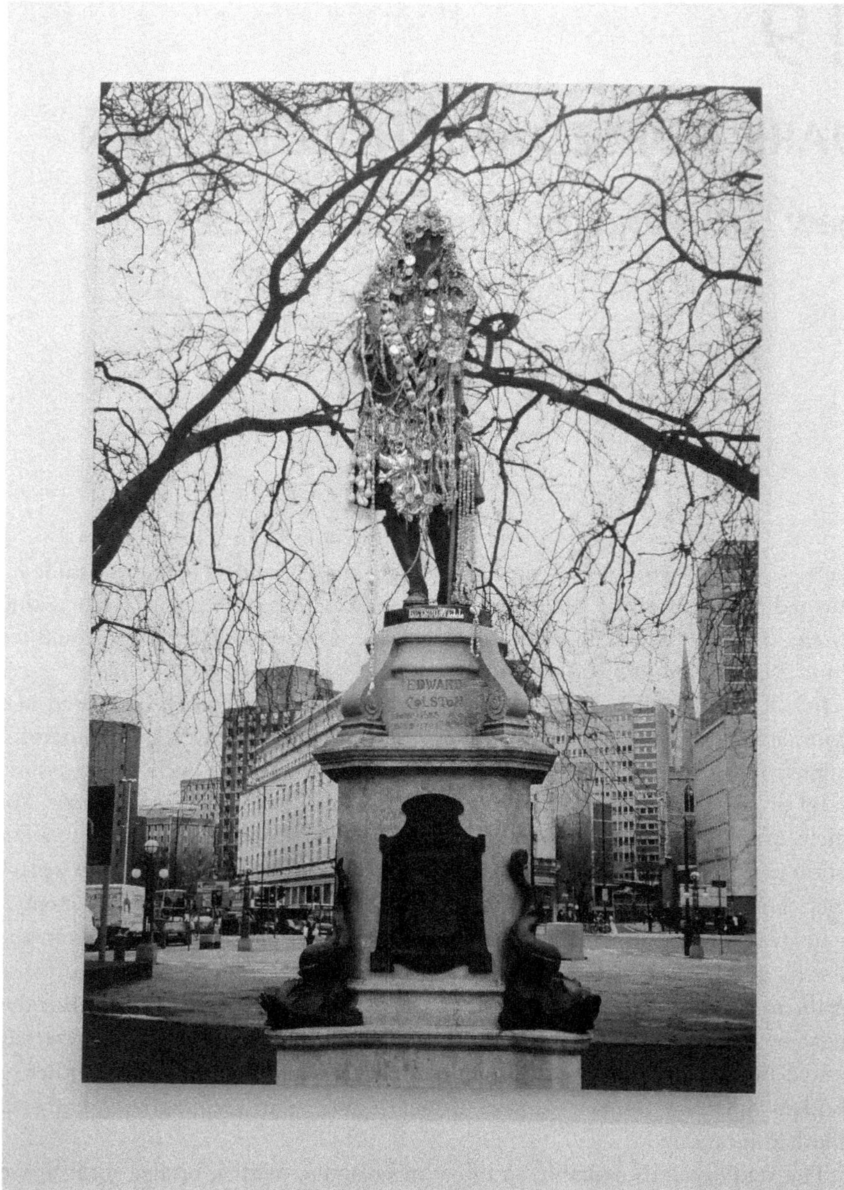

FIGURE 19.1 Hew Locke, *Colston* (from the series *Restoration*) 2006. Courtesy of the artist and DACS (Design and Artists Copyright Society).

soon throws up alternatives to what is generally called a conservative tradition. We might consider the way in which American Pop artist Claes Oldenburg, in the centre of Philadelphia, elevated a mere *Clothespin* (1976) to the status of a huge monument (a monument to the everyday perhaps). Zoom forward in time and we can find a millennial publication and group exhibition titled *Unmonumental* (2008) rooted in the New Museum, New York City.[3] The title of this show immediately suggests, even before seeing the work and reading its accompanying rationale, that the monumental tradition is and has been extended and challenged by contemporary artists. In fact, long before this exhibition and its title were conceived, artists, including Smithson, Oldenburg, and others, had been undermining and posing alternatives to the monumental tradition.

Oldenburg did this by replacing the usual important historical human figure with an everyday object (an object that is nevertheless 'important' enough, we might say, in its own context and in its own way). Smithson, in 1967, nominated readymade objects *as* monuments, thus suggesting something arbitrary and subjective about the choice of what is, should, or could be a monument. Fifteen years later a controversial monument to the American-Vietnam war in Washington D.C. was conceived by Maya Lin and utilised an unprecedented horizontal form that sank into the earth rather than towering over its surroundings.[4]

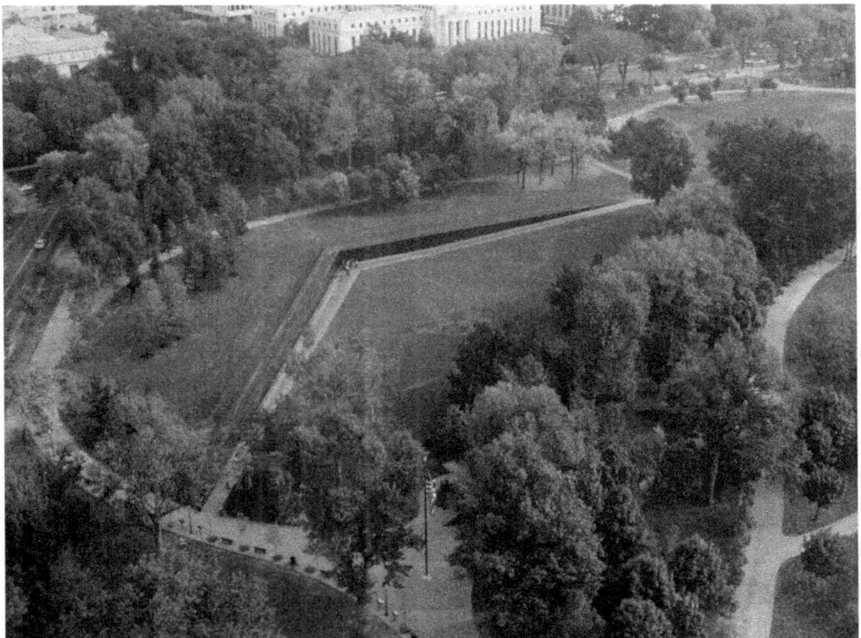

FIGURE 19.2 Maya Lin (architect) VVM Memorial. *Vietnam Veterans Memorial*, 1982 National Mall, Washington D.C. Public Domain and courtesy of Maya Lin Studio. Photographed by Terry Adams, National Parks Service.

Further research brings to light several exercises relating to the conundrum of how to appropriately mark the World War II holocaust of European Jews and other minorities.[5] The inversion strategy we see in Maya Lin's design also appears in works that, e.g., start out as vertical columns only to gradually retract into the earth, or invert in other ways, such as *Nameless Library* (2000), Rachel Whiteread's cast of a collection of books, installed in Vienna, which could be interpreted as symbolising the challenge to modern Enlightenment knowledge and cultural achievement posed by its antithesis in fascistic brutality and barbarism.

With the words 'anti-monument' and 'counter-monument' now entering our vocabulary we can start to trace some rich lines of thought on this theme by exploring, both in the library and in the city.

The 'lost wax' (itself a negative-sounding term) bronze casting method, responsible for so much of the martial monumental tradition, delivers a dark and resilient object, often involving, as we have said elsewhere, a resplendent figure and horse. In being hollow, a bronze cast is both practical and economical, i.e., for all its apparent bulk and stature it is relatively light and vulnerable, as statue-topplers have recently discovered to their collective delight.

A colleague and expert in the bronze-casting tradition pointed me to the advice of Cellini, the Italian Renaissance era master of sculptures in Bronze, who used measurements (when describing the excellence he aspired to in his own lost-wax bronze casting method) such as 'two fingers thick', or 'the thickness of an ordinary table knife's back'. These might draw us to consider the actual thickness of a completed bronze cast as surprisingly thin, best known only to the artists and technicians who make them, while leaving the general, passing public largely unaware of their finely balanced resilience and vulnerability.[6]

Many monuments mark, record, and establish the supposed virtues and achievements, not only of individual people or nations but also of the collective force referred to by Ariella Azoulay as 'empire', in the form of modern, European, expansive colonial dominance.[7] And so, along with the 1960s and 1970s generations' ironic plays and anti-monuments, we also see, alive and well today what might be called a counter-monumental movement, sometimes literally tearing down and/or defacing monuments, sometimes demanding *alter*-monuments that might begin to establish other figures or counter-national narratives, featuring different heroes and an alternative canon of 'formative' events.

What does this mean, not only for particular histories but also for history *per se*? For example, can or should history *ever* be marked or established, fixed in place, reified, concretised, and materialised, in and by a physical object in a physical space? Could or should history perhaps be left unmarked, its markers erased, leaving only intangible, mercurial and fickle, memories, stories and hearsay, as random ephemera?[8] Perhaps the internet-inspired model of 'trending' might satisfactorily supplant fixed notions of 'historical import' with an awareness of the ever-changing priorities of a dynamic and plural, Argus-like society whose perspective is always manifold and constantly shifting, thereby perhaps emulating the Deleuzian, neobaroque model (discussed in Chapter 18 of this book).

I also describe in Chapter 1 the focus in my early arts journalism on what I then called 'Black and Asian Artists in London'. One of the artists I met and wrote about during that period was Hew Locke.[9] For some time now Hew Locke has used photography and drawing to hypothetically address and 'dress' traditional monuments. At the time of writing (circa 2020), we hear quite regularly of the toppling of monuments that were designed to mark, establish, and conserve the legacy of what Azoulay calls 'empire'. Hew Locke's work on this theme did not in fact advocate (though the artist may well support) the literal toppling of monuments. Instead, Locke produced what I have come to think of as hypotheses. And so, first it might be worth considering the relative potency or ineffectuality of a hypothesis compared with the physical act of toppling a monument.

We know that a generation of conceptual artists reduced their works to ideas or concepts. Despite aspirations to entirely dematerialise art, these works often retained a modicum of material form, e.g., as typed pages, or black and white documentary photographic prints. Robert Smithson's *Passaic* piece utilises writing and photography as its materials in order to propose a form of hypothesis; in his case a 1960s equivalent of a Grand Tour on which objects might be turned into monuments at the artist's (or tourist's) bidding. Thus, Smithson, an established sculptor, hadn't changed the material make-up of the world to which he referred, but nevertheless showed that ideas, concepts, and hypotheses 'matter', they can change perceptions, and become effective works of art that bring possibility, question, and imagination into the world and into play. Hypotheses then, though relatively immaterial, nevertheless have – like a genie from a bottle – a certain immaterial power capable of changing the world.

Hew Locke has more recently hypothesised, e.g., in his *Patriots* series (2018), not that traditional, martial monuments be deposed (which might have seemed desirable but seemed hardly likely to the artist at the time he made these works) but that they be transformed by 'dressing' them in what we might call a carnivalesque manner.[10] Furthermore, Locke didn't dress the monuments directly but rather dressed and drew (hypothetically) onto photographs of the monuments. As with Smithson's *Passaic* work, a kind of nomination, a mediated proposition or hypothesis is thereby made, and yet, as above, the hypothesis, no matter how mediated, remains potent as a form of critical intervention, an idea that both endures and transforms.

Anyone who has visited Scotland will know that Edinburgh (incidentally Locke's birthplace) is a city unusually well-endowed with monuments, and these make a strong contribution to the city's special, ancient, and historical atmosphere. Meanwhile, Glasgow also boasts its fair share, including a famous equestrian monument of the Duke of Wellington that stands outside a building now home to the city's Gallery of Modern Art. Today, that statue is permanently dressed with the addition of a traffic cone placed on the Duke's head. Something that presumably began as a drunken Friday-night joke, or occurred during a political march, has become an informally agreed local tradition. It is also an implicit symbol of the city's progressive and multicultural community, which maintains a sceptical, ironic, and playful stance in relation to the city's official monumental history, much of

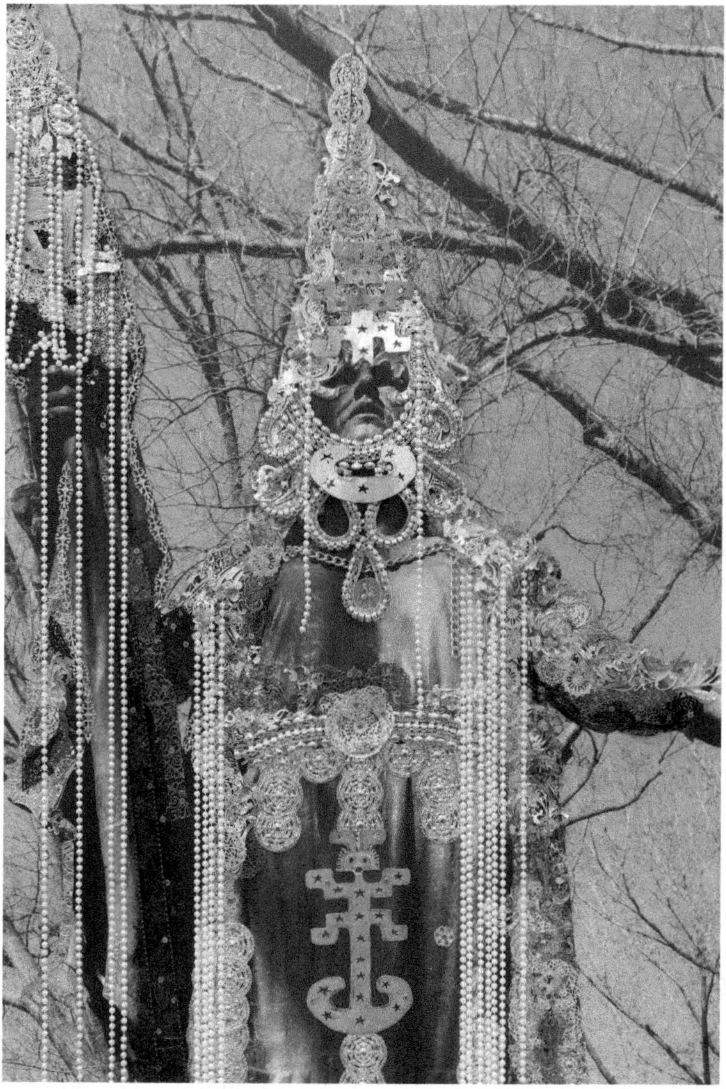

FIGURE 19.3 Hew Locke, *Columbus*, Central Park, 2018. Courtesy of the artist and DACS (Design and Artists Copyright Society).

it erected in the 19th century, and, like the Duke, often referring to Scotland's troublesome historical relationship with England.

We might again invoke here the concept of the carnivalesque to describe the irreverent gesture of placing and maintaining a traffic cone on a monument's head. And this playful irreverence also has the effect of suggesting an alternative, or indeed *inverted* value to that intended by the original monument. The addition of the traffic cone suggests that it is no longer royalty, rank, and military prowess that is celebrated here but rather the freedom of any ordinary citizen to question and critique those very institutions and values.

Hew Locke may be seen to do something similar, in spirit at least, though of course executed in a far more considered, conscientious and sophisticated fashion, when hypothetically dressing monuments in hand-drawn patterns and signs, or draping their image in festoons of cheap jewellery, in what amounts to a potent and gaudy decoration. Locke thereby transforms their image, meaning, message and purpose, brightening up but also implicitly mocking and weighing down these otherwise grim and dowdy dark horses and hollow men. Locke may even give them a second chance to interact anew with a world that has significantly and comprehensively changed since the lifetimes of those that the statues represent. Locke's overgenerous additions are a kind of overkill, an 'embarrassment of riches', a dubious kind of gift, that is also a kind of poison, and possibly a potlach.[11]

We all dress for special occasions, perhaps in comical ways for a party or political march, more glamorously for a wedding, or sombrely for a funeral. Dress temporarily marks and signals who we are, how we feel, and what we are part of. Dress is never permanent but invariably a hypothesis, a temporary and superficial assembly of signs and symbols that make and mark who we are, as a member of a family, community or event, sometimes only for an hour or a day, or perhaps in livery for the period of our employment.

Poet and critic Charles Baudelaire made observations about the ways in which fashions on the streets of Paris in the 19th century were as sure a sign of peoples' response to modernism as the paintings in the salons of the time. Similarly, Walter Benjamin, occasionally in his writings, appears fascinated by fashion and might even have regarded it as one of the most mysterious, yet powerful and pervasive manifestations of historical consciousness – an emphatic visual acknowledgement of constant cultural change.[12] Thus, dress may have a surprising amount to contribute to and extend this enquiry into history in contemporary art and culture.

In hypothetically dressing monuments, Locke also hypothesises the greater relevance of this 'superficial' (in a non-derogatory sense) and temporary (we might almost say 'virtual') gesture, over and above the assumed importance of intended monumental permanence underpinned by the traditional process of lost-wax bronze-casting. This might then leave us to once again consider whether, not only monuments but also history itself should be, could be, or needs to be more or less established, substantial enduring and permanent, or rather, fleeting, ephemeral, immaterial, and, like dress or fashion, ever-changing.

Notes

1 See https://holtsmithsonfoundation.org/monuments-passaic.

2 See www.diaart.org/exhibition/exhibitions-projects/thomas-hirschhorn-gramsci-monument-project.

Hirschhorn's series of 'monuments' dedicated to major writers and thinkers. Initiated in 1999 with *Spinoza Monument* (Amsterdam, the Netherlands), followed by *Deleuze Monument* (Avignon, France, 2000) and *Bataille Monument* (Kassel Germany, 2002).

3 Flood, R. (2007). See https://archive.newmuseum.org/exhibitions/918.
4 See www.mayalinstudio.com/memory-works/vietnam-veterans-memorial.
5 *The Counter Monument: Memory against Itself in Germany Today*, by James E. Young in: Mitchell, W.J.T. (1992) pp. 49–78.
6 Cellini, B. (1967) p. 112.
7 Azoulay, A.A. (2019).
8 'Unmarked' – a valuable concept, and the title of an influential book by Peggy Phelan marking the beginning of the historicisation of performance art. Phelan, P. (1993).
9 See www.hewlocke.net/Homepage2ndsite.html.
10 See www.hewlocke.net/patriots.html.
11 The word 'gift' in German means 'poison', and this subsequent play of language implicates a tradition whereby a gift, or any show of excessive generosity (as exemplified by central and North American indigenous peoples' traditions of 'potlach') can also and always be double-sided or two-faced, as the giver draws a special form of power from their own generosity and ultimately from the recipient.
12 Baudelaire, C. (1992) pp. 104–107; Ekardt, P. (2020).

Bibliography

Azoulay, A.A. (2019) *Potential History – Unlearning Imperialism*. London: Verso.
Baudelaire, C. (1992) *Selected Writings on Art & Literature*. London: Penguin.
Cellini, B. (1967) *The Treatises of Benvenuto Cellini on Goldsmithing and Sculpture*. New York: Dover Publications.
Ekardt, P. (2020) *Benjamin on Fashion* [electronic resource]. London: Bloomsbury.
Flood, R. (2007) *Unmonumental: The Object in the 21st Century*. New York, London: Phaidon.
Mitchell, W.J.T. (1992) *Art and the Public Sphere*. Chicago, IL: University of Chicago Press.
Phelan, P. (1993) *Unmarked – The Politics of Performance*. London: Routledge.

20

DARK HORSES AND HOLLOW MEN

Hew Locke and the monument – Part 2

In 2006 I found myself, not in front of a lectern, nor in an art college studio, but out and about in the city, contending with London's fickle climate, traffic, noise and fumes, walking around talking about monuments as well as negotiating the sometimes substantial physical distances between them.

Some years later, the City of London's commendable *Sculpture in the City* programme, which began c. 2010, allowed me to cash-in some of this experience. I came to enjoy walking and talking my way through appropriately designed and well-chosen contemporary artworks, carefully situated across the City of London region – the oldest part of London and famously delimited as 'the square mile'. Often this was with groups of students, many visiting London for the first time and who were able to learn about the city itself as a context for the artworks – an interesting alternative to the supposedly 'site-less' white cube context provided for so much of the contemporary art we encounter.[1]

In 2006, my role in the city, speaking of and to monuments, felt novel and what I might call 'interestingly uncomfortable', not least because many habitual methods of analysis, evolved within and pampered by the relatively luxurious, warm, clean, sheltered, well-lit and welcoming interiors of the city's blue-chip, white-cube galleries, were denied me. For contemporary artists, art lecturers and art students this discomfort can however be both welcome and promising as it provokes and insists upon other ways of looking at, evaluating, and perhaps making art. Discomfort often discourages us from remaining sedentary or standing still, like the lazy traditional monument itself. Discomfort keeps us moving, journeying, travelling and tripping, while looking, thinking, and experimenting with eyes and senses refreshed and stimulated by changed surroundings.

It is then worth once again noting here the discomfort we currently feel, not only with particular monuments that clash with our political and ethical allegiances, but also with the monumental tradition *per se*. This tradition might seem currently

DOI: 10.4324/9781003230632-23

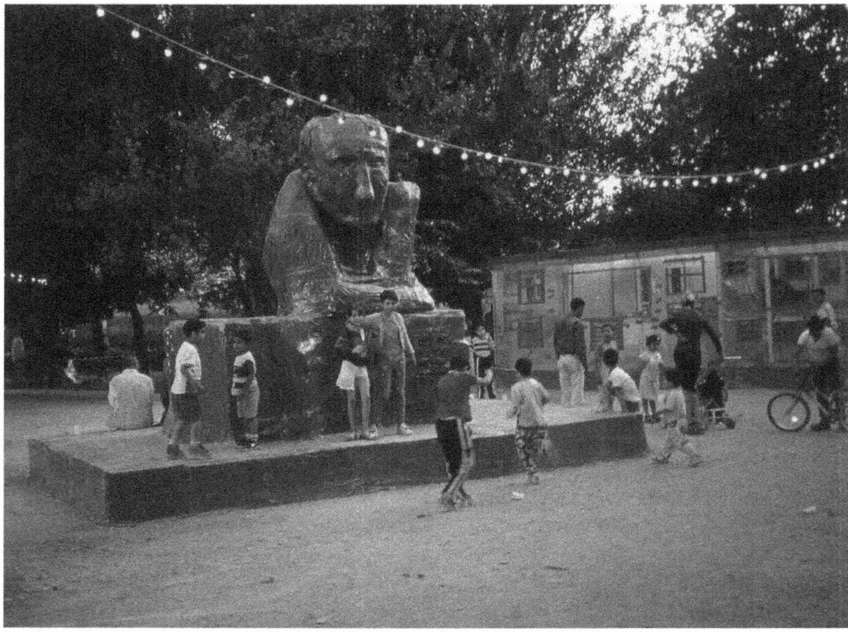

FIGURE 20.1 Thomas Hirschhorn, *Deleuze Monument*, 2000, sculpture. '*La Beauté*', Avignon, France. Courtesy of the artist and DRAC Provence-Alpes-Côte d'Azur, Aix-en-Provence.

cowed by our redoubled enthusiasm for change and renewal, and by our appeal for a 21st-century art that could perhaps catch up with the tumult of change experienced in so many aspects of our lives.

In 2006 I also gave an informal studio talk at Royal College of Art Sculpture department, titled *Dark Horses & Hollow Men*. That paper emerged from my role providing studio teaching and contextual studies for Camberwell College of Art & Design BA Fine Art Sculpture. The talk was based on monuments, but one of the idiosyncrasies of my paper was that it was also a piece of creative writing that described a walk across London, from South East to North West, on an unusually sunny Christmas day.

On that special day, when the city was transformed by its relative lack of use, dearth of residents and small number of visitors, the streets were almost deserted, and despite the bright sunshine an almost eerie atmosphere of empty stillness contributed a renewed sense of, and more intimate relationship with the monuments I encountered. The huge, lonely looking, frozen and weathered, bronze-black or stone-grey objects, usually obscured by workaday crowds and tourists hurrying-by, looked gloomier than ever, and even a little embarrassed to be so thoroughly exposed.

Here I'd like to steer and refer back to Part 1 of this chapter in order to continue to consider the siting of some temporary monuments by the artist Thomas

Hirschhorn (circa 2000). These were made in working-class housing estates, slightly remote and removed from the centres of cities (e.g., Kassel in Germany) where biennales or similar large-scale art events were being held. In one case, visitors to the event could access these monuments primarily, (or in effect, only) by using a local cab service contracted to serve this function.

These works interest me today, partly because I grew up on a similar housing estate about 20 miles from the centre of London. This means that I can recall a kind of adolescent yearning for the not-too-distant, not-quite-visible city, as well as recalling a thought that occurred to me at some point in my 20s or 30s when I became aware of the fact that the place where I grew up had 'no history'. At least, nobody of any celebrated cultural significance had ever grown up there, nothing of historical significance had ever happened there, and no one from there had ever died in a war, if only because the estate was new.

My housing estate could also be described as 'simulacral' in that it had not evolved organically from, or in response to, the land or locale, but was a pre-planned and prescribed *fait accompli* rapidly imposed on the unsuspecting Essex landscape sometime in the late 1950s (there may well be identical estates scattered around the UK, Europe and further afield). My generation were the first inhabitants of the estate's new world, a place without monuments or memorial plaques of the kind you find in older cities, towns and villages and thus, seemingly at least, it was a place without history.

Whether Thomas Hirschhorn had similar thoughts in mind regarding the impact of siting his monuments on suburban housing estates I cannot say, however, it might be relevant that on a housing estate close to where I now live (in the centre of London) I have found, not only an originally well-meaning, but now slightly incongruous Henry Moore figurative sculpture, but also a blue plaque dedicated to an ex-Arsenal and England footballer who excelled in the 1980s.[2] The Henry Moore sculpture seems to have recently grown more incongruous than when originally installed in 1962 as part of that estate's original utopian promise.[3] This might be an interesting line of historical thought to pursue and points to the idea that, at the time the estate and its Henry Moore sculpture were installed, the distinct cultures that the artwork and the estate now seem to represent might then have felt (or were perceived to be) more closely and harmoniously aligned than they are today.

So, something has happened in my lifetime (if my intuition about this changed relation is correct) that has failed a utopian promise and widened the cultural gap between the two cultures loosely represented by the council flats (on one hand) and the modernist sculpture (on another), and now the footballer's memorial (on yet another). There is surely more to explore here, but suffice to say, for the present at least, that this is another example of the ways in which material history and its theoretical questions surround us, always ready to open new avenues for our consideration.

As we have already established, monuments are not, primarily at least, a rural or suburban tradition. They tend to mark towns, cities, the nation's capital, and the very centre of the capital as the central site of historicisation of the nation; the place where the nation's 'great and good' are buried, remembered, and celebrated, along with events and figures said to have formed the nation.[4] This emphatic, and we might say obsessive centralisation, may seem an obvious and unavoidable fact, but it could be subjected to new scrutiny – along with other historicising tendencies and mechanisms – perhaps in terms of a current and growing desire for a more rational de-centralisation and re-regionalisation of the nation's assets, identity, treasures, and institutions.

Leaving the city, taking a bus or cab ride out of the city to a suburb or suburban estate, walking across the city on Christmas Day, all of these might allude to what the artist Robert Smithson called 'trips' (without intending, as far as I know, any reference to hallucinogenic drugs). Smithson was earnestly concerned with expanding the perhaps all-too-urban remit of modern sculpture, so as to include what he called 'sites' that are far from the city centre. He also (perhaps necessarily, and professionally) creates a dialogue between those sites and what he calls 'non-sites'. These 'non-sites' take the form of museologically ordered base elements (rocks, shale, etc.) taken from 'sites' and recontextualised in urban galleries.[5]

Meanwhile, Smithson is also interested in the trips taken *between* any non-site and its site (and even in the slightly arcane inversion of all this into what he called 'non-trips taken between a site and its non-site'). These are of course all trips between city and non-city, as famously documented in Smithson's *A Tour of the Monuments of Passaic, New Jersey* (interestingly dated, with unusual historical precision for an artwork, as Saturday, 30 September 1967). There, Smithson documents in subjective detail and in lyrical prose the lone trip or 'tour' that begins at a bus station and takes him out of New York City to the relatively barren, suburban county of Passaic, which has autobiographical relevance as the artist's birthplace.

As can be seen in Chapter 6 of this book, in 1998, 25 years after Smithson's premature and accidental death encountered while flying over a site in a light aircraft, the artist Tacita Dean created a sound piece in which she recorded herself and a colleague, searching, by means of a road trip in a car, and following official directions and instructions, in order to locate and witness the rumoured reappearance of Smithson's 1970 earthwork *Spiral Jetty*.[6] I am pleased to own a copy of the resulting artwork, archived in the form of a humble cassette tape. It records and traces the journey to its perhaps predictably disappointing conclusion.

Arriving at a destination only to find a much-anticipated phenomenon absent or invisible is what makes Dean's recorded journey the contemporary artwork that it is. It becomes symbolic of all our lives and all our ultimate and final journeys, beyond success and failure to eventually confront sublime absence. That absence is, we might argue, always and unavoidably, poorly compensated for by any fixed material tribute, no matter how resilient and enduring the tribute might be.

We may here have begun to perceive a certain train of thought emerging, involving journeys, trips, walks, drives, and flights, all of which can be seen as challenging to the fixity, site, stasis, and sedentary nature of the often bronze-cast, stone-carved and sculptural monumental tradition. It is often the monuments' fixity or stasis that we find ourselves contending with today, an incongruous fixity and stasis that contradicts or denies the unfolding of a new perception of history currently taking place – a perception that, in turn, cries out (as did Charles Baudelaire in 1846) for new and appropriate processes and forms to accommodate or represent fast changing lives and times.

How can a static bronze or stone monument relate to a person who; or a society that, since the 20th century, travels with such ease and speed over the ground and through the sky, and that, in 21st century style, is so influenced by virtual, digital technologies, which connect us in a flash of information that in turn calls on us to regard ourselves and our experiences as events rather than as things?

Would it not be appropriate perhaps for monuments – particularly those that mark events, but perhaps all those that commemorate any name accompanied by dates of birth and death (thus rendering us all *as* events) – to cease to be 'things' at all and to become events?

A nebulous notion, emerging from these thoughts might then be the supplanting of physical monuments with commemorative, annual or occasional walks, trips and drives, marches, pageants, parades, processions, and concerts, more akin to the eventful or eventual carnival tradition than that of fixed sculpture. We might also perhaps emulate those saints' day celebrations wherein an iconic object sees the light of day only rarely and briefly, glimpsed by a crowd as it is paraded and displayed before being returned to the darkness of an inaccessible vault.

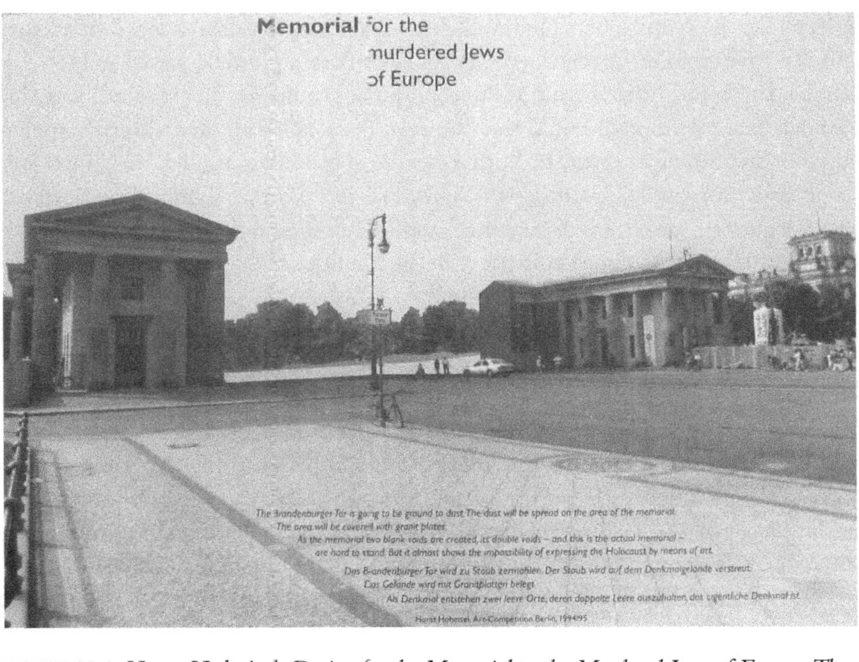

FIGURE 20.2 Horst Hoheisel, *Design for the Memorial to the Murdered Jews of Europe: The Crushed Brandenburg Gate I, Berlin*. Diptych. 1994–1995. Offset print, pencil, 118 × 82.5 cm; Jewish Museum Berlin, photographed by Jens Ziehe.

At an Association of International Art Critics (AICA) conference on art and populism held in Berlin in 2019, I gave a paper that played with the notion of revivifying certain carnival and pageant traditions, in such a way that they might provide an oblique means of political, social, and cultural representation, capable of including disenfranchised, regional, marginalised, and even extreme communities within a more expansive 21st century version of modern democracy.[7] On reflection, and for our purposes here, carnival – which Mikhail Bakhtin described as essentially an acknowledgement and ritual embodiment of unavoidable and inexorable change and renewal – might just provide a useful antithesis to the sculptural monumental tradition, as carnival is characterised by movement, passage, journey, transformation, and inversion.[8]

At the same Berlin conference, art historian, curator and salonnière Julia Pelta-Feldman contributed to a panel addressing the contemporary and notorious debate concerning Hannah Black's proposal to destroy a painting made by Dana Schutz of the corpse of murdered black teenager Emmett Till [9]. Interestingly for me, Pelta-Feldman invoked the work of Horst Hoheisel, one of the artists collected in my own research as an exemplary purveyor of post-World War II anti-, counter-, non-, negative, and un-monuments.

Pelta-Feldman compared Hannah Black's call to destroy Schutz' painting with a proposal made by Hoheisel in 1994 in response to a call for an appropriate way of memorialising the Holocaust within the city of Berlin. Hoheisel proposed that the entire Brandenburg Gate be ground to dust and scattered across the site it had long previously occupied and dominated as a classical symbol of victory and assertive marker of territory.[10] Pelta-Feldman's argument was that Hoheisel was all-but certain that his impossible proposal would *not be* accepted, and that Hannah Black's proposal could then be read as being made in a similarly speculative or hypothetical spirit. In both cases, Pelta-Feldman argued, the impossible or unlikely proposal or hypothesis was nevertheless worth making. Both deserved to be suggested, raised, aired, imagined, and discussed, if only to shape and further inform a debate that could consequently be confident that it had proceeded in a comprehensive manner.

We might then think of Hoheisel's proposal as a 'limit experience' concerning our musings on the possible relations between monument, site, and history.[11] Hoheisel's is a hypothesis in which the monument becomes, and is reduced to its own site, leaving us with a renewed, radicalised, and strangely inverted relationship of site to monument, one that might become appropriate to the relevant historical event (i.e., the holocaust) that the art and the artist were called upon to mark (or, in this case, perhaps *un*-mark). Here Hoheisel might even have gone beyond mere inversion, to turn a tradition, and his profession, inside out.

We can hopefully see in these implications of various hypothetical works and gestures a connection back to Smithson's (Duchampian) nominations, that do not change the world materially and physically, but enduringly influence it, albeit in the form of pictures, words, pages and now widely available PDFs.

We can also consider again those series of works made by artist Hew Locke, who, some years before toppling monuments became current, viable, and even commonplace, used photography and a personalised, somewhat carnivalesque approach to collage and drawing to hypothesise the transformation of monuments by means of a kind of 'dress' (perhaps comparable with certain rural traditions wherein, e.g., windmills and wells are 'dressed' at festive times of the year).

If so, then we can also trace connections between the thinking of Hoheisel, the work of Smithson and that of Locke to a wider tendency to dematerialisation informing the generations influenced by conceptual art (a tendency for which Fluxus thinking is also partly responsible).

Further examples of what I am here calling, and collecting as 'hypothetical works' might include Gino De Dominicis' (1969) *Attempt to Form Squares Instead of Circles around a Stone Falling into Water*; or Piero Manzoni's (1961) *Base of the World* (*Socle du Monde*), both of which provide further precedents for hypothetical art that make the apparently impossible at least *hypothesis-able*, by dispensing with the necessity for the art works materialisation (Joseph Beuys' 1965 performance *How to Explain Pictures to a Dead Hare* also comes to mind).

And here, and finally, these hypotheses also become synonymous with, or at least related to, some important attributes of the virtual, as immaterial yet latent, always de- and re-situated or un-sited, retaining the constant possibility of unfolding as event, as does this very virtual manuscript, along with every other file opened or unopened on my virtual desktop.

Notes

1 See www.sculptureinthecity.org.uk/
2 See www.blueplaques.net/show_images.php?search_id=id!3639.
3 See https://historicengland.org.uk/listing/the-list/list-entry/1385448.
4 Notwithstanding the fact that, in the UK, even small villages and boroughs tend to have some form of memorial to the local people who died as a result of the 20th century's two world wars.
5

> … Let us say that one goes on a fictitious trip if one decides to go to the site of the Nonsite. The 'trip' becomes invented, devised, artificial; therefore, one might call it a non- trip to a site from a Nonsite …

See https://holtsmithsonfoundation.org/provisional-theory-nonsites.

At this point we might also want to invoke the later, 1980s furore regarding the concept of 'site-specificity' relating to Richard Serra's *Tilted Arc*. Buskirk, M. & Serra, R. (1991).

6 See www.frithstreetgallery.com/audiovisual/tacita-dean-trying-to-find-spiral-jetty-1998.
7 See https://aicainternational.news/52-congress.
8 On Mikhail Bakhtin's *Carnival & Carnivalesque*, see: Storey, J. (1997) pp. 250–259.
9 See the complete edited papers of the AICA Berlin 2019 conference on art and populism here: https://books.ub.uni-heidelberg.de/arthistoricum/catalog/book/891

10 See www.knitz.net/index.php?option=com_content&task=view&id=27&Itemid=32&lang=en.

11 Associated with Georges Bataille, Maurice Blanchot, and Michel Foucault a 'limit-experience' is an experience that approaches the edge of living in terms of its intensity and seeming impossibility. It breaks the subject from itself.

Bibliography

Buskirk, M. & Serra, R. (1991) *The Destruction of Tilted Arc: Documents.* Cambridge, MA: MIT Press.

Storey, J. (1997) *An Introduction to Cultural Theory and Popular Culture* (second edition). London: Prentice Hall.

21

A PERSONAL HISTORY OF NEW SCHOOL HIP-HOP – PART 1

When it comes to popular music, our own point of view is paramount, and early 1980s music in the UK, from my point of view and that of some of my fellow connoisseurs at the time, was dire. We searched in vain on the airwaves and in the music press for signs of some new radical voice, wave, sound, persona, or style. Most of what we found there was manifestations of Bowie-envy, a few rock bands inflected by the ghost of punk, and the so-called New Romantics whose exuberant styling spoke of a decadent mannerism. On the brighter side (and to name but a few) Billy Mackenzie from Dundee briefly lit up our lives with his shockingly original operatic pop; Jerry Dammers' *The Specials* supplied sublime pop politics, and the maverick Kevin Rowland stuck his neck a long way out to try and convince a post-Thatcher generation that they might yet have a soulful flame to keep alive.

A friend and aficionado with excellent taste introduced me to Matt Johnson and his mysteriously named *THE THE* who showed some flinty integrity, as well as to a Swiss band called *Yello* whose weird mix of synth-pop was delivered with a haughtily aristocratic air. Meanwhile, the legendary DJ John Peel could be relied upon to keep a certain kind of musical radicalism alive (between 10 pm and midnight most nights of the week), but it sometimes seemed to be on life support.

Once our own bands had gravitated from playing in squats and pubs to reach London's West End clubs, we began to hear, appreciate, and eventually love a kind of music we had not really encountered or embraced before. In one West End club our band would not perform until after midnight, and so we'd find ourselves packing away amps, guitars and drums at around 1 or 2 a.m. As we did, what we could hear around us – as we repeatedly crossed the dance floor carrying something big, black, and heavy – were old rare grooves and new funky rap tracks built on samples of the same and utilising James Brown drum loops. They were played at body-shaking volume and featured massive bass lines.

DOI: 10.4324/9781003230632-24

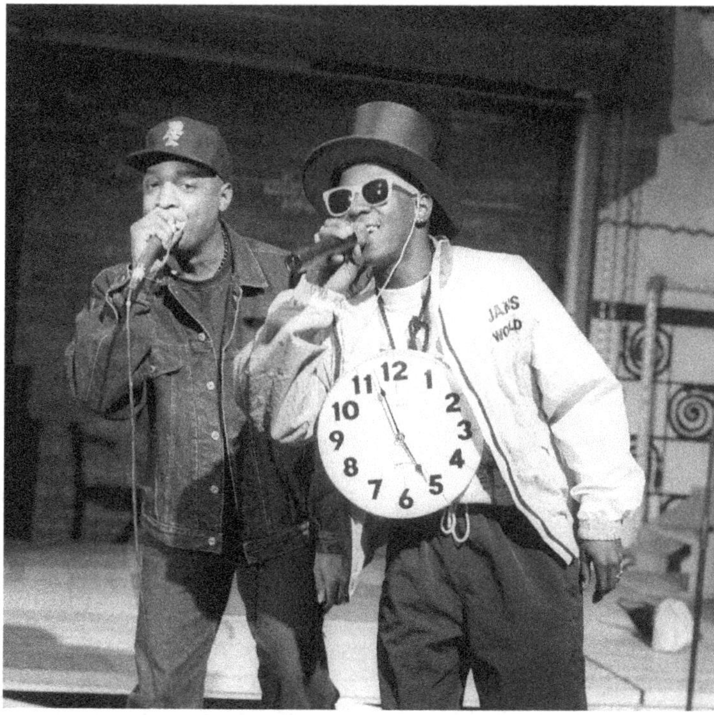

FIGURE 21.1 Public Enemy (Flavor Flav – aka William Jonathan Drayton Jr. and Chuck D – aka Carlton Douglas Ridenhour) appears on the Public Enemy Week segment of *Yo! MTV Raps* on September 19, 1991, in New York City. Photographed by Al Pereira/Getty Images/Michael Ochs Archives.

Furthermore, what we could see around us were people stylishly dressed and ecstatically dancing. They moved with passion, as if oblivious to the social injustices, assertive economic restructuring and political diabolism of the city and nation beyond the club's walls; as if unaware of the newly stark division of millions of real lives into either unemployed or tastelessly rich. And yet, if you listened closely, all that politics was in the music too. If not in the reality lyrics of rappers or soul singers (e.g., Rakim's *Paid in Full*, or *Money's Too Tight to Mention* by *The Valentine Brothers*, Gil Scott-Heron's *The Bottle*, or Gwen Guthrie's *Ain't Nothing Going On but the Rent*), then in the sonic message, the language and attitude of beats and basslines sampled, edited, and looped from old 1970s grooves.

When we reached home and packed away our gear it would be the small hours. Then, a late, last spin of the radio dial would conjure up all kinds of nocturnal pirate radio stations playing Electro or New School rap. Now, looking back, I can see how all this began to sow seeds in our minds about the truest and most positive directions and currencies in music at the time. However, what confirmed our ultimate conversion to this new music was (inevitably) the casual acquaintance and unintentional influence of a sharp and stylish girl we knew, who happened to be sharing the same 1980s typical, housing-benefit-ghetto-ised house as us. She was the only person we knew who actually had a job, and that occupation occasionally took her to New York and back. Each time she returned she would gift us cassette mix tapes recorded from the top NYC rap radio shows of the time.

The radio DJs then competing to be kings of the NYC airwaves were Marley Marl and DJ Red Alert and cassette tapes of their shows were, to us, electric and energising, fulfilling and inspiring. They contained all the newest tracks, as broadcast within the context of an NYC night's worth of radio listening, and they transported all that culture from The Bronx and Queens to our home in South London. They also featured interviews with artists dropping into the studio, supplying plenty of rap lingo, plus entertaining and inventive jingles made for the shows by the artists. Then there were the host DJs' raucous and witty patter and personae, their mixes and signature special effects. As such, there was just as much to fascinate us *between* the records as there was in the records themselves.

We became intoxicated by and indoctrinated into this new belief system and found ourselves trading guitars and amps for record decks, samplers, sequencers and microphones, jettisoning our lower Kings Rd (Worlds End) thrift store suits (that had evoked a non-committal, *a*historical 'no time') to buy the first sports shoes we had worn since school days. Soon we were embroiled in one of London's first Hip-Hop record labels, writing, making, producing, promoting, performing and distributing mostly rap tracks. Unfortunately, that initial heady period of generous exchange – as is often the case with hot creative ventures – didn't endure but quickly imploded as differential talents, interests, and directions began pulling apart what they might have pulled more constructively and enduringly together. Nevertheless, while it lasted, we did at least make a few respectable records. We even managed to visit New York together on a shoestring (or trainer lace perhaps) budget, where we showed what we were doing to the most critical and informed of all hip-hop audiences.

Among my strongest memories of that visit I recall a Manhattan dustman, in the morning, just outside my hotel, pointing at my gold and red Adidas Hi-Top sneakers and saying, 'Hey man, I thought you had boxing gloves on your feet'. I also recall walking home from a club at 4 a.m. and a homeless man offering to sell me a turquoise rectangle of cardboard, which I realised, as I passed, had once been the back of a book. For some reason, of all my rich experiences of New York City and various confrontations with urban poverty, this image remains exceptionally vivid and deeply ingrained. That man was, presumably, a citizen of the United States, and yet, right there in Manhattan, perhaps the richest place on earth, he newly introduced me to, and symbolised by his appearance, by his alienation, and by his strange gesture, all the poverty of America, and all the poverty in the supposedly modern world.

It's difficult now to find any appropriate or adequate way to express the passion, pride, and joy running through us and through New School Hip-Hop and rap at that time. I am really talking about a brief historical window, between 1986 and

1989, that I and many others have since come to think of as a golden age. New art forms or revolutions in the arts tend to follow a pattern of inspired emergence before lapsing into some form of mannerism. I have long harboured the notion that, during those initial inspired surges, when something elemental is occurring, it may be that all the eventual possibilities and tendencies of a new art form are discovered almost immediately, instantaneously, so that later developments are all merely extrusions of ideas and possibilities that were prototyped, hinted at, tried out, latent, or in some way or other enfolded and foreseen at the very outset.

The fundamental structures and methods of Hip-Hop had been laid down as far back as 1976 – a year that, coincidentally, also saw the uprising of Reggae onto an international stage, plus the joint apotheoses of Punk and Disco. However, what seemed to happen in the second half of the 1980s was that Hip-Hop shifted from being a relatively underground, urban, U.S. scene into a bankable international cultural form, which also brought Hip-Hop's art, style, and dance along with it. By that time, Jean Michel Basquiat, Keith Haring, and Malcolm Maclaren (with *Buffalo Gals*, 1982) had all helped in various ways shine some international light on it. Occasional crossover hits like *White Lines* (1981) or *The Message* (1982) by Grandmaster Flash and the Furious Five had cut through into mainstream consciousness, but somehow without yet significantly alerting a broad audience to the wider implications and promise of the Hip-Hop phenomenon.

Ultimately it was Def Jam recordings, and rap acts like Public enemy, Eric B & Rakim, LL Cool J, Rob Base & DJ E-Z Rock, Boogie Down Productions, Run DMC or JVC Force – to name just a few – who confirmed that a wholly new sound, new era, new market, and new attitude had arrived, had come to be conscious of itself and to be known as New School (or Nu Skool) Hip-Hop. New School, while losing none of the Old School's passion for craft, swagger, fun, funk, and braggadocio claimed the mic, decks, style, legacy, and fashion as vehicles for a newly focused and re-politicised realism. It now reached far beyond the block parties, dance floors, and projects where it had thus far acted as an adjunct to and extension of soul, funk, and disco, and developed into a broader, more expansive and inclusive, and yet more targeted, phenomenon.

Multiple styles and experimental differences began to vie for attention and Hip-Hop artists of all kinds began springing up around the world. This consolidated Hip-Hop as something persistent, permanent, and important, something now with its own history, an old and a new school, a substantial past and a lively, freshly emerging future. New School rap revealed new tendencies and possibilities for radical invention, making not only new political contributions but also numerous conceptual and stylistic innovations. At best it pursued a kind of adventurous avant-garde tendency, comparable to achievements that might be found in, e.g., Jazz or Dadaism. All of this made any attempted progress happening elsewhere, e.g., in the aforementioned guitar-based indie rock, look like tame and tiny steps in comparison with the arrival of New School rap that showed the world the full profundity of Hip-Hop as a paradigm shift in creativity and culture.

It is worth thinking a little longer about the huge socio-economic transformations taking place in the 1980s under the thumb of so-called Reaganomics and Thatcherism. It was black, urban Americans who were perhaps being crushed more than anybody at the bottom of new 1980s' socio-economic structures. And yet it was those same people who responded to those impositions most promptly, creatively, appropriately, and dynamically. New School rap constituted a wholesale revolution in the potential for fusing art and politics. It rapidly accelerated from a local to a global phenomenon, thus bringing what were previously relatively underground words, sounds, voices, styles, ideas, moves, concepts, news and history onto a more visible, now international stage.

Between 1986–1989, new rappers, inspired by a sense of *zeitgeist* and motivated by the opening of a window of opportunity seemed to be everywhere, producing mini-masterpieces and cleverly competing for attention, first on pirate and local radio shows and soon on national and international media. Their streetwise rhymes could be deadly earnest or focused on fun, but were always buoyant with innovative, playful charm and cool styles that demonstrated a willingness to display sometimes baroque levels of complexity. This was, after all, not just creatively exciting but a way to possibly get paid and recognised for talents that might otherwise, and at another time and place, have no such opportunity.

New School rappers and their DJ partners enthusiastically explored their elder relatives' record collections, reworking the previous generation's music history into a new future, glorifying and re-purposing sometimes little more than a tiny piece of a culture's much oppressed and marginalised past, scratching, looping and layering, weaving and fusing what a fine artist might call 'found objects' or 'readymades' in previously unheard-of ways that seemed to exceed levels of originality or virtuosity available to any guitar band and singer. It might even be argued that New School rap and Hip-Hop challenged all guitar-based music – mostly rooted in Afro-American blues – to subsequently review and re-envision itself in newly historicised terms.

In addition to scratched and looped music and beats, DJs and producers took influence from wild and free use of noises and effects developed as part of the 1970s reggae dub scene, so that weird whistles, tuneless sirens, repeated staccato announcements and shouts and hollers sometimes took the place of lyrics and melodies. Even basslines, so crucial to much soul/dance music, could sometimes be sacrificed in search of greater emphasis upon the ineradicable element of a stripped-down hypnotic beat, derived from a drum machine, a looped sample, or a mix of the two.

Anything, it seemed, could and would be scratched, sampled, and added to this mechanised modernity, the montage element adding to the realist atmosphere of the records. Building a futural soundscape out of bits and pieces of the past suddenly seemed to make the present newly alive with possibility (though it might have previously occurred to 1920s Dadaists, or early modernist movie editors like Vertov or Eisenstein), inviting swathes of new creators to play with a new toolbox and thus have a say. Like the body-popping dances associated with the Electro strain of Hip-Hop, an invisible current of invention ran a third rail through everyone and everything that touched New School Hip-Hop, promising to 'turn the tables' on established culture and turn underdogs into top-dogs (and one day even Snoopdogs).

New School supremo and Public Enemy's front-man Chuck D sometimes sounded capable of overthrowing all existing 'powers that be' (i.e., media, prejudice, propaganda, poverty and racism, capitalism, the state, the police, penal and justice system etc.) powers that kept black Americans from sharing in modernity's promise of equality, prosperity and democracy. Chuck D's potently pugilistic poetry promised all this could and would be overturned. His incitements to fight the above-mentioned powers through use of the punter's own positive state of mind – were always underpinned by and connected to a historically informed political legacy and agenda.

Meanwhile, Chris Parker, otherwise known as KRS ONE of *Boogie Down Productions*, had been a social worker and introduced himself on his records as both a philosopher and a teacher. He lost Scott La Rock, his DJ and closest colleague, to gun violence in the midst of the hugely creative period celebrated here, and subsequently set in motion the Stop the Violence movement, which, had it been more successful, might have extended the longevity of that golden age.

What to me was 'golden' about those few special years of invention and progress was the degree of inspired sophistication in both music-making and rhyming, which, while incorporating newly conscious and self-conscious levels and details of urban realism nevertheless maintained and developed important elements of the good times and party roots of Old-School rapping. And it was this benign force and legacy that ensured – for a time at least – that a rapper's bragging, pride, wit and passion; as well as their declarations of competitive antagonism, all necessarily remained (to some degree at least), tongue-in-cheek. It was all, at that time at least, a performance of pride and skill, but a performance nevertheless.

This self-consciousness of the performance of New School rap was evidence of its own historical consciousness, its self-awareness as the perpetuation of a tradition that had attained a new plateau. Pride in this craft, its progress and its growing legacy also encouraged its practitioners to make it artful and witty, and in this way incapable of becoming so blindly serious that it could simply advocate violence.

Many of the star rappers of that time, if viewed today, in retrospect, in their relatively cheap, hastily made videos, were far from muscle-bound, gold-laden and threatening, but (see, e.g., the original video for Rob Base & DJ EZ Rock's smash hit, *It Takes Two*) tended instead to be wiry wordsmiths and metropolitan masterminds who showed themselves surrounded by peers from their neighbourhoods all keen to get their faces, sneakers, track suits, haircuts, and if possible dance moves, into the frame, to share in a moment of fleeting and joyful success, in lives otherwise bound up in serpentine knots caused by a struggle to survive entwined with high creative aspirations.[1] Much of this material can now be seen, at least from my own mellowed perspective, as even endearing.

Rap was, then at least, still primarily rhetorical in the true and historic sense of the word, i.e., whatever its content, a rap was first and foremost a knowing performance of prowess, currency and skill, the demonstration of a craft by means of which the rapper aims to be admired or ends up humiliated, either gets paid or stays poor, is either promoted or eliminated from a competition, and – at that time anyway – this was still a competition directly among artists, DJs and crews, rather than among gun-wielding gangs or big-budget-wielding record companies.

Alongside this self-consciously rhetorical and performative core, rap was always, and nevertheless, a means to an end, primarily the aim of being seen, heard, understood, valued and appreciated; a way of participating in the world and of cultivating pride and ambition. This all arose from, and despite the most inauspicious socio-economic circumstances.

New School Hip-Hop music is an art form created, as it were, out of nothing but the misuse of basic DJ-ing equipment and the re-use of existing record collections (in fact the entire archive of black music history, if not the entire archive of recorded sound). Meanwhile its accompanying raps were nothing but inspired and intricate representations of immediate reality, drawn into playful and imaginative new relationships by the primary criteria and demands of rhythm and rhyme.

It is important to also repeat here that rap is an art form, based not only in a tradition of rhetoric but also, consequently and correspondingly, in a form of competitiveness which might blur a certain perceived boundary or distinction made in other cultures between art, sport, and street life. Furthermore, the careful appropriation and cultural redeployment of sports clothes, along with trophy-like golden chains and rings in Hip-Hop culture, also reflects this blurring. As in sport, judgements and valuations pertaining to rap are relatively unequivocal, so that booing and dissing of competitors is not only allowed but is an essential element, albeit often provided (and at best) in a relatively light-hearted manner.

At the heart of the New School version of rap, which, between 1986 and 1989, started to become a million-selling, worldwide record genre and industry, lies the simple, improvised battling of two or more MCs going literally head-to-head and 'coming off the top' (rhyming spontaneously), each trying to defeat the other by, if possible, 'traveling at the speed of thought' (as *The Ultramagnetic MCs* memorably put it). The aim is always to win the reputational laurels of best or better rhymer, and thus the support of an audience that might be convened in a club, sports hall event, social centre, park, or street corner.

Nuanced and dextrous invention, newly outrageous ways of boasting, etc., will always be applauded, but anything flat-footed, half-hearted, tentative or clichéd will be immediately identified and slapped down as 'wack'. As with any other art form, awareness of context is crucial, and so contemporary references and current debates – the newer and hotter the better – as well as plays on the latest developments in rap styles, slang, and language more broadly, are all essential to success. The point here is that New School rap directly translated, promoted, and internationally proliferated the language and values of the streets and impoverished projects from which it emerged. Any truly successful rapper knows how to frame that language and those values with a charm and invention that render them, simultaneously, deadly serious and clearly rhetorical.

Note

1 See www.youtube.com/watch?v=phOW-CZJWT0.

Bibliography

Eric B & Rakim (Barrier, E. & Griffin, W. writers) (1987a) *My Melody* (music recording). Universal Songs of Polygram International Inc., BMI.

Eric B & Rakim (Barrier, E. & Griffin, W. writers) (1987b) *Paid in Full* (music recording). Universal Songs of Polygram International Inc., BMI.

Gil Scott-Heron (Heron, G.S. & Jackson, B. writers) (1974) *The Bottle* (music recording). Peermusic Publishing.

Grandmaster Flash (Chase, C., Fletcher, E., Glover, M. & Robinson, S. writers) (1982) *The Message* (music recording). Universal Music – Z Songs, Sun Shining Inc., All Maf Productions Inc.

Gwen Guthrie (Guthrie, G. writer) (1986) *Ain't Nothing Going On but the Rent* (music recording). Universal Music Publishing Group, Sony/ATV Music Publishing LLC.

Malcolm Maclaren (McLaren, M., Horn, T., & Dudley, A. writers) (1982) *Buffalo Gals* (music recording). Universal Songs of Polygram International Inc., BMI.

The Valentine Brothers (1982) *Money's Too Tight to Mention* (music recording). Otis Music Publishing Company, Stan Flo Music Publishing Company.

22

A PERSONAL HISTORY OF NEW SCHOOL HIP-HOP – PART 2

Building on but also away from the Black Is Beautiful and Black Power movements of the 1960s and 1970s, the Hip-Hop of the late 1980s did not embody the overt politics of a minority culture's demands. While Martin Luther King, in one of his most influential speeches, had repeatedly cried 'Now Is The Time!' only for those revolutionary words to undergo deferral and disappointment, Flava Flav, Public Enemy's trickster-like sidekick to front man Chuck D, repeatedly interrupt his lead rapper's politicised flow with his own weirdly insistent question: 'What Time Is It?' meanwhile wearing a timepiece the size of a kitchen clock draped around his neck.

Public Enemy's DJ, Terminator X, would simultaneously locate and cut up slices of black music history to produce loops, scratches and samples that provided an adamant, driving yet funky beat enhanced with an eerie, uncanny, discordant and experimental halo. Add to these plays with time and history the then pervasive image of a baseball cap worn reversed, and the whole takes on potential symbolism as a refusal of any simplistic or teleological sense of progress, any presumption of a forward-going and auspicious direction.

So, when Flava Flav kept saying 'What Time Is It?' while wearing that clock and a baseball cap turned backwards, you got the unnerving, but simultaneously liberating feeling that language, time, meaning, and history were being jumbled and rejigged, unfixed from their usual use and context, like a Mercedes or VW sign levered off the bonnet of a car, to thereby and thereafter float free of any given and established order and context. Words, however apparently authoritative, were re-deployed poetically, re-ordered, turned inside out or upside down if necessary, by a generation, a culture, who may just have entirely new uses for them.

Meanwhile, Hip-Hop dancers body-popped or spun in distorted circles often on their heads, and developed variations on the moonwalk – according to which a simultaneously mimetic and robotic human appears to travel both forwards and backwards. In many ways these dancers proclaimed a carnivalesque inversion, refusal

DOI: 10.4324/9781003230632-25

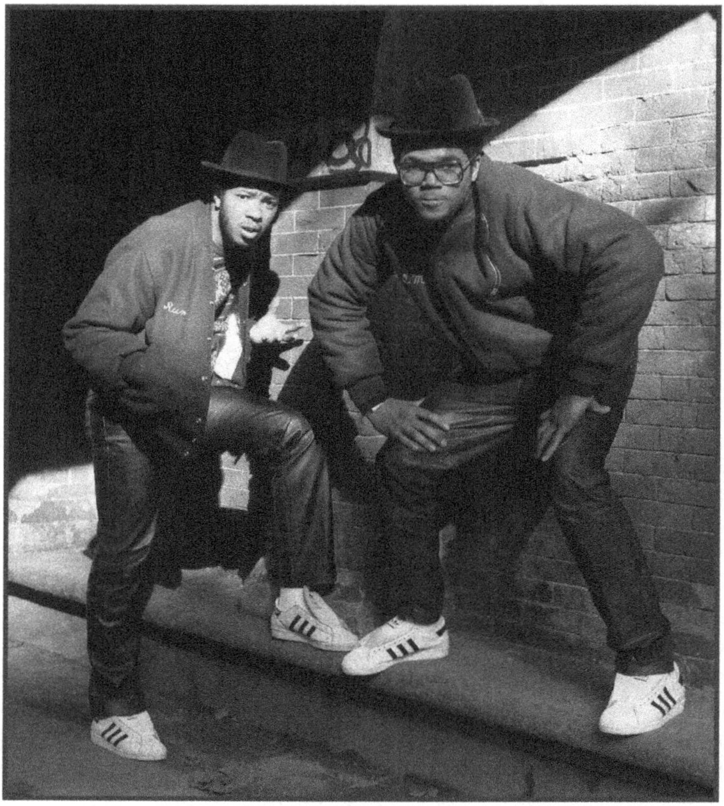

FIGURE 22.1 Run DMC's Joseph 'Run' Simmons and Darryl 'D.M.C.' McDaniels pose in Central Park, New York, 1984. Photographed by Oliver Morris/Getty Images.

and dissent, performing emphatic disruptions and radical acts, in response to which the original European *avant-garde* and jazz generations might have been awed and envious.

Such disorientations, contradictions, refusals and paradoxes might render all equal, in that these very forces are able to reveal a pre- or post-linguistic, pre- or post-syntagmatic, pre- or post-grammatical state in which actions, words and their meaning are rendered out of order and up for grabs – as they might well be for the poet or rhetorician. Words, for the poet, rapper or rhetorician (who may also adopt new words for their own assumed stage name) are materials to mould into an image of truth and reality, and simultaneously an acknowledgement of the arbitrariness of any externally imposed or given notion of truth and reality.

Those most oppressed and who might seem to have least access to the luxurious academic commodities of 'critique and debate', so familiar to the privileged, middle, or 'chattering' classes, might be forced to think and act hyper-creatively, in ways that necessarily go beyond known, dialectical and otherwise teleological structures, indeed, beyond altercation itself and beyond established discourse, truth and meaning, to think and act within the broad and artful realm of rhetoric where words and signs can be scrambled and disoriented, performed, hyperbolised and rendered parodic.[1]

And all this to survive and possibly escape the otherwise debilitating and demeaning structural paradoxes, contradictions, and disorientations imposed by the combined powers of poverty, oppression and injustice. For example, the idea that if I protest or revolt I may make things worse for myself. Or, no matter how I try to climb socially I can never thereby escape the condition of an *arriviste*. Or, in accepting assistance to escape my inferior position in a hierarchy I become yet more dependent and thus more inferior, etc. Such are the paradoxes of poverty, or just a few at least.

Scrambling all established orientations, dancing on your head, walking both forwards and backwards simultaneously, reversing your hat, insisting that bad means good, wearing affordable sportswear as a street champion's robes, spray painting and writing esoteric tags and signs, mixing apparently incongruous records, making unexpected rhymes, all of these are ways of refusing and dissenting that, nevertheless, and simultaneously, serve to create and form a subculture's own rules, laws, and language. But they have wider implications for the cultural theorist or social philosopher messing with habitual forms and with relations of history and futurity.

When the DJ, misusing the technologies of record deck, mixer and sampler, spins, rewinds, repeats and loops a single bar of a beat, a futuristic art form (and we might say the future itself) is born and heard. And yet the material of which that future is made is the past. New School Hip-Hop thereby insists upon rethinking our habitual representation, or logic of the relationship between past and future, in ways that might also suggest a political upheaval.

1980s Hip-Hop convinces us, albeit rhetorically, that if we use idiosyncratic and experimental, verbal or visual language (consider the difficulty of reading graffiti tags for the uninitiated), with a certain degree of emphasis, gusto, and confidence, while taking cultural practices to courageous and inventive limits, we may yet be able to twist the bars of cages from which there is no option but to escape, bars rendered malleable by the heat of creative energies. If so, the artist cannot be said to be simply doing wrong, nor committing a crime, but rather confusing, bewildering, and questioning whether the existing notion of 'the wrong' might itself be wrong.

It is at this point that we might operate at a truly radical, progressive, and perhaps avant-garde level, disturbing the roots of our context while reframing our plight as a newly heroic and inventive adventure. In doing so, we aim to leave the prison guards or police (as silent movie clowns often did, and as attendees of carnival still do) taking off their helmets and scratching their heads. We might puzzle the law, confuse the court, and shake justice by pointing out that bad can mean good, as it does on every occasion on which we rightfully demonstrate or protest in a way that others regard as transgressive.

For Hip-Hop graffiti artists of the 1980s, the walls, streets, and sides of trains were galleries, but they were spaces taken, occupied, territorialised and never requested. The artists' fame was bravely claimed and marked out, their work exhibited without

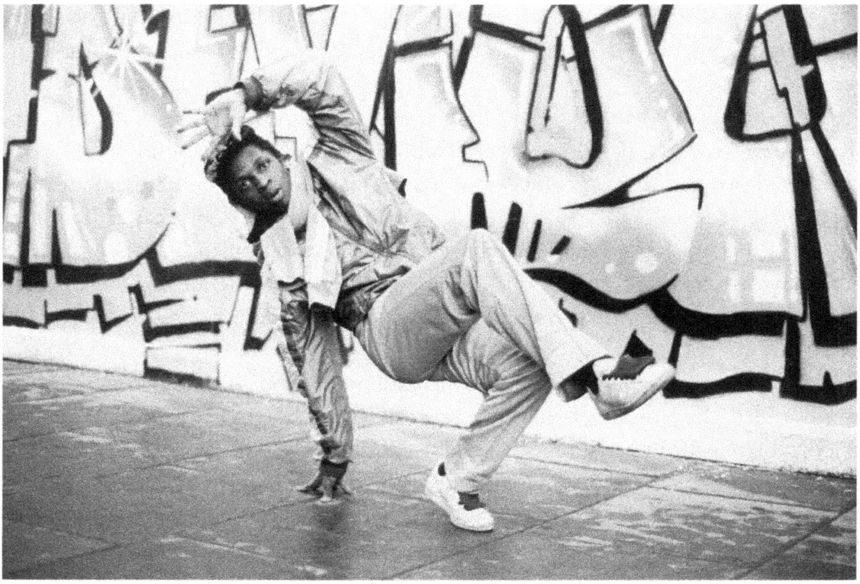

FIGURE 22.2 A breakdancer in action against a graffiti backdrop, Covent Garden, London, 1985. Photographed by Leon Morris/Hulton Archive/Getty Images.

waiting for recognition by a paternalistic commercial gallery system of 'middlemen', who might one day deign to allow a few outsiders in and through.

Hip-Hop artists 'bombed' trains using stolen spray cans, working at night after breaking into locked sidings. Come the morning, those trains had become canvas and gallery for a painter's signature style, and thus for the culture of Hip-Hop as a whole. Then, those massive, mobile artworks, layered with designs and declarations, slid out of Brooklyn or Queens at dawn to spend the day riding into and through Manhattan for everyone, cleaners and clerks, baristas and bankers, to see.

Any form of dissent here is wrapped in a productive artfulness, while political action, in this and many of the examples used here, invariably means not waiting or deferring, not mediating, nor handing responsibility for your life, your problem, or your dream to some other power or person; to the state, or to any established political system; nor even to any abstract and debatable notion of historical progress. Compared to Hip-Hop, all those options would merely be more or less obedient forms of relative inaction and complicity.

Emerging within impoverished, black, urban communities, 1980s Hip-Hop may have seemed, to a critic steeped in a left-wing political tradition, to act with a certain capitalist complicity – 'Just Do-ing It', as a popular Nike slogan emerging at that time declared. And yet, inexorably, and ultimately successfully, Hip-Hop carved out a cultural space, territory, industry and economy, perhaps most significantly by using art as the centre of, and as the key to its community, its power, its politics, its economy, its history, and perhaps even its law.

Hip-Hop always seemed to go forward by going back. DJs mixed and looped old records by radically misusing record decks and mixers, along with the latest samplers and a pantheon of vintage drum machines. However, as well as going forwards by going backwards Hip-Hop also seemed to raise itself upward by going downward, its dancers exceeding bodily limitations, not through transcendent attempts at balletic flight but rather by means of a newly emphatic relationship with the ground, seemingly embracing the undeniability of gravity, an immanent force which, like capitalism, Hip-Hop never refuted, denied, or contested, but rather tended to over-affirm and over-determine, perhaps as a way and a means of avoiding being crushed by it. We could therefore think of the New School Hip-Hop strategy as a kind of radical complicity.

To attempt an analogy, boxers sometimes hug their assailant tightly as a way of disarming and tiring their power while cramping their fighting style. Perhaps this would be a useful image to help someone like myself growing up with left-wing political thinking, to understand the way in which Hip-Hop seemed to explicitly embrace the very capitalism that oppressed it, seeing wealth, or at least 'getting paid' (paid for the first time *in generations*, paid in fact for the first time *ever*) as at least a first step towards a broader form of emancipation.

Much like their 1960s forerunners in Motown, who took the motor-car production line as a model for making successful and lucrative soul records, Hip-Hop's dancers reflected an era in which both new technology and a new economy were increasingly bearing down upon humanity, inevitably having the crudest and most immediate impact on the poorest members of the richest societies. Hip-Hop's dancers Body-Popped like futuristic robots, and impossibly contorted themselves like living manikins undergoing manipulation by unseen hands. They span on their heads like human drills trying to get further underground or to escape poverty-bound bodies by means of a strangely inverted Sufi-like disorientation.

If Hip-Hop's approach to politics avoided any simplistic idea of linear directionality it also had no direct or apparent association with the liberative Marxist project that informed so much of my own left-leaning art, life, philosophy, and politics. While the reggae of the Bob Marley era had tended to cultivate a marginal, alternative culture and belief system, challenging the rampant 'Babylon' of consumerism, media, and the unjustly policed modern state, 1980s Hip-Hop rather 'bought' capitalism, at least in that, for the most part, one of the central and explicit aims of its artists was always to get paid – albeit perhaps as a parodic mirror of the 'no-alternative' Reaganomic and Thatcherite creed then aggressively transforming the so-called 'leading nations' while bearing down upon and threatening the poor, the weak and the vulnerable.

Though perhaps more aware of capitalism's heinous roots, methods, and violent injustices than anyone in the so-called leading nations, the young black Americans who invented and evolved Hip-Hop did not suggest or promote any utopia, judgement day or deliverance; any alternative society or economy. Nor did they set out to challenge mainstream, consumerist, capitalist society's fundamental tenets. Rather, these all tended to be incorporated, accepted, and referred to as a crucial aspect of a given, unchangeable – for the time being at least – reality. However, when rappers bragged about getting paid, wore clothes as commodities, wore gold or golden chains, boasted of drinking champagne, driving luxury cars etc., they may, nevertheless, have strived to out-capitalise capitalism itself, i.e., parodying or developing a pumped-up, rhetorical image of the central aim for their lives, their art, and their society.

That aim was to first, foremost, and finally obtain sufficient wealth to demonstrate the possibility of escape from generations of lives led in ghettoised and over-policed poverty just a few wrong steps away from exclusion from school, broken home, unemployment and imprisonment, and all this despite being shoved up close and hard against one of the richest and most privileged societies on earth. The aim, furthermore, was not to make an escape 'by any means necessary'[2] but rather to prevail by means of art, craft, skill, style and fashion.

The actions exampled here, in New School rap and 1980s Hip-Hop (while some also appear in Punk, Rock & Roll, Jazz, etc.), are innately disobedient. They necessarily refuse and evade established, polite, discursive and refined procedures, so as to maintain a culture's own vitality and to avoid being compromised, diluted, mis-translated, and thereby demotivated and dissipated by established, external structures.

Perhaps, only by insisting on a fundamental, historically deep-bitten refusal to comply (even while maintaining the guise of an apparent, magnanimously expressed complicity) could such a truly new creative cultural paradigm (not a new work or new style but a new *paradigm*) survive and thrive adequately to serve this dynamic subculture or minority; informing its art and its politics and succeeding in the ultimate, urgent, necessarily positive aim of improving its lot, against all odds and at an impossible moment, while delivering a more self-respecting future – all (and this is surely crucial) by its own means, and on its own terms.

For those few golden years, Hip-Hop seemed to provide the world with a new way of talking, walking, dressing, dancing and making art; a way that was both highly pro-active and simultaneously dissenting; a way, perhaps, of fighting power by embracing it, while expressing a dynamic culture that leapt fearlessly beyond all usual assumptions about how art and politics might be conducted or inform each other.

For me, 1980s New School Hip-Hop took a different approach to any relationship between history, art, culture, economics, and politics that I had previously encountered. New School rap resisted politically by expanding social, cultural, and economic territory, fighting power by being creatively powerful, and responding to poverty, prejudice, segregation and oppression, not with stones, placards, and speeches; not with academically conducted arguments and ballot boxes; and not even by suggesting an alternative socio-economic system, but through the apparently infinite resource of a fulsome and central art form, one that was a way of life in itself, an economy, a politics, a *milieu,* and a belief system informing and pervading every aspect of the society from which it emerged and which it proudly served.

If, in rap, politics becomes (or returns) to rhetoric (in the most positive sense of that word), i.e., a performative wielding of amplified, more or less convincing, signs and codes, we might say the same for Hip-Hop's economics. Even as rap pertains to, and arises from the pressing political issues of poverty, racism, prejudice, and an overbearing, industrial-scale penal system, it nevertheless avoids a direct clash with external truth-claims, by ceaselessly acknowledging the truth of its artfulness, of its craft, rhythm, imagery, wit, etc. That *is* rhetoric.

Economically, a huge gold or golden chain becomes a rhetorical and hyperbolic counterweight to real poverty and to ancestral generations of poverty, stretching far back into the past, back to colonialism and slavery of course, and a poverty that – unless something is done (Just Do It) stretches away into the future too.

The New School rap performer invariably goes under an adopted name and often wears clothing and jewellery that are a dramatic amplification of established coded signs and symbols. While for the jazz musicians of the 1920s and 1930s some kind of pawned, second-hand suit might, despite their perilous poverty, have been necessary to maintain standards of smartness associated with professional credibility, for this 1980s generation, sneakers and sports clothes were a form of affordable smart attire, within reach of the famously, fastidious and self-consciously stylish, yet also notoriously poor black American community.

My Adidas (1986), one of Hip-Hop act Run DMC's biggest hits, focused its attention on the wearing of clean, bright, new sneakers, visually amplified by being worn loose, open, idiosyncratically laced or unlaced, thereby increasing the sneakers' apparent volume and symbolism as a kind of hyper-commodity.[3] Thus, something commonplace, essential, and relatively cheap was simply but significantly subverted into an unmistakable subcultural sign, not revered as an out-of-reach aspiration or deferred desire, but displayed as a territorial claim, immediately made.

Another of Run DMC's hits featured the line 'Not Bad Meaning Bad, But Bad Meaning Good', a seeming declaration that, in Hip-Hop's new paradigm and in the world of New School rap, language, logic, or grammar could not be imposed as and by any external master's voice.[4] Rather – like an inherited record collection, the contents of a sportswear shop, or of a used electronic equipment store – words exist as a kind of archive, there to be discovered, woven, broken, used, misused, reused, reclaimed, reworked, and reversed if necessary, giving wordsmiths maximum freedom to play their part in creating a new cultural paradigm.

Sports clothes, while broadcasting messages relating to competition, also come with implications of futurity due to their associations with technology, progress, and excellence. Sport is always pushing into the future, achieving objectively verifiable excellence, breaking records, changing possibility and extending what human beings and human bodies are capable of. Track suit and sneakers, while affordable attire, were redeployed by New School Hip-Hop, becoming the ideal outfit in which to programme a drum-machine, to perform a human beat-box, to body-pop, or to rhyme inventively about being better than the rest.

To wear sports clothes, in pristine commodity form, yet slightly subverted and re-cultured, by, e.g., reversing caps or swelling-up sneakers by artful misuse of their laces; and to then further amplify the outfit with more or less, real or fake, outsized watches and chains, makes of the self an instant hero, a *Hercules* of stage or street, and all in a kind of unmediated, un-deferred – perhaps we could even say 'immanent' gesture.[5]

Thus, this success, this economy, of style and of fashion, is as rhetorical as is much else in rap, i.e., it is performed, claimed, and contrived as a convincing image, and yet an image which nevertheless serves, through its conviction, as the most likely vehicle by means of which to achieve the real, actual and indisputable success of 'getting paid', here and now, and not in some promised, hypothetical, ideological, and political promised land. For New School Hip-Hop, the future (like the latest sneaker; or a rhyme coming spontaneously 'off the top'; or like a spray-painted graffiti flourish exercised in a hurry before running from a subway guard) is certainly, and always, precisely, now.

In that brief golden period circa 1986–1989, Hip-Hop and New School rap broke out of their local scenes, projects and ghettos onto a world stage, thus creating a whole new wing of the music industry, one that is now a bigger and more lucrative market than that established in the 1960s and 1970s by rock music. Its popularity and influence are still clearly growing, year by year becoming ever more influential to new, increasingly artful, inventive and successful artists, generations, and communities.

For some, rap and Hip-Hop may have also become relatively decadent, overblown, and corrupted by the trappings of its immense success, all further encouraged by the hyper-visibility of the luxuriant pop-video format, etc. Nevertheless, despite such huge and apparently capitalism-complicit achievements, it maintains the status of a subcultural movement, one which has fulfilled much of its initial political and economic mission to 'get paid' while never ceasing to entertain, to compete creatively, and to innovate, always with wit and invention, and nevertheless, and thereby, always also fighting power.

Today there is a global, billion-dollar rap industry (one to which, I admit, I now pay less attention), producing wealth and employment, nurturing professionalism and thus providing avenues to middle-class lifestyles for new generations of previously impoverished people. 1980s Hip-Hop and New School rap might justifiably claim to have done what it saw as the most basic and important part of its duties, without overtly embroiling itself in more arcane, idealistic, visionary, or abstract historical debates about social progress and ultimate justice.

Hip-Hop's achievement was made with an unusual mix of consensus and dissent, radical complicity and outrage, a mix of charming and offensive qualities, all of which may have served to avoid a more direct, potentially more ill-fated confrontation with the massive, ever-present, and intimidating penal system ranked against young black Americans in the 1980s and of course still now.[6] Hip-Hop and New School rap succeeded by means of a crafted, rhetorical, often jocular, and always to some degree tongue-in-cheek inventiveness, allied to radical experimentation. This combination kept the genre underground and marginal while nevertheless proliferating exponentially and succeeding worldwide.

Late 1980s Hip-Hop achieved a thorough political and aesthetic transformation by means of non-dialectical, non-confrontational, creative and innovative, rhetorical, mischievous and spirited strategies that might appear to remain complicit with all that antagonised it. A great many artists and rhetoricians, compelled to example an effective form of dissenting political action, showed themselves capable of creating a new paradigm, language or reality of their own, one that detached itself from any consensual or complicit aspiration to logic and truth (representatives of the good), and instead went further than these existing values, refuting them, inverting them, exceeding their own logic and truth, to claim a new and alternative language and signification. And this is a point where progress becomes a cultural paradigm shift, where bad comes to mean good.

By means of New School rap and Hip-Hop's paradigm shift, the past is also rendered futuristic. This may sound illogical, but it is rather a fact manufactured from a new logic. Given New School Hip-Hop's paradigm shift, the response to poverty can be to over-embrace, to the point of parody, the most feared and dominant forces – capitalism, gold, greed – rather than explicitly opposing or running away from them in the possibly misguided direction of a teleologically promised better world.

New School Hip-Hop always insisted that anything better must be here, now, and must come from yourself. Thus, funky diva Lyn Collins on the intro to '*Think (about it)*' (1972) comes irresistibly to mind, proudly proclaiming: ' … we gonna use what we've got, to get what we want'. All of Hip-Hop's positivity and reality seems to be there, at the start of a track that numerous rappers and DJs of the next, 1980s, generation (including Rob Base and DJ E-Z Rock) sampled, looped, and rapped over to create masterful hits of their own.

Notes

1 We might invoke Gilles Deleuze's *The Logic of Sense* here too.
2 The famous axiom associated with Malcolm X – though purportedly coined by Jean Paul Sartre.
3 Run DMC (1986).
4 Run DMC (1986).
5 Title of one of the author's favourite, formative, much looped and sampled tracks, performed and recorded by Aaron Neville. The classical image of Hercules here becomes a model of the heroic mentality needed in order to survive and maintain pride and self-respect amid the day-to-day challenges of the 1970s black ghetto life. *Hercules*, (perf. Aaron Neville) written by Alan Toussaint (1973), Warner Tamerlane Publishing Corp.
6 Wang, J. (2018).

Bibliography

Eric B & Rakim (Barrier, E. & Griffin, W. writers) (1987a) *My Melody* (music recording). Universal Songs of Polygram International Inc., BMI.

Eric B & Rakim (Barrier, E. & Griffin, W. writers) (1987b) *Paid In Full* (music recording). Universal Songs of Polygram International Inc., BMI.

Grandmaster Flash (Chase, C., Fletcher, E., Glover, M. & Robinson, S. writers) (1982) *The Message* (music recording). Universal Music – Z Songs, Sun Shining Inc., All Maf Productions Inc.

Malcolm Maclaren (McLaren, M., Horn, T. & Dudley, A. writers) (1982) *Buffalo Gals* (music recording). Universal Songs of Polygram International Inc., BMI.

Run DMC (Daniels, M.C. & Matthews, D. writers) (1986) *My Adidas* (music recording). Protoons Inc.

Run DMC (Daniels, M.C. & Matthews, D. writers) (1986) *Peter Piper* (music recording). Protoons Inc.

The Valentine Brothers (Valentine, J., Valentine, W. & Wiggins, C.J. writers) (1982) *Money's Too Tight to Mention* (music recording). Otis Music Publishing Company, Stan Flo Music Publishing Company.

Toussaint, A. (perf. Aaron Neville) (1973) *Hercules* (music recording). Warner Tamerlane Publishing.

Wang, J. (2018) *Carceral Capitalism*. Los Angeles, CA: Semiotext(e).

23

GIVING FORM TO HISTORY

History and story, Johannes Phokela, and the Soweto museums[1]

> A dad once asked his son 'The story or the warrior, who do you think is stronger?' 'The warrior' replied the son. 'You are wrong' said the father, 'the warrior might win a thousand battles but the story survives to tell the exploits of the warrior'.
>
> *Traditional Nigerian tale, relayed by Chike Chinazom*

Making History, a 2007 exhibition showcasing the Society of Antiquaries at London's Royal Academy, reminds us of a Biblical timeframe for history which still held sway in Enlightened and modernising Europe deep into the 19th century, and working on the assumption that the world is a just a few thousand years old.[2] A complicated genealogy or family tree in the same exhibition (*The Roll Chronicle* 1422–1471) attempts to justify the reign of King Henry VI by tracing his lineage and authority back to Adam and Eve.[3] This is hand-painted in red and winding, river-like or tree-like lines, on a textile of which only a few meters of the much longer scroll is unrolled and made visible for the exhibition.

A more manageable form – albeit for a much greater period – appears in a National Aeronautics and Space Administration (NASA) map, using a graphic that can be usefully and easily represented in the ubiquitous 21st-century medium and context of A4 paper, or shown easily on PowerPoint. Here, NASA, representing the USA, emulates Henry VI in the way that it plots its own divine right, now back to the big bang while inspired formally, not by tree or river-like shapes but by something akin to a disposable coffee cup.

What is perhaps most interesting in these examples is that what we call knowledge of time and history is changing so rapidly that it seems inherently unreliable. And, as a response to this uncertainty, every era and culture imposes form upon that time *as* history, in order to gain a perspectival control, which in turn awards legitimacy and justifies power.

DOI: 10.4324/9781003230632-26

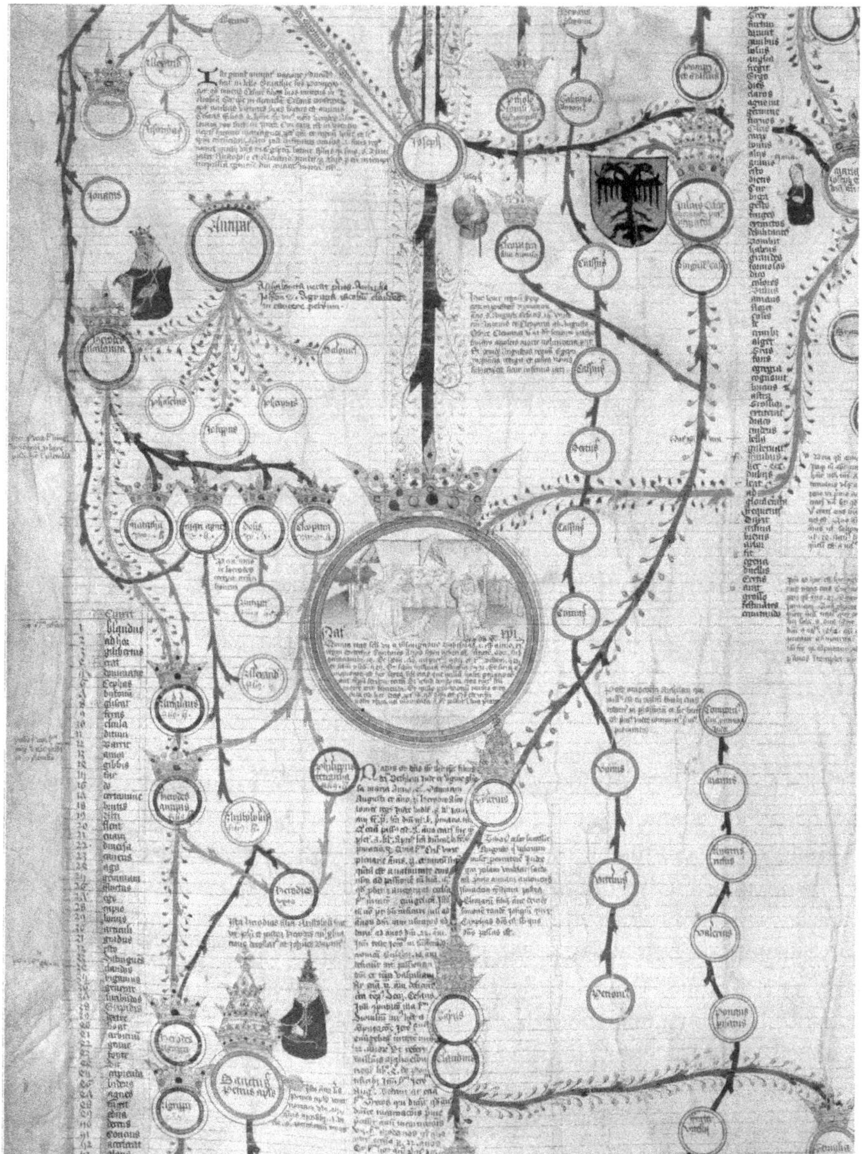

FIGURE 23.1 Part of *The Roll Chronicle* (left) and detail (right). Compiled to chart the descent of Henry VI (1422–1471) from Adam and Eve. Courtesy of the Society of Antiquaries of London. MSS/0501: Membrane 2: Adam and Eve The Temptation. © The Society of Antiquaries of London. And MSS/0501: Membrane 10 © The Society of Antiquaries of London.

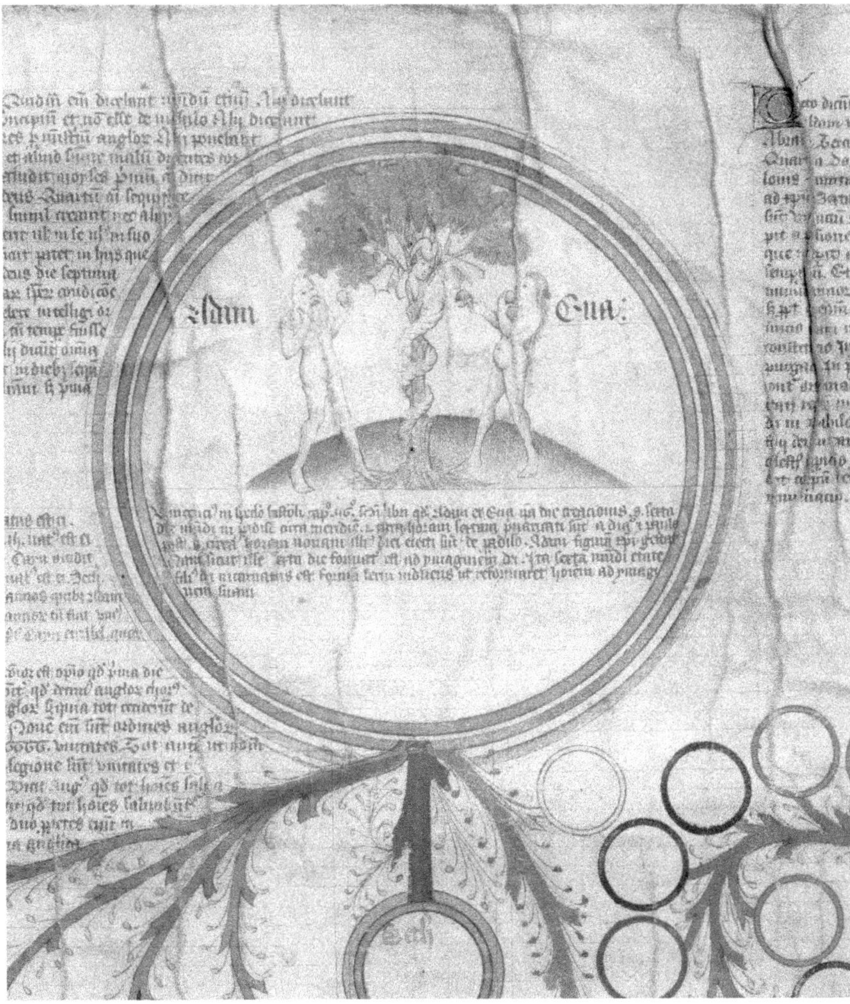

FIGURE 23.1 (Continued)

What is true of history may well be true of art history. We can look back into art history today and see powerful individuals crafting and bending history as they go. London's Courtauld Galleries display not only prime examples of post-Impressionist painting but also the story of how Roger Fry and Samuel Courtauld between them put the term 'post-Impressionism' on the art history map as part of a project to celebrate and establish the value of Cezanne's work (subsequently seen as pivotal in modern art history).

Anyone who has seen the above-mentioned family tree of Henry VI might agree that it bears similarities to a diagram made by Alfred H. Barr, director of the New York city Museum of Modern Art during the 1930s, as part of the scramble,

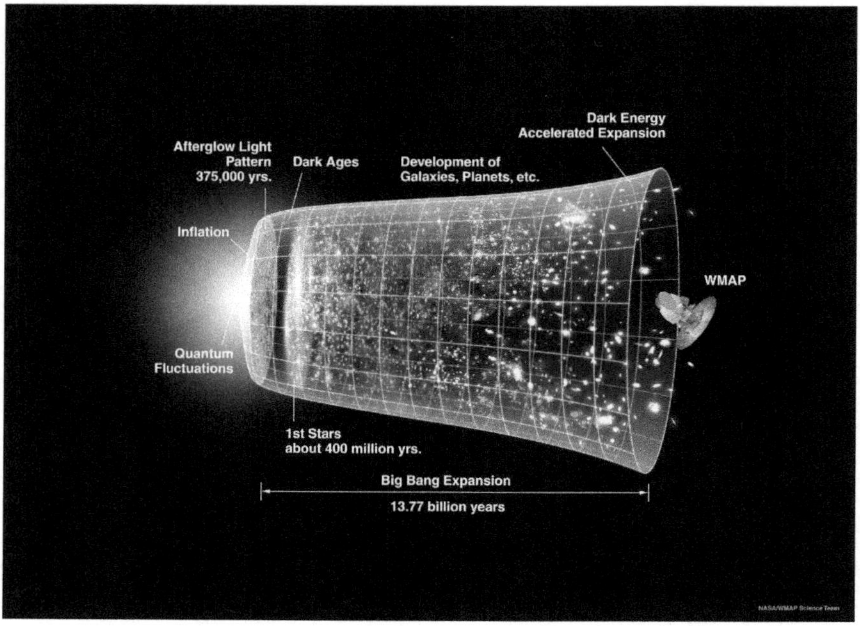

FIGURE 23.2 NASA. The timeline of the universe image (the 'coffee cup' image). A representation of the evolution of the universe over 13.77 billion years. The far left depicts the earliest moment we can now probe. Public domain. Credit: NASA/WMAP Science Team.

partially inspired by Fry and Courtauld, to claim an understanding of the dynamically unfolding phenomenon of modern art.

In this diagram, arrows sweep and swerve like plans for an occupation; causal connections are made as the story is woven together into a satisfying piece of knowledge, into history as fact. Ultimately, the dragon of uncertainty is slain by modern graphics and everything is clearly labelled by *sans serif* fonts until the nervous curator and historian can rest assured that, despite the complex revolutionary eruptions of modernism, everything does have a place in time and remains in place.

The form given by Marcel Duchamp to his own personal art history, during the forbidding years of the late 1930s with European futures in increasing doubt, is the *boite en valise* – now often considered an archival, museological, or curatorial exercise.[4] Here, Duchamp ironically 'hand-made' miniatures of his 'readymades' and found appropriate ways to represent his manifold and varied approaches to art. As an eccentric pragmatist more attuned to the 20th century's capitalist paradigm than to its opponents and alternatives, Duchamp modestly reduced his *oeuvre* to a selection of handy salesman's samples, ever ready to travel lightly (like many exiles and entrepreneurial adventurers from 1930s Europe) and potentially useful in the seduction of buyers and dealers.

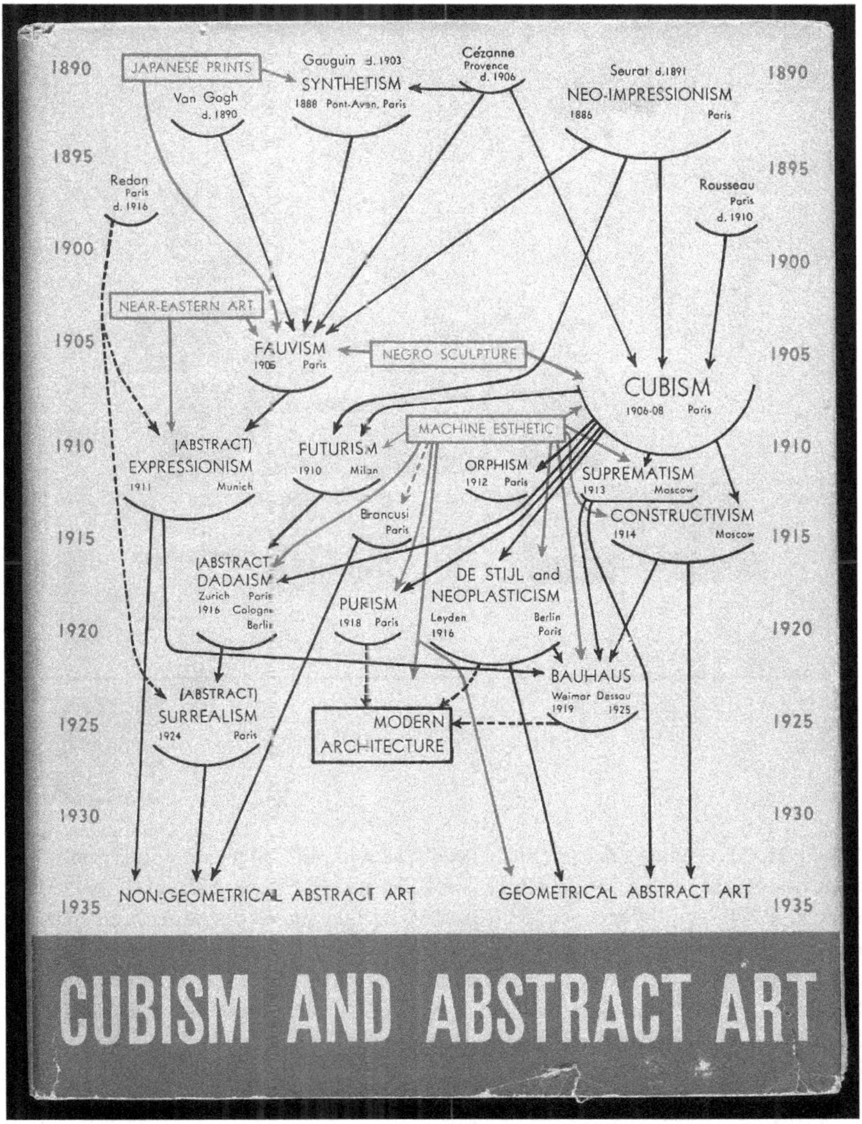

FIGURE 23.3 Barr, Alfred Hamilton Jr. (1902–1981). Cover of the exhibition catalogue. *Cubism and Abstract Art.*, MoMA 1936. New York, Museum of Modern Art (MoMA). Offset, printed in colour (19.7 cm ×26 cm). The Museum of Modern Art Library, New York. MA143© 2021. Digital image, The Museum of Modern Art, New York / Scala, Florence.

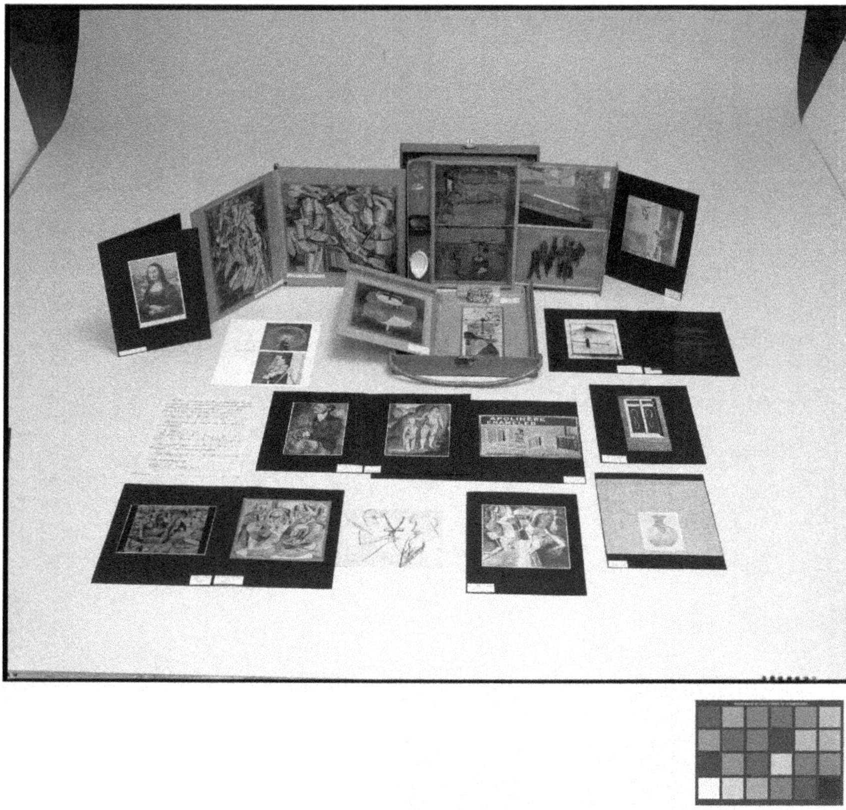

FIGURE 23.4 Duchamp, Marcel (1887–1968): *Boite-en-valise*. Duchamp ou Rrose Selavy) – *Box in a Valise* (From or by Marcel Duchamp or Rrose Selavy), 1935–1941. New York, Museum of Modern Art (MoMA). Leather valise containing miniature replicas, photographs, colour reproductions of works by Duchamp, and one 'original' drawing (Large Glass, collotype on celluloid, (119 cm × 23.5 cm) (40.7 cm × 38.1 cm × 10.2 cm). James Thrall Soby Fund. Acc. n.: 67.1943.a-rrr.© 2021. Digital image, The Museum of Modern Art, New York/Scala, Florence.

According to Duchamp's re-reasoning of the operations of artworks, each of these miniatures can expand – under scrutiny, and with imagination (like memory itself) – back to their original scale, incorporating all the primary ideas and crucial concepts that give the works value, and that remain, even though size, craft, and materials (all rendered secondary by Duchamp's cerebral revolution) have changed. We can perhaps take this as a model of a way in which to represent history by making of it something manageably distilled into a reassuring story, one that we can carry with us, even while subject to modern disorientation and violently changing modern times.[5]

A history of art might seem relatively benign, it might give unity to a diverse *oeuvre*, it might affect art's value or the taste of the art audience, it might make certain artists and styles prominent while obscuring others, and at its most serious it might promote a particular cultural or nation-al perspective at the cost of obscuring others. While Duchamp's is a self-reflexive, intimately subjective history, Barr, Fry, and Courtauld, caught up in the conspiracy of forming the burgeoning modern narrative, are perhaps unaware of just how selective and empowering their overarching perspectives are, and for this ignorance we might today criticise them, or, with mock-Christian generosity, forgive them for they knew not what they did.

If we turn away from art history and towards art's view of history itself, we may assume that the stakes become higher. In postmodern or post-postmodern times, when every phenomenon has the potential to claim a meta status, to occupy a hyper-reality, and to take its place within a relativism resulting from a critique of value difference, Barr's map looks naïve, almost arbitrary. It uses some now anachronistic and inappropriate terminology and seems so much less authoritative than it presumably did in its, and Barr's, heyday. From a feminist perspective, a post-colonial perspective, a multicultural, Hi-Lo or *a*historical perspective, Barr's graphic and linear attempts to command, direct, and establish complex narratives and relationships appear merely local and overly perspectival.

The artist Simon Patterson once lampooned all such procedures by subverting, in his 1992 work *The Great Bear*, the London Underground map and awarding lines and stations to intersecting cultural categories – e.g., European philosophers or Renaissance painters for one line, famous footballers for another. He thus implicitly allowed these varied historical figures to potentially encounter each other at major junctions where surprising possibilities might result from their insertion into this subverted modern classic of organisational form: a form which – it is worth noting at this point – we know to be untrue, and which is yet an extremely useful representation, perhaps most useful in being most inaccurate.[6]

To diverge further from art and come closer to history itself, we can now explore forms and history in relation to a specific cultural and national history, i.e., the history of South Africa and its now disassembled apartheid regime. Since the euphoria of the early 1990s, when Nelson Mandela was released from prison, won a democratic election, and formed a soul-searching and forgiving rainbow government, incorporating all tribes, cultures, minorities, etc., the government has come under perhaps inevitable criticism for the slow pace of significant social and economic change. However, something on which little expense has been spared – and this is *not* a criticism – is history pivoted perhaps, around two state-of-the-art museums in the township of Soweto.

In Soweto, The Apartheid Museum and nearby Hector Pieterson Museum tell the same history, as a story, and in slightly different ways, to visiting schoolchildren, local residents, visitors from Johannesburg and the rest of the country, and to travellers from all over the world who are increasingly interested in sites of historical and political trauma and significance as tourist destinations (a phenomenon that Walter Benjamin or Jean Baudrillard would surely have been interested to witness and reflect upon).[7] The Apartheid Museum gives us the emotive story of how the

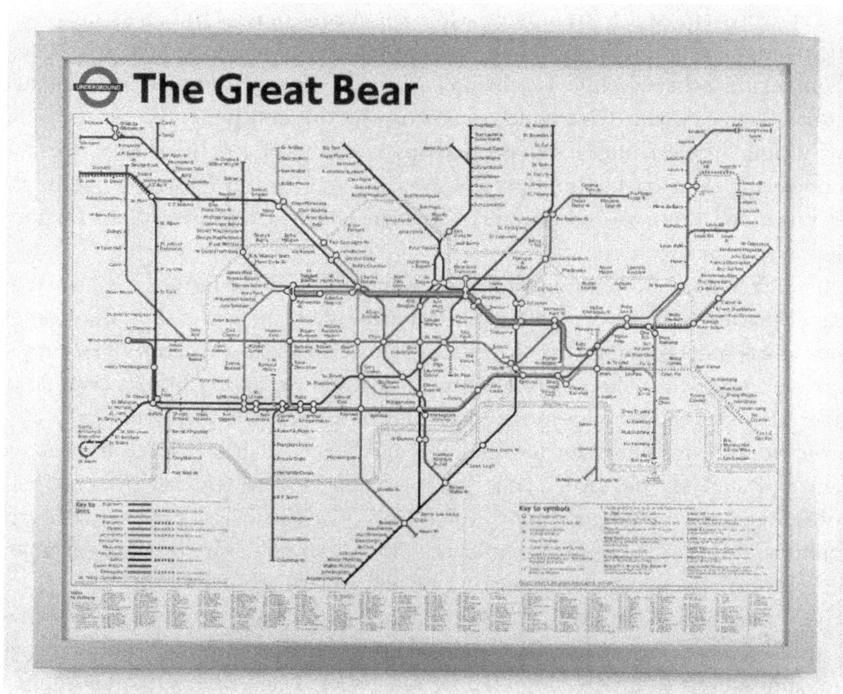

FIGURE 23.5 Simon Patterson, *The Great Bear*, 1992. Four-colour lithographic print in an anodised aluminium quad royal wall panel with glass and silicon seal. Edition of 50. Dimensions: 43" ×53"/109.2 cm × 134.6 scm. Copyright Simon Patterson and Transport for London. Photographed by Stephen White.

apartheid regime came into existence, how it thrived, then eventually succumbed to forces of social justice and racial equality. The Hector Pieterson Museum focuses on what might be called a turning point or fulcrum of that story.

The story is highly emotive and the Apartheid Museum is cleverly designed, using a blend of Hi-Technology and Brutalist architecture, to lead visitors up, down, around, and through dark and sometimes dismal spaces, while video recordings spark tears, anger, and disbelief before offering ultimate relief, joy, and comprehension as the story of a horrifying and disturbingly recent oppression turns to one of victory, and as we are delivered into the light of brighter, more open spaces by the thoughtful architecture.

In Johannesburg's currently wary and sceptical climate, a cynic might say that the museums are slightly heavy-handed in their formation of this history, but, given their temporal and physical proximity to the traumatic events they describe, and the deeply felt emotions that motivate their project, it is hard to imagine how else this story can be told, at this time at least. Nevertheless, the story is here convincingly pinned into form and into place by intelligently staged, designed, and selected information, artefacts and tableaux.

But let's now briefly *tell* the story. It is a 'good' story (formally) in the sense that it is worth hearing, though it is a story of something extremely bad that leads to something better. And that leading *is* the story, the story that led the country from something bad to something better over a period of almost 50 years, and which the visitor now takes in, by scrutinising and imaginatively unfolding often miniaturised representations in one or two hours.

Note that the all-important story not only outlives and records the events that inspire it, but also in some ways precedes, inspires, or gives rise to those events, i.e., we could say that it is the story that *led* the country even before the story itself was completed and formed. What we might call the spirit of the revolution, of any revolution, the spirit of necessary change and progress (perhaps invoking Hegel here) is itself a story, albeit latent or in outline, a story whose form cries out for appropriate events, as content, to fill and fulfil it. In this respect we might also say that the story and its events (destined to be historicised) seem to be made for the museum rather than the other way around.

However, the story also has independence from the state-funded museum, and remains in the mouths, hearts, and minds of the people; in lived experience, living memories, and in a state of flux which is maybe its truest and most accurate (albeit formless) form. Like all good stories it can be told from memory, and like all such stories it has been told before, and each time it is told it is a little different, a little less accurate perhaps as, even if the words remain the same, and even if a museum or book has pinned them into a certain order and into place, the world in which they are spoken will have changed.[8] The clearer the form of the story becomes, the more convincing its contents and meaning become, and therefore we could also say that, like the London Underground map, a story can become increasingly useful and reliable the more stylised and less 'accurate' it becomes.

A policy of apartheid (or separateness) was installed as what the South African government, in 1947 (i.e., with knowledge of Nazi atrocities) openly referred to as a 'final solution'.[9] This justified the destruction of black and mixed urban communities and the construction of vast suburban townships like Soweto where people were forced to live in tiny, uniform houses without electricity or any public transport other than a limited train service which could bring necessary labour into the city in the morning and then out again in the evening. There was a curfew for black people in the all white city, and so, to not comply with this strict mechanistic schedule was dangerous, and could even be fatal as many black people died mysteriously during apartheid once they found themselves in police custody.

Where black and mixed communities had previously thrived within the city, houses were bulldozed, making space to build leafy white developments with wide drives and large private houses. Meanwhile, in Soweto, every house was (and largely remains) the same, or very similar, stretching out as far as the eye can see, mostly consisting of four walls, four small rooms, a roof, and an outside toilet, all of which, from the outset of this unprecedented example of social and racial engineering, became overcrowded.

Education for black people under apartheid was also strategically minimal, the prime minister himself stated that it should purposefully qualify black people only for 'a menial role in society', there being no desire on the part of the ruling whites for black people to be in any way mobile, i.e., neither in terms of social aspiration nor geographic location.[10] Furthermore, when children *were* taught, they were taught in the Afrikaans language of the oppressive minority, a version of Flemish or Dutch; not in English, and not in any of the many indigenous languages of the region.

In 1976, after nearly 30 years of apartheid rule, children in Soweto schools, aged between 8 and 18 years, requested that they be taught in English, in this way hoping to find a way to communicate with the world beyond the confining culture of apartheid. They made several small, unsuccessful protests in their schools, but on the night of 15 June 1976, pupils of several schools secretly made placards for a march the following day, about which they informed neither their parents nor their teachers. They would march to *insist upon* being taught in English.

On the morning of 16 June, in the Soweto schools, when it was time to sing a daily hymn in the Afrikaans language, the children instead began singing a black African song, and this was the secretly arranged signal between them that the march would indeed take place. By the end of that day, several of the children had been shot dead by the police. Hector Pieterson, aged 13, was the first, or one of the first, to die. The place where he fell is now marked with a substantial monument and the museum named after him is nearby.

The events of that day are seen as pivotal, in that this children's crusade began the newly focused and assertive struggle against apartheid which eventually resulted in South Africa being expelled from the British Commonwealth, suffering sanctions imposed by United Nations countries, and becoming embroiled in a guerrilla war (with an international dimension) led by the African National Congress (ANC), who finally overcame apartheid by forcing the Afrikaans into a democratic election nearly 50 years after apartheid began, and 15 years after the children's march of June 1976.

This is the story told today in Soweto's new museums. We have briefly retold the story, which is just one of the many that you might hear today in South Africa, all of which are part of the one big story that in one way or another no one seems to stop talking about or thinking about, as the country searches to find its own form and future, and to heal deep and bitter wounds.

White Afrikaans have their own stories of course, which also give form to history. Some may best be forgotten and, under the unprecedented reconciliatory terms of the transition of power, may also be forgiven. However, to take just one small example that *is* perhaps worth remembering (in light, at least, of our theme here), we can make reference to a book, titled *Genealogical Register of the South African People*, published in 1966:

> ... it researched the limits of the South African nation in terms of intermarriage and genealogy [...] it draws a *white* limit, a racial boundary, despite the

apparently inclusive term South African people. There is palpable relief in South African Prime Minister Hendrik Verwoerd's preface to the book: 'That the people remained white', he marvels, 'in spite of exceptional circumstances, is [...] remarkable'.[11]

Though its aims are repugnant, and its conviction apparently deluded, this genealogy can be seen to serve the same *formal* purpose as several of the other examples in this chapter. This 'genealogical register', like the family tree, the Biblical history, the NASA map, the museum's story, Barr's diagram, or Duchamp's *boite en valise*, is yet another form given to another history, and designed with the intention of legitimising a present and presenting a legitimacy – even though it is based on the howling *illegitimacy* of a tiny percentage of colonising oppressors describing themselves as '*the* (South African) people' (my italics), and thereby insisting that everyone else in the country, despite their indigenous heritage, is either not part of its people, or simply not people. Again, we are reminded that inaccuracy is no bar to usefulness.

Historians must always hesitate before the responsibility and authority they wield in writing history, because history is made by, and remains in (or perhaps 'on') their hands. Every history needs its form or its debate with form, a shape and style that make its contents plausible and repeatable. The apartheid museum needs its architects and designers, along with the influence of numerous video and installation artists, to make its stories clear and to make its points with impact. There is a level of history that is scientific, involving research and a search for objectivity, but there is also its form, and the crucial art by means of which it is formed.

The forms we give to history will, it may seem from our examples, always be influenced by the empirical world, whether it be the influence of the forms of rivers or trees, of briefcases, coffee cups or maps. We have already seen how artists have played a role in influencing our perception of history by lending to it their own changing ideas of form. Here, before concluding, we can detail a few artists who might have perpetuated this legacy.

In *Hako*, a 2007 installation at London's Chisenhale Gallery, artist Hiraki Sawa used digital video to break an enigmatic story into a number of sub-narratives. The viewer formed these into one only by moving about the large room, occasionally making narrative connections via a kind of parallax, whereby apparently disparate sub-narratives would momentarily align and synchronise across several rectangular screens.[12]

Each of the looped video sub-narratives also momentarily came to a rest between their repeated loops. At this point the physical apparatus of the screen on which they were projected was explicitly acknowledged by the purposeful projection of white, moulded wallpaper. This momentarily replaced the sub-narrative's illusion of other times and places and snapped the viewer back into the presence and awareness of the mechanism responsible for the images. This brief reminder, of the event that we actually and presently occupy while viewing, and of the practicalities behind the technology, eventually gave way once more to the return of the looped sub-narratives.

Composed of several rectangular screens, Sawa's installation dispersed and temporalised what would otherwise have been a controlling grid. In doing so he perhaps helps us to visualise a way in which a historicising parallax invariably allows our present perspectives to align sub-narratives of the past and history and subsume them into the overarching narrative that is always our conception of our historical present.

Meanwhile, Sawa's work insists that however we are caught up in the stories that we make and tell, the here and now and the actuality of our presence should never be forgotten, even if it may not yet have its own story or form within which we can lose or divert ourselves.

The artist Saskia Olde Wolbers, blatantly, yet nonetheless mysteriously juxtaposes forms and stories in her work, using a strange dialectic. The visual forms often appear abstract, complex, and subject to morphological dynamics, while the spoken narratives that accompany them evolve in parallel, clearly and simply, and the two offer each other an elusive, yet somehow satisfying relationship. It is as if the story offers itself to the form and the form to the story, while each exists autonomously without the need of the other, and they are brought together almost arbitrarily by the artist, as if to insist that neither element – form or story – should be complacent about its identity but should always be open and ready to be questioned by its other.

In *Placebo* (2002) Olde Wolbers used a found object which is essentially a grille or grid (a birdcage in fact) and repeatedly immersed it in paint, filming in close-up the resulting encounter between static grid (as an *arch* form) and fluid paint (formlessness), thus also alluding to the history of painting's surfaces, abstractions, actions, monochromes, and geometries.[13]

But what is perhaps most useful for us here is that the forms Olde Wolbers proffers – made via unexpected subversions of everyday materials – appear far more complex and motile than expected and might therefore provide history with appropriate models to replace those outmoded by the passing of modernism and the 20th century.

The fact that Olde Wolbers not only used 20th-century strategies (e.g., Dada) of using found or readymade objects, but also used moving image to present these possible forms, echoes Gilles Deleuze's reminder that new technologies, such as cinema, give us not only new kinds of image but also new possibilities for, and new forms of, thought – and here we are claiming the same point for the possibilities of thinking history.

Jeff Wall, trained as an art historian, whose art was loudly affirmed by leading critics in the early 1990s, has repeatedly replayed art history's own stories and linked their forms to enduring and contemporary political issues.[14] As he does so, he appears to support the idea that while the motive for the production of history is always political (in that it concerns both people and the present), the forms given to history, to stories, and to events have always been and continue to be the responsibility of some form of art. We might even say, having encountered Wall's works, that art history is always a history of the art of history.

The artist Thomas Struth, in his well-known museum photographs, shows how we offer our own forms, literally and symbolically to history by inhabiting and perusing its spectacle as somewhat awed Lilliputian subjects and voracious postmodern consumers of multi-cultural artefacts.[15] The perspectives of figures in Struth's pictures (who are us of course) might differ from those of earlier protagonists of modernism and Enlightenment who may have regarded history as a force to be harnessed, steered and shaped, and knowledge as an external object that might eventually be grasped in its entirety.

Today, in Struth's museum photographs, we, the public, seem to crawl around on the body of history while living out relatively *a*historical, consumerist, and touristic lives. As we have seen above, history, no matter how harrowing, can today become an aspect of spectacular leisure and prurient pleasure, and, despite the professed aims of the contemporary museum to widen participation, enlarge audiences, etc., the more we make a spectacle of history the more we may diminish its reality, relevance, and its relation to our awareness of our present, which might be correspondingly diminished.

What is *not* diminished in this procedure is of course spectacle, consumerism, and tourism themselves, all of which only grow in stature by proving themselves capable of encompassing any challenge (whether from present or the past) to their monopolistic colonisation of the popular imagination.

Johannes Phokela, a South African artist who grew up in Soweto in the 1970s, and had to learn to read, write, and paint by candlelight, today repeatedly illuminates matters of form and history while re-painting and remixing those 17th-century Dutch and Flemish painters whose works shared the period in which the first Dutch and Flemish settlers began the colonial expropriations that would lead to apartheid South Africa.[16] Phokela's work therefore short-circuits history's pre-formed narratives, refusing to allow the established perspective of Western art history to obscure distasteful political factors that made its own apotheoses possible. Instead, Phokela actively reawakens these political factors in the form of counter-narratives, and as part of the unfinished business of a long search for justice.

There are of course many more artists, dealing with history whom we could cite or provide a cameo for here (e.g., Jeremy Deller, Thomas Demand, Rita Keegan, Godfried Donkor, Tavares Strachan, Cameron Rowland, and Johan Grimonprez are just a few names that readily come to mind). However, suffice to say that all those to whom we have referred above engage in history, like myself, from the special and oblique perspective of artists and not historians. In doing so they tend to remind us, and often adamantly so, that history has always been formed, is always an image, and that there are infinite and imaginative ways by which to form and reform history.

Meanwhile, the contemporary artist's special contribution might also and always be to provide a reminder that the purpose of every history is ultimately to clarify the forms and images informing our present perspective on historical events.

An important point to which we have alluded above remains yet unresolved or inadequately considered, and that is the question of the increased conviction and reliability given to history by forms that are nonetheless *in*accurate. Perhaps the best

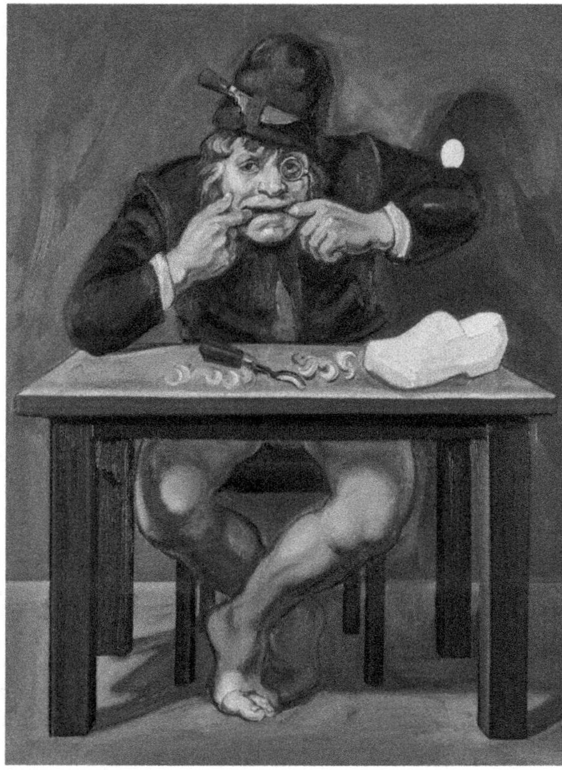

FIGURE 23.6 Johannes Phokela, *Monocle Sam – (Sabot's Tough)*, oil on canvas, 122 × 91 cm, 2021. Monocle Sam is an imaginary comical character who supposedly, invented wooden shoes often worn by European peasants from the middle ages (known as Clogs or Sabots in France). The idea of the work came from toying with the etymology of the word 'sabotage'. With kind permission of the artist.

way to develop this is to shoulder responsibility for the fact that, when we speak of forms in relation to history, we not only invoke the concept of the story, but also, in other ways, depart from any more scientific vision of the discipline (or the disciplined vision of the science). Where art forms history, it is clearly a rhetorical and formal device, with no commitment, in itself, to truth or veracity. Nevertheless, without the form given to history by art, and even by artifice, history will have no conviction, no sense of legitimacy by which to convince us of its truth.

Where we speak of form, we speak of the art that will always in some way inform any science. For example, we could consider the numerous crafted, idiosyncratic objects used over the centuries as essential to the proving of scientific hypotheses, or the very syntax and grammar within which, and by which, scientific discoveries are made convincing when published.[17] Art, though it may flirt with ideals, is never unduly concerned with accuracy and veracity, but sees its primary duty in finding the best or most appropriate means by which to convince. In its dialogue with materials and processes, art is continuously forced to acknowledge – and in a way that easily and often becomes self-reflexive – the inventiveness and possible arbitrariness of the forms it gives to ideas.

In the relation of forms to history, art will always then be a kind of *rhetoric* – visual or verbal – helping the scientific expert and specialist historian to sustain, however momentarily, or enduringly, the illusion of an accurate and reliable truth that can be used to orient us within an otherwise frighteningly formless environment.

This orientation allows us to proceed, and perhaps even to progress, if only from one inaccurate (the term is not pejorative here) form (and its corresponding sensation of orientation) to another. It is not therefore necessary that the forms we give to history be judged accurate or not. Our present perspective must – by definition – be always incongruous to the past it represents. What is crucial, and has hopefully been demonstrated in the examples above (whereby, in each, a form has been chosen and given to history), is that in and for their time, forms utilise appropriate reference to the contemporary environment, in such a way as to make whichever legitimising history that wishes to be told, sufficiently current, and thereby credible.

Notes

1 This is an edited and updated version of a chapter from my doctoral dissertation titled *A Hesitation of Things*, University of London, 2009. O'Kane, P. (2009).

2 *Making History: Antiquaries in Britain*, 1707–2007 a touring exhibition, was held at London's Royal Academy, 15 September–2 December 2007. Gaimster, D. et al. (2007).

3 www.sal.org.uk/collections/explore-our-collections/collections-highlights/roll-chronicle/.

4 See www.moma.org/interactives/exhibitions/1999/muse/artist_pages/duchamp_boite.html.

5 The 20th-century Freudian subject also relies upon personal history with which to form, reform, and reconsider the disassembled ruptured and traumatised self. Here we also invoke the memory of the briefcase carried by Walter Benjamin in 1940 on his last journey across French mountains to the Spanish border, and which was said by Benjamin to contain documents important to history but which subsequently disappeared.

6 See www.tate.org.uk/art/artworks/patterson-the-great-bear-p77880.

7 See www.apartheidmuseum.org/. See also reference to J.D. Salinger's *Catcher in the Rye*, the museum-visit section, cited in chapter 3 of this book. Also refer to the museum visit in Chris Marker's *La Jetée* cited in chapter 14 of this book.

8 Here again unconscious echoes emerge, of the 'museum' excerpt from J.D. Salinger's 'Catcher in the Rye' seen in Chapter 3 of this book.

9 Within the apartheid Museum exhibition a video recording of a speech being made by Mr Verwoerd during his 1947 election campaign shows that he was elected on a promise of implanting a 'final solution'.

10

> They were "riots looking for a place to happen" in the words of a *Sunday Times* editorial; and stemmed from a spirit of revolt among youth which was partly rooted in their dislike of the Bantu Education system, to which Dr Verwoerd had publicly and very explicitly referred in earlier years as education for a menial place in society. Davenport, T.H.R. & Saunders, C. (2000) pp. 449.

11 Hendrik Frensch Verwoerd writing in – *Genealogical Register of the South African People*, published in 1966 by Malherbe, D.F. du Stellenbosch, and quoted in Chipkin, I. (2007) pp. 29–30. Verwoerd, H. F., (1966) pp. 29–30.
12 Held between 5th September and 14th October 2007. See https://chisenhale.org.uk/exhibition/hiraki-sawa/.
13 See www.saskiaoldewolbers.com/works/placebo-video-stills-synopsis/.
14 See https://gagosian.com/artists/jeff-wall/.
15 See www.thomasstruth32.com/smallsize/photographs/audiences/index.html.
See www.thomasstruth32.com/smallsize/photographs/museum_photographs_1/index.html.
16 See www.artnet.com/artists/johannes-phokela/.
17 Oxford's *Museum of Scientific Instruments* provides excellent evidence of this dependent relationship of art, science, object, and idea.

Bibliography

Benjamin, W. (1999) *The Arcades Project*. Cambridge, Mass & London: Belknap.

Chipkin, I., (2007) *Do South Africans Exist?* Johannesburg, SA: Wits University Press.

Davenport, T.H.R. & Saunders, C. (2000) *South Africa – A Modern History*. UK: Macmillan.

Gaimster, D., Nurse, B., McCarthy, S. (eds.) & Starkey, D. (Intro.) (2007) *Making History – Antiquaries in Britain, 1707–2007*. London: Royal Academy.

O'Kane, P. (2009) *A Hesitation of Things* (PhD) University of London.

Verwoerd, H.F. (1966) *Genealogical Register of the South African People*. Malherbe: D.F. du Stellenbosch.

24

ELIZABETH PRICE AND THE POPULAR PAST

Amateurism, fetish, and juvenilia – Part 1[1]

Today, despite a constant call to fixate our gaze upon the new, the present, or the contemporary, it might be in history that we find the most surprising adventures and discoveries.

There we can exercise our imaginations most fully and locate the tools and materials we need to enable us to engage with, disrupt, and transform any established and habitual understanding of the present. Furthermore, that same retroactivity might afford us a certain disruptive and critical agency that is hard to find if we are consciously fixated on and in the present.[2]

Pinned on my studio/office wall I keep a brown daub made on sugar paper by my nephew when he was three or four years old. The picture has a strangely satisfactory sense of completion and conviction, the kind we might be looking for later in our lives and careers as artists and writers. It is imbued with the value of a certain unconscious audacity, an omnipotence born of naivety. As a hoarder as much as an archivist, I also find it all but impossible to discard my own earliest artworks and writings, anything I have completed that is made by my own hands and might be called my 'juvenilia'. I believe that these early works may contain treasures that are inaccessible to me now and may deserve to be re-evaluated one day by myself or some responsible and hopefully empathetic other.

Even though my own professional status and influence is not particularly high, I am convinced that these often inspired and unbound beginnings should not simply be regarded as the crude and tentative overtures of an oeuvre that became increasingly bold, refined, and professional, but should be seen simply as other and different works arising at other and different (not better or worse) moments, in a story that is not necessarily one of linear progress.

Another way of approaching a fruitful dialogue with history is for me to recall the significance of the first time a colleague pointed out to me the possibility of using a digital scanner to transpose my medium-format photographic negatives

DOI: 10.4324/9781003230632-27

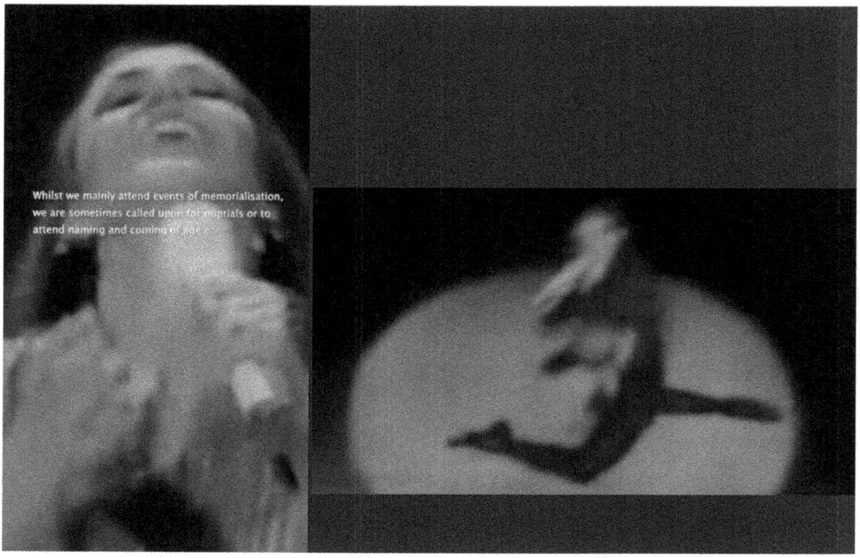

FIGURE 24.1 Elizabeth Price, still, two channels. *K*, 2015. Courtesy of the artist.

from the 'analog' realm into the digital realm. In this process I experienced a certain technological jolt and began to revisit the past in a new way, bringing it rapidly into the present where these old images now share the more mobile, more easily multipliable, distributable and malleable benefits of digital files. I soon found myself also transcribing cassette tapes to digital files, creating a similar effect for the history of my modest musical output. It seemed to me there and then that a transvaluation like that promised by Nietzsche revealed itself, as past and present mingled and merged in ways that suggested a new-found equality. This seemed profound, disruptive, if not revolutionary.

An artist who has not, or has not yet been able to live on the professional proceeds of their creative work might, quietly at least, address themselves as 'amateur', a culturally derogatory but otherwise merely technical term. Meanwhile, the word 'amateur' clearly contains traces of amorousness and insists that, at a certain stage of an artist's career (and of an artist's life seen in professional terms) the artist is undeniably involved in a 'labour of love'.[3]

As the amateur phase develops into the professional (for the luckiest, most privileged, persistent, or talented), past and present are conveniently divided into a standardised relationship and corresponding evaluation. The more-or-less successful professional artist begins to be paid and may even be able to live on the proceedings of their creative work. The most fortunate few might even accumulate wealth by means of the peculiar machinations of the art market or 'creative industries', which can be just as exorbitantly abundant as they can be punitively parsimonious.

That same market will not hesitate to forage into a professional artist's juvenilia if profitable value and interesting novelty might be found therein. Curators and historical revisionists tend to attend to such juvenilia with avaricious glee. A certain organisation, of old and new, late and early, amateur and professional status, thus becomes blurred as the story of the artist's progress is adapted and extended to accommodate newly valued and valuable items, once hidden and perhaps strategically secreted by the artist themselves, who may have preferred to parade only those items regarded as indicative of the progress of their late and latest works.

In his 1929 essay on Surrealism, Walter Benjamin writes:

> (Andre Breton) can boast an extraordinary discovery. He was the first to perceive the revolutionary energies that appear in the outmoded, in the first iron constructions, the first factory buildings, the earliest photos, the objects that have begun to be extinct, grand pianos, the dresses of five years ago, fashionable restaurants when the vogue has begun to ebb from them. The relation of these things to revolution.[4]

Following Benjamin's and Breton's cue here, we might use examples of artists and their works to explore the special potency and revolutionary potential of the enormous archive of cultural imagery, and particularly that which has amassed because of mechanical and digital reproduction technologies, in and as what we might call 'the popular past'. The special pathos of this material appeals emotively and increasingly to the present, compelling a sense of responsibility to both history and humanity.

Blurred faces, abstracted into grainy black-and-white tones, look into a lens, out of a past that inevitably appears relatively youthful, inept, and even innocent. Transported by means of various recording apparatuses they all arrive in the present, coming down to us subject to the compromising effects of layers of preservative reproduction.

Turner Prize-winning artist Elizabeth Price has repeatedly deployed these emotive archival materials (as in her two-channel video installation simply titled *K*), juxtaposing hi-def, hi-tech imagery with archival black-and-white images, and in a way that illustrates our current cultural condition, dangling as we are between a rapidly emerging future and a past that swells exponentially behind and beneath us, like Hokusai's famous wave. Ironically, the proliferation and sophistication of new technologies delivers us into a mutually consuming repast with the past, one that might allow us to justifiably refer to our own time as 'the age of the archive'.

Price eschews revelation of any intimate self that might be operating within or behind the scenes of her video art and Hi-Tech installations. She juxtaposes grainy found footage of 1960s pop singers against a digitally animated image (whose own provenance is unclear) of a strange machine for weaving stockings. These two very different images – the former undeniably historical and the latter so 'new' that it appears inaccessibly futuristic – may at first seem incongruous, but as we watch the video and listen to its soundtrack (which includes some vaguely didactic lines of text spoken by a robotic voice) we feel that a synthesis is possible after all.

There is little or no sign of humour here, but there are entertainments of other kinds. We are, e.g., reminded of the ancient cultural roots of the pop singer's role as Price's text invites us to see her performers as 'professional mourners' who perpetuate a shamanic function, both for the society of their heyday and for our own age of the digital archive that enables their resurrection.

The fact that the singers in '*K*' are not contemporary (not, e.g., 'K-Pop') but images of singers who may themselves be already dead and mourned, is part of their sensual appeal. The past casts a particular spell over the image, and thus over the viewer, especially when presented as a sequence of artfully chosen clips and edits enhanced by carefully composed, captivating sounds, words, and music.

Price's video reminds us of how we fetishise the past as an object, along with any object of the past. The outcome is a kind of unrequited longing. We treasure what we find in the past as a valued connection to, and compensation for irretrievably lost time, and in this way each historical object becomes a fetish. The museum, with its tradition of displaying treasured objects at arm's length in vitrines, clearly serves this function, but Price's work might remind us that the invention of photography, then cinema, leading in turn to video, the digital, and to her own digital video art, has exponentially multiplied the quantity of objects (albeit in the form of their mechanically, then digitally reproduced images) to which we now have increasingly easy access, and which provide a connection between us and the otherwise irretrievable past.[5]

The digital age, initially so futural, turns out to be equally archival, an age in which our access to images of the past is increasing exponentially, both in terms of scale and of ease, a development which might be seen to expand both André Malraux's photographic 'museum without walls' and Douglas Crimp's postmodern theorisation of 'the museum's ruins', into a reading of our entire epoch as an age of the digital, image-based, archive.

Meanwhile, an exponential archival increase in availability and visibility might serve to quantitatively balance the disorientingly futural and inhuman qualities of the digital realm that we might find it difficult to visualise, grasp, or inhabit.

As our digitised archives grow, and as they themselves begin to age (always under the threat of being surpassed by yet newer technological processes), so the proximity, prevalence, and pathos of the past increase and become a defining aspect of our environment.

The exponential enlargement and increased prevalence of the reproduced past render the present, by comparison, more effervescent, ephemeral, unquantifiable, and difficult to evaluate. While the present is reduced to the merest crest of a breaking temporal wave that denotes the very limit of an increasingly voluminous past, the future simultaneously becomes void, a no-go zone into which humanity peers only to find it difficult to discern or imagine anything. This is a realm perhaps known and visible only to the digital itself.

However, it is there, in a digital future apparently uninhabited by humanity, that Price's strange stocking manufactory whirrs away. Occupying one screen of her two-channel video it works relentlessly, all but effortlessly, and with no apparent need for human assistance or interference, even as its purpose seems to be to produce articles

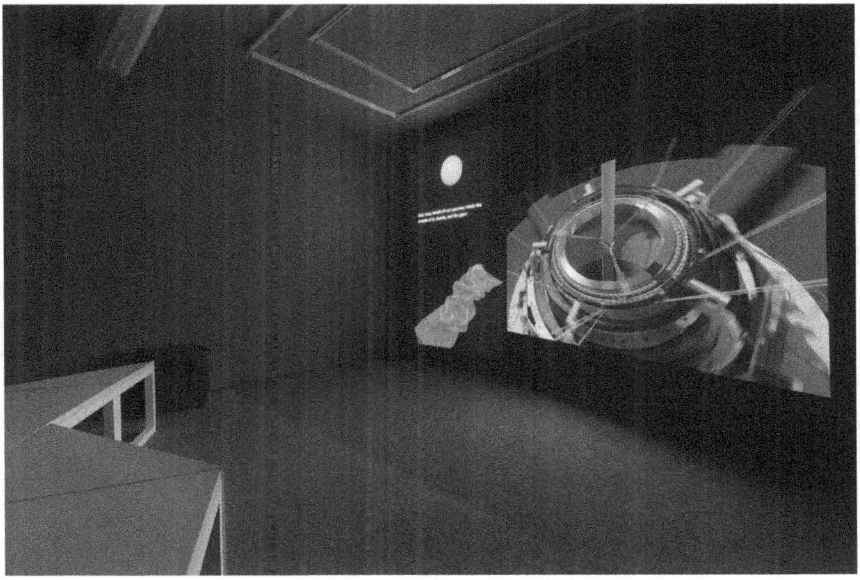

FIGURE 24.2 Elizabeth Price, *K*, 2015, installation view, Wyoming Project, Beijing, 20 Apr 2018–28 May 2018 – 002. Courtesy of the artist.

of clothing to adorn human bodies. The spoken text that accompanies the video speaks of an 'Orphic gloom' that pervades both the realm occupied by the machine and that from which the clips of 1960s pop singers emerge. However, this 'gloom' also corresponds to the darkened room in which the video '*K*' is shown to the public (according to strict installation parameters set by the artist), thus extending the subtly ritualistic and hypnotic experience of the work as a whole. The 'gloom' thus becomes a reference to form as much as to content.

Price's compelling rendition of the contemporary possibilities of meticulously installed video art, places audiences in a quasi-religious scenario, like worshippers at a shrine humbled by a bright electric beam of light that produces magical images. Writer and critic Mathilde Roman could perhaps be prompted here to expand her thesis '*On Stage: The Theatrical Dimension of Video Image*' and might agree that the age of video art is also an age of newly hallowed spaces, unlike our ever more brightly lit white cubes.[6]

Towards the end of '*K*', a single stocking is ejected by the machine, almost as if the device were playing stripper. Like the finest of gauntlets, in being dropped before the audience it makes a subtle provocation. Its singularity (one divided from a pair) calls upon each individual subjectivity that makes up the audience, while emphasising the empathic quality essential to any fetish.

But the object here is neither the stocking itself nor any specific erotic object or experience associated with it; rather it is all the sensual promise and allusion that resides within the past, within the image of the past, within images *from* the past, within our exponentially growing archive of past and passing images, and within the otherwise irretrievable past that images can only ever partially re-present.[7]

The archive today maintains a strange allure and sensuality, and even the potential futurity of the digital is constantly seduced into service of the past. We find we have a quasi-erotic attraction to long-surpassed technologies and their antiquated images, including the clichéd, ubiquitous, yet no-less mysterious and inexplicable example of that nostalgic value stimulated within us by early black and white photographic, cinematic and television images.

Perhaps this yearning confirms Nietzsche's image of a life and a world that is always returning (see Chapter 9 of this book). These images affect us by triggering some inescapably passionate response at the sight of the loss of our younger selves as well as our earlier modernity, to which we feel we belong if only because we share, as indexically connected 'family members', that age of photography, of cinema – the childhood of the age of the archive.

This is perhaps what Walter Benjamin means, in his *Theses on the Philosophy of History*, when he simply but profoundly states:

> The past carries with it a temporal index by which it is referred to redemption. There is a secret agreement between past generations and the present one. Our coming was expected on earth.[8]

Because here lies an understanding of existence, and of our responsibilities to time and history, that might only be made in the age of the archive, the age of mechanical reproduction, and the modern epoch of history's dominance as a master narrative.

How we love to peer and peek (as did Benjamin into, e.g., Atget's photographs) into ancestral moments when modernity was both more novel and more imbued than it is today with hope, confidence, belief, and adventure – noting that we are unable to connect in quite the same way to any time prior to the invention of the early 19th century's newly indexical photographic image.[9]

Might it be possible then that the strange device we see weaving away in Elizabeth Price's '*K*' represents the process of history itself, history as a digital machine, weaving from threads and strands of some mysterious base polymer (which might be time itself), objects destined to be manifest only ever as fetishes, and with no use or destination other than to act as mnemonic signs of all that exists in the past, out of reach and irretrievable.

The arch-fetishistic image of the stocking leads us to regard museologised objects as things that exist or persist in the present, while acting as fetishes and mnemonics for the past itself; the past from whence they come but to which we have no real access. This 'history machine' confronts us with an uncannily inhuman image of mechanical autonomy, possibly reminiscent of history's spiritualisation by Hegel (subsequently materialised by Marx and now, here, again dematerialised, albeit also virtualised, at least by these theories and by we, would-be theorists of the digital).[10]

The objects made by Price's machine are highly commodified, with smart packaging that features crisp graphics and the intriguing (possibly Kafkaesque) moniker

'*K*' (the brand-like title of the piece as a whole), all of which are devices that consumers find hard to resist desiring, obtaining, unsealing, and thereby claiming and owning. Popularly regarded as an arch image of a certain modern mode of erotic fetishism (for the 20th century at least), sheer stockings mark themselves out as modern while nevertheless referring to the past. They mark the past as other and refer to the erotic and inviting untouchability of past time and of all objects made more delicate and precious by their increasing age.

Marx reinterpreted the ancient and shamanic fetish function as having been translated, in modernism, into commodity form. There it exacerbates desire and cultivates the salivating atmosphere of consumerism. Meanwhile, his fellow guru of modernism, Sigmund Freud, implied that fetishism, in and for a modern society, transforms from a religious object associated with the magic of the gods into a *memorial* object whose mystique and power is derived from modernism's crucial and particular relationship to a past against which it necessarily distinguishes and defines itself.

The past thus becomes modernism's overarching, omnipresent, and omnipotent other, its spirit or spectre; hence, the modern museum (along with the railway station, department store, and later the cinema) replaces church, temple, cathedral and shrine (in terms of spectacle, grandeur and worship) as the primary locus of history – modernism's master narrative and central belief system.[11]

The antique eroticism of the stockinged, gartered, and corseted, Georgian, Victorian, and Edwardian eras in the history of women's wear, spans the rise of the modern bourgeois culture that Freud is credited with liberating from its debilitating, anachronistic and unsuitable sexual repression. The persistence of the stocking, throughout this dynamic period of change, and even though technologically surpassed by the more modern, functional, newly technologised (and Americanised) vogue for 'nylons', 'tights' or 'hose', renders the stocking an arch modern fetish.[12] It becomes untimely and thereby takes on that 'revolutionary' quality found by Benjamin and Breton in 'the outmoded' (see above).[13]

In Price's video, the classic or vintage stocking not only survives decades, even centuries of modern fashion history, but surpasses the present to appear in a depopulated digital future gloom where all light is artificial (a mere image of light, a dim memory of a light, to which we might no longer have natural or immediate access).[14] Price's mysterious machine operates in a re-imagined future; the place and time of the digital only, a crepuscular realm created to counterbalance the overpopulated and increasingly unwieldy, digitally archived past.

Notes

1 Parts of this essay were previously used in an article for *The Science Museum Journal*, titled '*Technologies of Romance*: looking for 'object love' in three works of video art', published in Autumn 2019, Issue 12. See http://journal.sciencemuseum.ac.uk/browse/issue-12/looking-for-object-love-in-three-works/?fbclid=IwAR24hOewXUeEimni_5vR3K5P8_hktBMc0HE78jcW6d34Ay17_r9PRaPRkd0.

2 'Retroactivity' is the framing word used by Craig staff in his own published enquiry into our theme –'Retroactivity and Contemporary Art'. Staff, C. (2018).
3 What I am tempted to call, in light of some of my own recent publications, a 'technology of romance'.
4 Benjamin, W. (2000) p. 229.
5 Chris Marker's video artwork *La Jetée* might be said to encapsulate these claims. It is born of the threshold between the still photographic and moving image and relays an arcane tale of a man sent back in time to transform the future. N.B. It is also a love story that places the image of a museum at the heart of its dream-like narrative.
6 Bar the crepuscular environments contrived for Rothko's late and grandiose works.
7 It is perhaps significant and symbolic of our current culture that, in recent years, polite speech has avoided direct reference to death, supplanting it with the word 'passing' as in: 'I am sorry to hear about your mother's passing'.
8 Benjamin, W. (1968) pp. 253–264.
9 Ruttman, W. (dir.) (1927). At 59 minutes, a young newspaper seller momentarily gazes into the lens of the camera and thus appears to momentarily and perhaps eternally link our time to his, without interruption.
10 Which was subsequently materialised by Marx, and then comprehensively scrambled by Benjamin in his aphoristic, koan-like *Theses on the Philosophy of History.*
11 Associations made by modernising 19th-century Parisians, according to examples provided by T. J. Clark in his classic study: Clark, T.J. (1985).
12 Benjamin, of course, saw fashion as always and inevitably historical. Even in its most modern moments (and Benjamin's 1920s and 1930s were surely daring in this regard). Benjamin called fashion a 'Tiger's leap into the past'.

Benjamin on fashion in: Ekardt, P. (2020). Also: Mitchell, W.J. T. *Revolution and Your Wardrobe – Fashion and Politics in the Photography of Jane Stravs,* in: Stravs, J. (2002) pp. 79–82.
13 Benjamin, W. (2000) p. 229.
14 Price features in this work, and elsewhere in her oeuvre, a 'sun' installed discretely in the image and made up of numerous photographed, 20th-century suns montaged into a moving image.

Bibliography

Benjamin, W. (1968) *Illuminations.* New York: Schocken Books.

Benjamin, W. (2000) *One Way Street and Other Writings.* London: Verso.

Clark, T.J. (1985) *The Painting of Modern Life – Paris in the Art of Manet and His Followers.* London: Thames & Hudson.

Ekardt, P. (2020) *Benjamin on Fashion* [electronic resource]. London: Bloomsbury.

O'Kane, P. (2019) Technologies of Romance – Looking for 'Object Love' in Three Works of Video Art. *Science Museum Journal* (online) Issue 12 (Autumn). http://journal.sciencemuseum.ac.uk/browse/issue-12/looking-for-object-love-in-three-works/?fbclid=IwAR24hOewXUeEimni_5vR3K5P8_hktBMc0HE78jcW6d34Ay17_r9PRaPRkd0.

Roman, M. (2016) *On Stage: The Theatrical Dimension of Video Image.* Bristol, UK Intellect.

Ruttman, W. (dir.) (1927) *Berlin Symphony of a City.* 20th Century Fox.

Staff, C. (2018) *Retroactivity and Contemporary Art.* London: Bloomsbury Academic.

Stravs, J. (2002) *Photographic Incarnations.* Ljublana: Scientific Research Centre of the Slovenian Academy of Science and Arts.

25

ELIZABETH PRICE AND THE POPULAR PAST

Amateurism, fetish, and juvenilia – Part 2[1]

Understanding of our current relationship with history might be found in further consideration of the concept of juvenilia referred to at the start of Part 1 of this chapter. The term generally refers to those products of an artist's career deemed to have appeared prior to that artist's full maturation and professionalisation. However, if this is indeed an age of the archive, it subjects potentially anything and everything to review, revision, relativism, re-evaluation, or Nietzschean transvaluation. Thus, we might come to question our ability to make clear distinctions between an artist's mature works and their 'juvenilia', thereby devaluing the past and the early in favour of the new and the late (not forgetting that Nietzsche, according to his philosophy of life, also championed the child as a model of all that adults should aspire to).

What would become of our culture and our values if all of our past became equal to all of our present, and if our childhoods were equal to our maturities in every way? What would be the effect of such a flattening of the habitual hierarchy between old and young, between naivety (habitually considered derogatory) and sophistication (habitually considered praiseworthy)? Here we might be drawn back to Douglas Crimp's postmodern theorisation of 'the museum's ruins' and the eponymous essay in which he theorises the work of Robert Rauschenberg wherein (Crimp discerns) the lithographic printing process became a great equaliser, a democratising plane on which all kinds of cultural images – high and low, old and new – freely associate, disrupting hierarchy and meaning, and thereby perhaps (for our argument here) transvaluing values.[2]

Similarly, Andre Malraux claimed that photography provided us with a 'museum without walls', i.e., a non-exclusive visual record of everyone and everything, collected without judgement, organised without hierarchy and made freely inviting and available to all.

Today, as can be seen in the references in Part 1 of this essay to the work of Elizabeth Price, these ideas are far from exhausted. Of course, the scanner, and

DOI: 10.4324/9781003230632-28

FIGURE 25.1 Walter Ruttman, *Berlin: Symphony of a Great City* (1927). Screenshot at 1:01: 36 / 1:04:35.

various software, applications and devices, as well as social media platforms like Instagram, Pinterest, etc., have made the radical proliferation of what we might call 'the popular past' more intense and pervasive. Furthermore, on these social media sites, not only do unprecedented quantities of images and unparalleled degrees of eclecticism reign, but the professional and amateur also rub shoulders and compete for attention in unprecedented ways.

In his influential essay *The Work of Art in the Age of Mechanical Reproduction,* Walter Benjamin showed a prescient interest in the ways in which readers of modern newspapers began to feel free to contribute their own letters and ideas to the columns of the newspapers that they read.[3] Today, we all have a ready confidence to do likewise, having noted that, given the opportunity, the template, and the platform, our own wit, wisdom and news can look just as well on the screen as that of officially authorised and qualified journalists, commentators, and comedians.

Hence, there arises an uncomfortable and controversial divide between the populist, the amateur, and the expert, even a crisis of expertise *per se* as we begin to wonder: should we view this as a progressive, democratic, and liberating tendency (another aspect of a Nietzschean transvaluation of values), or should we fear its barbaric, possibly proto-fascist and post-Enlightenment implications, as 'the crowd' (sometimes referred to as a 'mob') is elevated, not so much by politics as by technology, to the status of a democratically empowered, potentially dominant force, albeit one without any recognisable leader or ideology?

What might happen if the unsupervised amateur, or juvenile, following the logical procedures of democracy, now ascends to take charge of the next phase of our modernism? Should we worry? After all, did previously powerless adolescents not threaten to, and to some extent succeed in perpetuating a similar form of 'barbarism' in the 1950s, 1960s, and 1970s? The prospect of a 21st-century children's and amateur's crusade nevertheless threatens potential Armageddon for the currently empowered, central, dominant, socio-economic class, whose status and role is justified (in their own eyes at least) precisely by their special skill, experience, education, culture, established moral standards, tolerance, and generally moderate behaviour.

Rather than pursuing this volatile political question to its ends here, we can instead return to Benjamin's observations of Breton (again see Part 1 of this essay) and to further scrutiny of the special value awarded to early photographic, cinematic, and televisual images.[4]

In the early 20th century, photography and film were marked out in their infancy (once again we might be tempted to call them juvenile) as the inspiring new technologies of their day. *Berlin, Symphony of a Great City*, a 1927 film by Walter Ruttman, made in and around Berlin, documents a day and a night in the life of the city.[5] The work is typically modern and typically photographic, at least with regard to the special qualities that Walter Benjamin discerned within the photographs of Eugene Atget – i.e., photographic images are not works of art according to any established understanding of the work of art up to their moment, but are, rather, a newly political aesthetic form that provides historical 'evidence'.

The photographic, and later the cinematic (especially perhaps when applied to the streets of the modern city), allows the ordinary, the evident, the immanent, the 'there', the *already* there (not the invented, created and contrived), to take a place in art and (for Benjamin) to take the place *of* art. The photographic or cine camera frames the ordinary and thereby honours and elevates potentially anything. Existing values are thereby transvalued.

Today, those at pains to make distinctions between the digital and analogue epochs of photography might be led to acknowledge that photography's most profound contribution to our culture undergoes only a quantitative (and not any truly qualitative) difference as it crosses this generational, millennial boundary. The digital realm is, it might be argued, (only) an exponentially enlarged 'museum without walls'. Correspondingly, the first cameras could be retro-interpreted as early forms of 'scanner', beginning – in the 19th century – the work of our 21st century 'age of the archive', as they initiated the mass gleaning, storage, and organisation of the popular past.

As Benjamin says in his comments on Breton (above), the revolutionary power of the outmoded includes 'the first photographs', i.e., the juvenilia of the medium of photography itself, the juvenilia of modernism, the juvenilia of Paris, Berlin, London, etc., the first modern cities. All of these are specially, strangely, and newly valued by Breton/Benjamin, not just because they are new and thus modern, but because already (by 1929 when Benjamin's *Surrealism* essay was written) 'the vogue has begun to ebb from them' – i.e., because these apparently young, new, and modern phenomena are unexpectedly revealed as being already old (perhaps modernism is travelling faster than planned). And here, not only does the relative value of the young become available to transvaluation, but any habitual or standardised relation of old to young has also become scrambled.

The photographic or cinematic artist (e.g., Eugene Atget or Walter Ruttman) no longer cooks up an image of life from base materials in the way that a painter does, but rather (as much curator as artist) nominates that which is deemed worthy of retaining and remaining. The photographic or cinematic artist frames choices, snaps 'shots', and makes 'takes' selected from the extant visible world. For Benjamin, recording in this way distances art from presumptuous 'creativity' and equates it with forensics. As such, images (again) become historical '*evidence*', and not merely historical illustration (as in e.g., the tradition of 'history painting').

A truly and appropriately modern art is thus born, just in time to record the emerging modern world. The two reciprocate, flatter, influence, and complement one another. Certain images seem to lend themselves to the photographic or cinematographic: the comings and goings of trains and trams, neon advertisements reflected in wet, tarmacadamed streets, fashionably dressed crowds entering a theatre, or working women leaving a factory – all are elevated simply by being selected, not only by art but also by history.[6] And thus, they become embroiled in a conspiracy of the two, elevated as spectacles of novelty and of note, while simultaneously laid down into the archive like new wine that yearns to be old, irrepressibly destined to 'develop', with age, into its full sensory potential.

The photographic and cinematic image turns art into history and creativity into curating ('curativity' perhaps?). History, in turn, is rendered a quasi-photographic process. Benjamin called his essay on Surrealism a 'snapshot' (despite its length) and cited other aspects of photographic and cinematic capability (including the close-up, X-Ray, and slow motion) as alternative means by which to picture and give form to progress, time, and history.[7] Photography's and cinema's newly indexical image also created a new sense of evident continuity between past and present, the kind over which Roland Barthes famously emoted in his *Camera Lucida* (1980) where he seems to seek an indexically intimate reunion with a loved one who has recently departed into the otherwise inaccessible past.[8]

Today we can look back and see the birth of our societies and our cities, the birth of our own modernism, aided by photography and cinema, in such a way that we also see that old world as young, and as innocent at least of those crimes we know that only subsequent events will bestow. Louis Daguerre, in his image *Boulevard du Temple* (1838), delivered (apparently by accident) the first human being to be recorded in this way. Walter Ruttman added another significant figure to a modern pantheon of empty streets and urban loners in one fleeting moment from *Berlin, Symphony of a Great City* (about one hour and one minute in) when an adolescent-looking boy or girl, who may be selling newspapers along the tramlines, glances for a fleeting moment into the filmmaker's lens.

This ordinary event and anonymous young person may have come to occupy a realm and a status once reserved for the sacred and rare, but what might also interest us is this child's particular face, chosen (according to the logic of Roland Barthes's 'punctum') as something that jumps unexpectedly out of the past to pierce the heart of the present, not with love for a particular person whom we will never know, nor even with empathy for the society and humanity of 1920s Berlin (and corresponding concern for all we know that it will eventually endure) but as affected by the sublime indexicality which links us materially, physically, unarguably and sensually to this particular boy and thus all those people and events that, once 'contemporary', have now passed into the past, but also into their future, which is our here and now; and even as they, in one way or another, prepared and provided this future for us to inhabit; this future in which we are able to, partially at least, 'meet' them.[9]

Following Barthes, but also, and again, echoing Giorgio Agamben in his essay *Judgement Day* written in response to Daguerre's *Boulevard du Temple* (its image and figure), the youth in Ruttman's movie never ceases to gaze into my own eyes, however briefly, and to call upon me and upon us, the people of now, the people of that child's future.[10] The call of the people of the past is unavoidably emotive and demanding. They call to be respected, remembered, and preserved if possible, to be allowed into the archive, if there is room for them.

Meanwhile, the past necessarily appears younger, more innocent than ourselves. The people we find there are innocent of their own future, a future that we know and that we also are. Thus, the mechanically reproduced image of the past becomes as morally indexical as it is physically indexical, and in this way becomes, as Benjamin suggests, a primarily ethical and political (rather than primarily aesthetic) image.

Both the amateur and the juvenile are relatively inept, but also relatively innocent, at least of cynical, strategic, mature professionalism, with its hard-headed

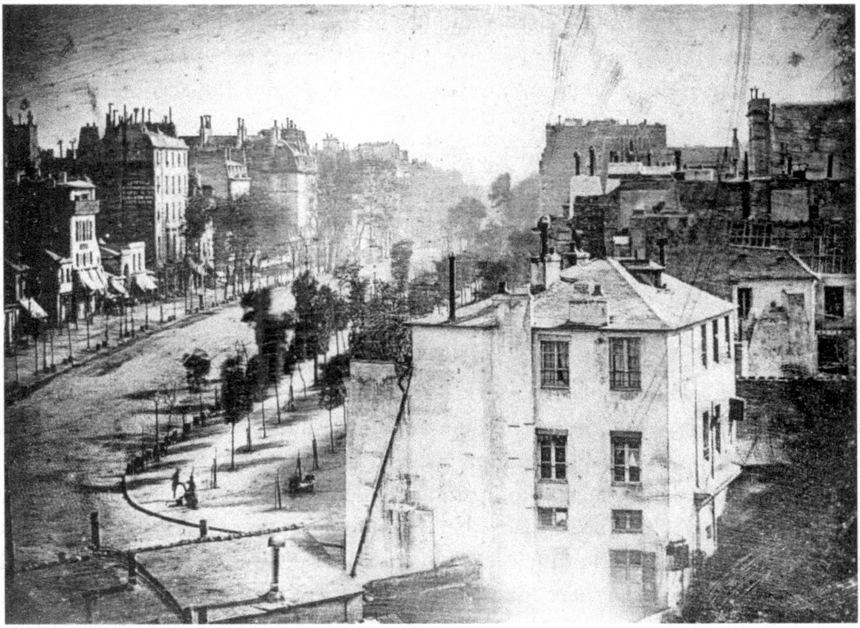

FIGURE 25.2 Louis Daguerre, *Boulevard du Temple* photograph of 1838 (or possibly 1839). One of the earliest daguerreotypes and considered to be the first photograph to include an image of a human being. Media Commons.

strategies and sharp elbows. The amateur and the juvenile are both innocent of mature professionalism's conspiracy to prioritise achievement over more delicate, dainty, or wayward aims. In Zen Buddhism, we come across an alternative, in those tales of spiritual enlightenment in which it is precisely the novice and the newcomer who can see the highest possibility of thought and action, to which those more sumptuously (and therefore *presumptuously*) qualified are blinded by their own sense of status and accompanying hubris.

In this case, we might suspect that the highest achievements of art and craft, as of thought and life, might not after all be available to the most experienced and self-assured, but are, on the contrary, the privilege of the open-hearted, unambitious, unconscious, wayward, and wide-eyed; of the novice, the juvenile, the amateur; as well, perhaps, as the outsider, newcomer, or migrant.

We might presume to hold dear the values of age, experience, and maturity, as well as the values of progress, skill and craft that, according to a certain history of art, seem to go hand-in-hand. Meanwhile we know that modern art, from the outset consistently challenged and changed such values, whether they were inherited from elite academies (i.e., from 'above') or from the artisan's traditions (from 'below').

From Coleridge and Wordsworth, publishing in their 20s their initially, shockingly, relatively rustic and informal *Lyrical Ballads*; through to Manet achieving notoriety in his 30s by paradoxically succeeding in a 'salon of the refused'; and then on further, through to the glorious insolence of post-World War II teenage rock 'n' roll, pop, punk and Hip-Hop; avant-garde cultural and creative activities have long asserted that the locus of modern value lies in the spirit of unencumbered youth and unfettered innovation, wrapped in emphatic belligerence and a kind of creative ignorance, that is, by definition, unavailable to the mature, the accomplished, and the established.[11]

Values in modernism are no longer what they used to be. Our Nietzschean touchstone, occasionally referred to here, inspires a deconstructive 'philosophising with a hammer' whereby values are transvalued by becoming targets and sites of renewal rather than authoritative standards carved into stone.[12] It is only by testing, tapping, and breaking open assumptions that we might become Nietzsche's celebrated child, or what Bob Dylan called *Forever Young*.

Thus, we might finally return to Nietzsche's assertion of a transvaluation of values, and of questions of value *per se*. What would a world without such values, or without values, look like? Are values an all-too-human conceit that machines do not share? And is transvaluation precisely what the amateur, novice, juvenile, or outsider promises and brings as a disruptive gift to all and to any established sense of achievement? Is this not in fact 'the new' itself, coming Christ-like (Christ as the hero of the 'new', and of the New Testament), or coming as a redemptive child who innocently (and perhaps ignorantly) rejuvenates life and our understanding of it, even in, or precisely in, the child's barbaric and bombastic, inarticulate, and unrefined manner?

From out of the past peer appealing faces, photographed, filmed and archived. We might even hear their voices, sustained and carried into the present by mechanical, then digital reproduction. They become our concern, we have responsibility for and to them, if only because they prepared the world for us; because, as Benjamin says: 'our coming was expected on earth'.[13]

We can interpret this short but profound phrase to mean that the lives of previous generations were governed partly by this parameter, that a subsequent generation was and is always 'expected'. Any life is, and must be, led, however consciously or unconsciously, with respect for and with knowledge of generations to come. We might do this most obviously today by trying to preserve the planet as an environment fit for human habitation, but might suspect that Benjamin also meant something less obvious, less concrete, i.e., that every life is led in ways governed and limited by the fact that others have preceded us and will proceed after us and succeed us. And this is a way in which a life can be said to be lived historically.

We never live only now, but always and also 'then' in the past and 'then' in the future; live there and then in a continuum that does not divide past from present from future. The past, 'old' as it supposedly is, will also always be young, always both older and younger than ourselves. New technologies, and our age of the archive, mean that the past will henceforth be increasingly populated, and thus popular. The past is a cornucopia to rival the all-too-new, shining and gift-wrapped constant 'present' of consumerism and of 'the contemporary'. History is a 'continent yet to be explored' (Nicolas Bourriaud) and one that we visit, not only to find previously unknown objects, but also to renew the already affirmed and known, considered and cared for – the 'pre-loved'.

Meanwhile, each journey to the past invites us to redraw the very backdrop against which all historical objects have thus far been set. The new, the future, the current, the present, and ourselves too, all arrive in 'the' world, 'a' world, or 'this' world, inexorably, as 'expected'. And yet we do so as barbarians, speaking first in incoherent noises, then in new voices, new words and accents, championing new rights and values, inevitably tending to induce some degree of fear, along with keen anticipation of all our promise.

And yet, as the poet Constantine Cavafy has eloquently implied, every mature and established authority knows that every barbarian comes as a kind of necessity, as a gift, a deliverance, not only as expected but as needed and necessary; as the future for which those who came before us have consciously or unconsciously prepared. Every barbarian comes as what Cavafy calls, in the last line of his poem *Waiting for the Barbarians*, 'a kind of solution'.[14]

Once we have announced and embraced the fact that 'our coming was expected on earth', we might look at the popular past and the age of the archive anew and see not only an emotive appeal made to us by the past, but also a kind of pact, a paternal reassurance that our own experience is, and always was, served, supported, and shaped by the past, and by the entirety of the past, without division. In return, the past requires us, and each generation, to take care of it and to care for it, like a child, even as we also acknowledge the past's parental role in preparing the world for our own coming.

Taking greater heed, taking greater care, and caring more by way of gratitude for the past, we might then come to realise that we serve the same function for future generations, expecting them, just as we ourselves were 'expected on earth'. Consequently, we might begin to live more consciously and explicitly *for* them, empathising with those others who preceded us and who will follow us, as much as we live for ourselves. And this might constitute what Breton referred to as a 'revolution'.

Notes

1 Parts of this essay were previously used in an article for *The Science Museum Journal*, titled '*Technologies of Romance*: looking for "object love" in three works of video art', published in Autumn 2019, Issue 12. See http://journal.sciencemuseum.ac.uk/browse/issue-12/looking-for-object-love-in-three-works/?fbclid=IwAR24hOewXUeEimni_5vR3K5P8_hktBMc0HE78jcW6d34Ay17_r9PRaPRkd0.
2 Crimp, D. (1980) pp. 41–57; Crimp, D. (1993).
3 Benjamin, W. (1968) pp. 217–251.
4 I have published on populism and popularity elsewhere, e.g., http://thirdtext.org/OKane-carnival and http://thirdtext.org/okane-maskocracy.
5 Ruttman, W. (dir.) (1927).
6 See Harun Farocki's *Workers Leaving the Factory in 11 Decades* (2006) once installed in London's Tate Modern. It features 11 decades of moving images of women leaving a factory, the first of which is considered to be the first cinematic film, *Workers Leaving the Lumiére Factory in Lyon* 1895 by Louis and Auguste Lumiére. See www.tate.org.uk/art/artworks/farocki-workers-leaving-the-factory-in-11-decades-t14332.
7 *Surrealism – The Last Snapshot of the European Intelligentsia*, in: Benjamin, W. (2000).
8 Barthes, R. (1982).
9 Something similar happens at the close of Francois Truffaut's 1959 movie *The 400 Blows*.
10 Agamben, G. (2007) pp. 23–27.
11 Coleridge, S.T. & Wordsworth, W. (2005).
12 Philosophising with a hammer is an image and idea conjured by Nietzsche, not least in the title of his book *Twilight of the Idols, or, How to Philosophize with a Hammer*. Like most of Nietzsche's striking imagery, it remains for us to interpret. It could refer to the violent breaking of tablets, but equally (as my PhD supervisor Howard Caygill once suggested), to the kind of detailed testing and assembling carried out by watchmakers using miniature hammers, or doctors gently seeking a reflexive response from a patient's knee.
13 *Theses on the Philosophy of* History in: Benjamin, W. (1968) p. 254.
14 Cavafy, C. (2007) pp. 53–55.

Bibliography

Agamben, G. (2007) *Profanations*. New York: Zone Books.
Barthes, R. (1982) *Camera Lucida – Reflections on Photography*. London: Cape.
Benjamin, W. (1968) *Illuminations*. New York: Schocken Books.
Benjamin, W. (2000) *One Way Street and Other Writings*. London: Verso.
Cavafy, C. (2007) *The Canon – The Original One Hundred and Fifty-Four Poems* (second edition). Washington, DC: Centre for Hellenic Studies, Trustees for Harvard University.
Coleridge, S.T. & Wordsworth, W. (2005) *Lyrical Ballads*. UK: Routledge.

Crimp, D. (1980) *On the Museum's Ruins*. October journal, summer (No. 13).
Crimp, D. (1993) *On the Museum's Ruins*. Cambridge, MA: MIT Press.
O'Kane, P. (2019) *Technologies of Romance – Looking for 'Object Love' in Three Works of Video Art.* The Science Museum Journal, (online) Issue 12 (Autumn).
Ruttman, W. (dir.) (1927) *Berlin – Symphony of a Great City*. 20th Century Fox.

26

REVERB

A passion for the past in popular music – Part 1

The Community Centre was the first place I ever heard pop music played at high volume. It was the first place I witnessed people dancing – which I still sometimes think might be humanity's greatest achievement. The Community Centre was also the first place I'd ever been moved to dance myself, though intensely shy and never gifted in that sense I may have barely tapped a foot. The Community Centre was certainly the first place I'd ever seen a DJ, with crates of records, an oil wheel, and a mirror ball.

Though its title sounds contrived, official, and far from glamorous, the Community Centre provided an important fulcrum of cultural development for residents of the housing estate where I grew up, and who had access to what might be considered a limited range of cultural experiences. Affectionate memories come to mind now when I think of that building and a few smaller, sporadically placed, more provisional buildings gathered around it on the edge of what we called 'the wasteground'.

At the Community Center's 'Disco Night', DJs played the latest (early 1970s) hits, enthusiastically juxtaposing pop, rock, glam, soul, and early disco music. Pop records seemed to confirm my place in the world, and I would have climbed inside the system's big black speakers if in doing so I might have come closer to the source of the vibrant culture blasting out of them. It's not difficult now to bring back to mind the insistent riff of David Bowie's *Jean Genie* making my nervously coiled teenage body want to jump around in time with it like an adulatory frog[1].

Meanwhile, I have an enduring, vivid, and surely nostalgically enhanced memory of the first time I experienced George McCrae's *Rock Your Baby*, introduced, not only sonically but also visually as a spot-lit mirror ball began effortlessly turning, powered by an invisible electric force, just as the record's percussion box intro was faded up by the DJ[2].

Viewed critically, and through an academic filter, all this may sound a little kitsch, corny and clichéd, but for me this image retains the essence of something

DOI: 10.4324/9781003230632-29

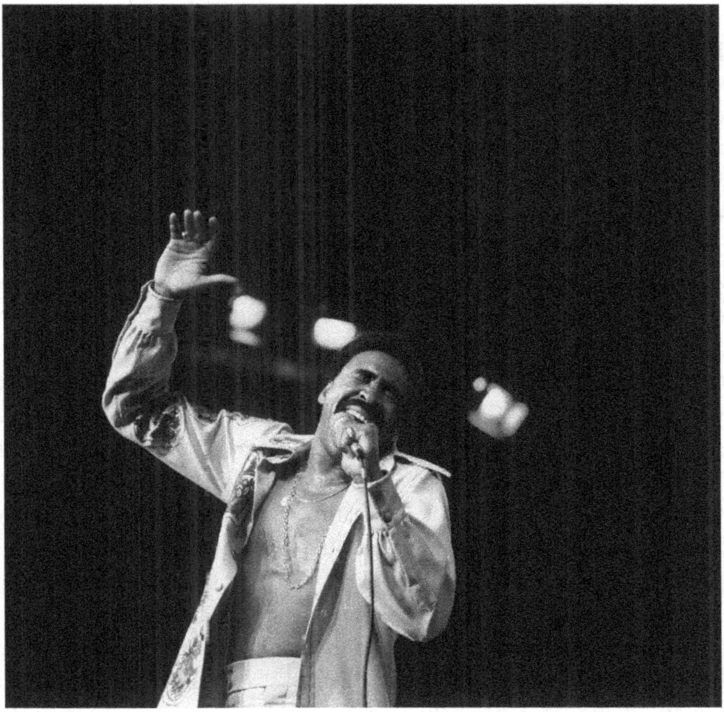

FIGURE 26.1 American soul and disco singer George McCrae performs live on stage, circa 1974. Photograph by David Redfern/Redferns.

that much of my writing, art, teaching, and in a way my life is about. So-called 'popular culture' is a term that refers to ways of living, and of thinking about and feeling those ways of living, that are no less important or valuable than supposedly higher cultures.

Furthermore, seemingly cold mechanical devices, consisting of nuts and bolts, transistors, light bulbs, resistors and wires, coils, circuits, pick-ups and plugs, chains, and wires, can all create sublime experiences. They can provide some form of transcendence, raise goose-bumps, send shivers down spines and together create lasting memories, even shaping a character, while making feet tap, voices sing and bodies move more proudly, less shamefully, freeing themselves in music[3].

Thus, for a few minutes, as George McCrae's gently shuffling disco beat slipped into synch with the slowly turning mirror ball's circling reflections, our otherwise dull and utilitarian Community Centre (also used for scout meetings, jumble sales and shotgun-wedding receptions) was transformed into a teenager's palace, momentarily playing host to the precious energies of an assembled crowd of adolescents who opened hearts and minds to the influence of music and light.

George McCrae's hit, featuring members of what came to be KC & The Sunshine Band, is said to have been composed and recorded hastily. The famous percussion machine was added to the multi-track recording last of all, and in a crude fashion, by simply pointing a microphone at the speaker of an organ equipped with a built-in beat box. Today it is important, both to me personally and for the purposes of the wider project here, that the gentle but persistent percussion pattern that hooked me and my peers into a transformative emotional experience was not performed in the recording studio by a skilled percussionist but by a pre-programmed machine.

Of course, a real, human percussionist may, at some stage, have programmed the machine's rhythms to provide them as presets, but the fact that it was a machine and not a person on the recording was surely a decisive factor in connecting the sound so effectively to us and to the vision of the mechanistic turning of the mirror ball. This combination of mechanised forces, this technologised art, communicated itself to the tentative motion of our shoes and thus travelled out into the wider, late 20th-century world where the song was an enormous hit.

The wooden huts assembled just outside the brick-built Community Centre seemed to have been left over from the recent building of the estate. A forward-thinking councillor may have predicted that they might serve a social function and rescued them from demolition. Consequently, various small clubs and playgroups now used them and local bands hired them for rehearsals. On one particular Disco Night, after leaving the Community Centre accompanied only by my tuned-up senses, I was stopped in my tracks by the sound of a band rehearsing somewhere within those huts. The musicians sounded better than average for the standards on our estate, and they were repeatedly practising the opening bars of Stevie Wonder's *Superstition*[4].

I could work out only roughly where the sound might be coming from, and perhaps because I couldn't see the source of the music I looked up as I listened. Beyond the sulphurous glare of the concrete lampposts I saw the black sky, and, by squinting and focusing my eyes, began to pick out stars. Meanwhile, I concentrated on the sound of the band. I noticed that the riff was being boldly picked out on an electric guitar fed through a Wah Wah pedal, rather than played on a Clavinet keyboard as used on the original recording[5]. But the guitar and its effects only seemed to give the funky riff extra attitude as it jumped around over the drummer's interpretation of the simple but emphatic beat that helps Stevie Wonder's song sound so upright and proud.

As I gazed at the sky and listened to the band, musical machines were again working their magic on me. I knew that the guitar I heard was connected by a wire through a series of effects to an amplifier, probably with a built-in reverb. Pop and technology had conspired to change music forever, creating new pathways and possibilities in people's lives, new narratives, new forms of romance. The pop 'star' and 'rock star' were more prevalent in popular experience than the few real stars that could barely be picked out in the night sky between the lampposts' orange glare[6].

Stevie Wonder's song constitutes a warning. The warning concerns adherence to an anachronistic, potentially disempowering belief system. And it is directed at a community (initially black America, although vulnerable and oppressed peoples more generally are implicated) that needs all the power, belief, aspiration, and confidence it can get in order to survive its often ignominious, unfair, and oppressed state and status. But Stevie Wonder also knows (it's there in his stage name) that the same strata of society nevertheless need recourse to a certain magic, soul, spirit, and inspiration – irrational and un-modern as some of these forces might seem.

The Romantic philosopher Schiller, followed in the 20th century by Max Weber, wrote of a modernity defined and enabled by disenchantment[7]. In the scenario described above, the collision of 'wonder' and 'superstition' might speak of and to this proposition, possibly leading us to propose in turn the notion that enchantment, as a form of romantic inoculation, mediation, transcendence, or redemption, is difficult to eradicate from human experience, i.e., no matter how modern we become, humanity will always find new forms and new vehicles for transcendence and redemption. This reflex might be evidence of a survival instinct, or a way in which we continue to adapt our ancient arts to emerging technologies, and romanticise this journey as an adventure.

According to rock mythology, Heavy Metal music takes its name from the industry of the English midlands, in and around which some of the genre's most famous stars were raised or once employed. The mythology of popular music history suggests that their music was made to emulate, compete with, and ultimately escape from thundering presses and fluorescent forges churning out the base materials of modern life. Meanwhile, 'Motown', a nickname for the motor car manufacturing city of Detroit, became the name of a record company that turned out moving and uplifting soul records that sold by the million, including Stevie Wonder's *Superstition*. Thus, creativity inspires us and reminds us that hope and inspiration can and will spring from the most inauspicious cracks and crevices of a barren, impoverished, even incarcerated existence.

While machines apparently imprison those who work away in the engine rooms of capitalism, eking out a precarious life at the butt-end of the socio-economic structure, those same technologies can nevertheless provide some compensatory hope and colour to the same difficult lives. They provide simple pleasure and relief in the form of affordable, mass-produced entertainment ('kitsch' as Clement Greenberg described it in 1939).[8] As black American culture (Stevie Wonder's primary audience) has consistently proven throughout the history of modernism, human beings, even at their poorest, most oppressed and disheartened, can, through art, rally and redeem, by means of creative invention and the crafting of whatever time, space, and material there is to hand.

'Stevie Wonder' was an appropriate stage name, adopted by an exceptional – and exceptionally young – showman. Despite social and cultural disadvantages associated with both his blackness (in a white-dominated nation, society, and music business) and his blindness, he soon amazed and entertained a huge audience with his supreme creative talent. Whenever I've listened to Stevie Wonder's *Superstition* riff, first as a teenager and right through to now in my middle age; and whether on the radio, vinyl record, CD or via streaming; or even when an amateur band repeatedly played the riff that night in the huts by the Community Centre, it has always stirred something within me that encourages hope. Something of Stevie Wonder's own sense of sovereignty, his own overt insistence on achievement against the odds, always travels across space and time, to get in my system and under my skin, helping me believe that, despite my own relative powerlessness, and despite the awareness of cultural difference and injustice that began to engrain itself in my own psyche as a teenager, I can regard myself as valuable and redeemable.

In any historical period of musical instrument manufacture, the term 'technology' might refer to innovation, to prostheses, or implicate what Marshall McLuhan called 'extensions of man'.[9] It is therefore worth noting that many of the technological possibilities mentioned thus far are ramifications of a man named Les Paul who, in the 1930s, added a pick-up to an acoustic guitar. Legend has it that he initially extended the wires of a gramophone's stylus and stuck the stylus to the soundboard of an acoustic guitar. But the 1920s and 1930s had also seen the inventions of the electric piano and Hammond organ, as well as the steady development of orchestral and military drums into the compact kit first used by jazz bands and later by rock and pop groups.

In the post-World War II era, entirely new instruments and effects appeared; gadgets with previously unheard, yet strangely welcome sounds and names, like the Fender Rhodes electric piano, the Fender Stratocaster guitar, the Moog synthesiser, the Mellotron and the Hohner Clavinet. Then there were effects like the Wah Wah pedal, Phaser, Fuzz Box, Watkins Copicat, and a procession of drum machines including Roland's Rhythm Ace, 606, 707, 808, and 909 models.

All of these instruments and machines were enthusiastically concocted from wires, patch-boards, circuits, knobs, valves or early digital technology, then mass produced and ultimately destined to shape what became the signature sounds of the musicians and bands who featured them on their hits. Much of this inventive fallout derived of course from the earlier invention of the microphone, the radio, and the recording cylinder, which led in turn to headphones, vinyl records, and then the music cassette; plus in-car stereo, portable transistor radio, Walkman, iPod, streaming, etc. All of these have conspired in the proliferation of the great, emotive, cultural nexus we call pop.

By the time I became a teenager, even on our uninspiring housing estate, almost anyone could beg, steal, borrow, pool resources, obtain a guarantor for credit, or nobly work enough overtime to obtain a record player, some records, a guitar and amplifier, plus perhaps some form of microphone and PA system and a few effects. Despite having no musical education, and (we realised only much later) almost no education of any kind, you might be able to mimic a simple riff or learn the basic chord sequence to a well-known song.[10] Then, if you made your own variation, repeated it for a while, and played it with attitude and at volume, it began to sound convincing. If you could also keep reasonable time and even simultaneously shout a few lines of rhyming lyrics into a microphone, then you and a few other like-minded, long-haired housing estate heroes might just outgrow your bedrooms, hire a hut, an after-school classroom or farmer's barn, and now rehearse for hours without being repeatedly told to 'KEEP IT DOWN!' or having your electricity supply switched-off by your parents.

After a miraculously short time and according to the mysteriously unlimited potential of unbridled youths, who exceed their assumed limitations simply because they are not aware of them, you might then compile a set of songs, including some standards, 'covers', and a few of your own. This repertoire, in turn, made you feel enfranchised and able to rightfully demand that the world listen to what you had to say and play. Thus, technology allows and enables dreams as you gradually come to inhabit a rare and audacious fantasy of potential success, which, without your electrified guitar, amplifier and microphone, would be unthinkable and unavailable anywhere else within the limitations of your housing estate life.

Pop music, though seemingly revolutionary and unprecedented, is in fact only the modern incarnation of some ancient expression of social cohesion cultivated through shared experience of song and dance. Despite its reputation as the hugely exploitative modern 'music industry' (which one seasoned jazz musician referred to recently as a 'plantation') we could argue that pop has helped and enabled billions to negotiate the otherwise unbearable disenchantment of their modern lives and environment.

As the contemporary artist Cao Fei implied in her video *Whose Utopia?* (2006), pop allows and actively encourages us to retrieve a smile, a tear, a move, or some other human act or emotion from, e.g., an otherwise relatively inhuman office or factory routine. It enables us to retain our pride even when we don the incarcerating livery of servitude or when our own clothes become tarnished by our day jobs. Pop might help us endure a 12-hour multi-drop delivery shift dogged by monstrous traffic jams, pressed by the boss's schedule, and polluted by diesel fumes.

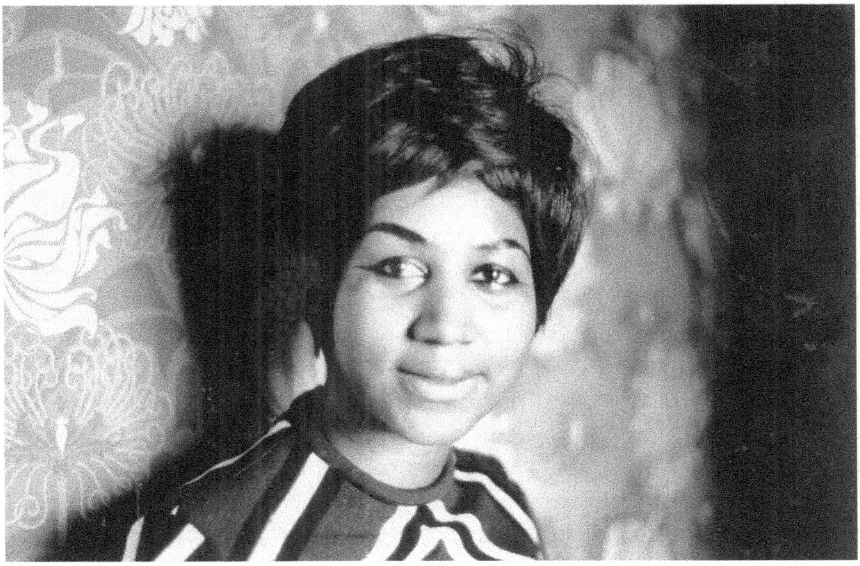

FIGURE 26.2 American soul singer Aretha Franklin, a star on the Atlantic record label. Photograph by Express Newspapers/Getty Images.

Pop can romanticise what might be an otherwise unbearable task, injecting a little spirit into the limbs of those who '... run for the bus dear...' (to briefly invoke Aretha Franklin).[11] Pop inspires feet to tap and heads to nod even when exhausted by a lifestyle built on insecure, irregular, and unpredictable contracts, or on a poorly remunerated '9 to 5' augmented by the additional hours of an exhausting daily commute.

Supposedly 'low-cultural' pop, rock, and later punk, reggae, Hip-Hop, etc., provided, for most of my own youth, a viable model of artistic excellence and aspiration. By the age of 13, moral guidance was no longer provided for me by the Stations of the Cross hung on the walls of our local church but by posters on my bedroom wall featuring pop and rock stars in outrageous costumes and provocative poses. I made myself late for school one day because, as I rushed out of the house I heard Gladys Knight singing *Midnight Train to Georgia* (1973) on the radio and rushed back in to hear it in its entirety, to feel it nurturing me, even just for those few minutes, right up to the last second before the DJ dared to speak over its fading refrain.[12] There and then I instinctively felt that this experience, and its very own excellence, was more important, valuable, and inspiring to me than the poor and painful, educational and social experiences I was having at school.

A circular, seven-inch disk, of thin, industrially pressed black vinyl, with a small hole at the centre of its stylish label, might contain what has been called a 'three-minute opera' – an appropriate description of the compressed emotional roller coaster that many a classic pop song can provide; meticulously crafted, produced, and performed, as many are, according to a special brevity, tailored to the needs of DJs, of commerce, and of the harried modern lives of all who scrape a living from the harsh, imbalanced and unjust socio-economic nexus of capitalism and consumerism.

Lovers of pop music take their favourite songs to the grave with them, preferring their secular blessing, as a summary of a life lived, to religious hymns and prayers. Meanwhile, the archive of pop's supposedly disposable (despite being so memorable) lyrics, and cheaply bought tracks, piles up with the passing of generations into high towers of 'low' culture, a proud pantheon of collective memory that stands as a monumental 'record' of the sensibilities of all those masses who make, and have made modernism, not by wielding and profiting from its harsh economic system; not by exploiting others for profit; but simply by enduring and surviving as best we can.

Pop music allowed me, and millions of others (the 'us' with whom I was remotely and technologically connected by mass-produced popular songs), to look, to dream, and to feel something beyond the hard facts of our unpromising circumstances; beyond a social structure that meant we never ceased to feel the debilitating and intimidating gaze of all those 'better' than us – in terms of wealth, inheritance, housing, and education; in terms of confidence, manners, and articulation; in terms of 'culture', prospects, and opportunities. Pop allowed us to dream beyond the significant socio-economic barriers that we felt strongly but could neither see nor explain; that we knew thoroughly but didn't understand.

Pop enabled us to look up and out into a wider sky of imagination and potential. Its high-spirited notes, lyrics, back beats, and bass-lines embodied possibility, urged action, and provided some sense of social empathy and cohesion, even in those who might be rendered justifiably inert by life's compound difficulties and consistent disappointments; in those aspirationally stunted by the lack of any other proffered or inherited 'ladder', by means of which to explore, realise, and direct all the brimming potential we felt inside. Pop encouraged us to reach out and try to achieve status and respect of a kind that might be somehow comparable with the professional world that we otherwise only glimpsed but could never expect to attain.

Nevertheless, in my early teens I had little knowledge of the way in which society was economically organised.[13] It may in fact be symptomatic of a non-professional environment that the majority of its youthful products, while as bedazzled as the rest of society by the spectacle of professional achievement, grow up with no comprehension of the realistic timeframes and pragmatically organised structures and procedures necessary to realise such outcomes. This ignorance surely contributes to much disillusionment, bewilderment, frustration, anger, loss of self-belief and lack of confidence.

But pop still encouraged us to look inside ourselves, where there secretly resided a sensitive yet expansive, unfettered, unstructured and ultimately sovereign self, who, once touched by a chord, melody, rhythm, or lyric, could, like our own internal Hercules, exponentially expand, ultimately allowing us to believe that no force, external or internal, could wholly crush or corrupt us.

Notes

1 Bowie, D. (1972).
2 McCrae, G. (Casey, H.W. & Finch, R. writers) (1974).
3 To provide another example: recently I saw a shoestring production of a Chinese play in a tiny theatre. The 'grand finale' featured the youthful cast of three or four singing while a poorly secreted hairdryer blew hundreds of hand-made paper butterflies in the direction of the audience. It was, in a way, pathetic (in the best sense of the word), but as a result, strangely moving.
4 Wonder, S. (1972).
5 Stevie Wonder is said to have written the song initially for guitarist Jeff Beck, who, after Wonder had made a huge hit of it, recorded a version using guitar rather than clavinet for the main riff.
6 Eventually followed by the Video star, Rap star, Games star, MySpace and You Tube star, Ted Talk star, Vlogger, Podcast star, etc.
7 Weber, M. (1965, 2001).
However, also noting that Goethe's novel *Elective Affinities* (1809), on which Benjamin wrote in great detail, also features debate and discussion of the part played by superstition in increasingly modernised lives. Goethe, J.W.V. (2008).
8 Greenberg, C. (1965).
9 McLuhan, M. (2001).

10 Van Morrison's classic *Gloria* (1964), for example, used the same riff throughout almost the entire song and just required impassioned dynamics to sustain interest (see also David Bowie's version of *Rebel Rebel*).
11 Warwick, D. (Bacharach, B. & David, H. writers) (1966); Franklin, A. (Bacharach, B. & David, H. writers) (1968).
12 Knight, G. (Weatherly, J. writer) (1973).
13 *Candy Floss & Diesel* in: O'Kane, P. (2017) pp. 84–93.

Bibliography

Aretha Franklin (Bacharach, B. & David, H. writers) (1968) *I Say A Little Prayer for You* (music recording). BMG Rights Management Ltd.
Benjamin, W. (2000) *One Way Street and Other Writings*. London: Verso.
David Bowie (1972) *Jean Genie* (music recording). EMI Music Publishing Ltd.
Dionne Warwick (Bacharach, B. & David, H. writers) (1966) *I Say a Little Prayer for You* (music recording). BMG Rights Management Ltd.
George McCrae (Casey, H.W. & Finch, R. writers) (1974) *Rock Your Baby* (music recording). BMG Rights Management Ltd.
Gladys Knight & The Pips (Weatherly, J. writer) (1973) *Midnight Train to Georgia* (music recording). Universal Polygram International Publishing Inc.
Goethe, J.W.V. (2008) *Elective Affinities – A Novel*. Oxford: Oxford University Press.
Greenberg, C. (1965) *Art and Culture: Critical Essays*. Boston, MA: Beacon Press.
McLuhan, M. (2001) *Understanding Media: The Extensions of Man*. London: Routledge.
Morrison, V (1964) *Gloria* (music recording). Carlin Music Corp.
O'Kane, P. (2017) *Technologies of Romance Part: I*. London: eeodo.
Weber, M. (1965) *The Sociology of Religion*. London: Methuen.
Weber, M. (2001) *The Protestant Ethic and the Spirit of Capitalism*. London: Routledge.
Wonder, S. (1972) *Superstition* (music recording). Jobette Music Co Inc, Black Bull Music Inc.

27

REVERB

A passion for the past in popular music – Part 2

The reverb sound effect was invented, along with many of pop's aforementioned technologies, in the 1930s. It is used today on almost all pop music recordings and generously in karaoke booths worldwide. It made a strong impact on some of the earliest rock and roll hits, constituting a key element of their innovative sound and thereby coming to be forever associated with pop.[1]

Reverb provides an imitation of the acoustics of a large concert hall and thus creates an illusory popularity or instant stardom, when added – at the touch of a button, pull of a slider or turn of a knob – to any vocal performance, guitar solo or the general ambience of an otherwise 'dry' studio recording. Reverb is fame on tap, an added sense of mythic grandeur, the instant aura of a sonic halo. Reverb makes a sound, a song, or a sentiment linger in the air, just as it might within a cave, cathedral, or concert hall. Reverb extends presence in time while creating a sense of spatial distance, and thereby strangely increases value.

While reverb, as a sound effect, has a history, it may be possible that certain aspects of history also constitute a form of reverb. For example, the popular variant of history known as 'nostalgia' involves a tendency to enhance, colour and glorify the past, to provide the past with a halo of added value, amplifying what might otherwise be bare historical facts with a positive aura.[2]

However, any object of historical interest (which might of course be almost any object) occupies at least two worlds and two times; that in which it originated, perhaps its heyday, and the time in which it is now regarded and re-evaluated. Just as reverb appears to swell, prolong and extend a sound further into time and beyond its original event, so the enduring presence of – and corresponding fascination we have for– objects from, of and in the past, might qualify as a form of 'reverb'.

Furthermore, just as a photographer or cinematographer might increase the glow or ease the edge of a portrait's profile so as to flatter or render it more attractive, so the cultural profiles of past objects, images and events may be softened and graced

DOI: 10.4324/9781003230632-30

by their distance from us in time. As if proving the popular English axiom that 'time heals all wounds', even the most shocking and evil of deeds may lose some of the harsh-edged newness of their original eventuality as they are assimilated into history, as phenomena that, by means of reflection, we gradually feel more able to comprehend and assimilate.

But even as an object or event falls into a history that is more than willing to accommodate it, we might become aware of a certain inaccuracy caused by a certain effect which, like reverb, or the portrait photographer's flattering art, distorts our perception in the process of rendering that same object or event both more acceptable and more useful to our current purposes and perspectives.

We might here recall Cervantes' *Don Quixote*, a figure besotted by the particular technology of the book, within which he discovered the alternative, mythologised culture and value system of a bygone age.[3] Don Quixote's apparent folly is, in part, a manifestation of anachronism, as he insists upon living a now-redundant way of life within a more modern present. Perhaps this too could be described as a form of 'reverb', after all Don Quixote is captivated by his own image, both flattered and distorted by what we might call the mirror of history, a condition not unlike that of the experience of any karaoke singer who, despite an untrained and unappealing voice, magnifies and enhances their image and proficiency, not only by means of the microphone and the reverb effect, but aided by a professionally performed and recorded instrumental backing track, of a song long established as a classic in the history of popular culture.[4]

Conversely then, the karaoke singer is also like Don Quixote in that both replay, rather poorly, the achievements of older, greater others, bathing their own relative ineptitude in the glow, the auratic reverb, of past glory.

For Don Quixote, the relatively modern technology of the printed, bound, distributed, and widely read book, not only proliferated but also glorified and promoted certain narratives according to the specific and fixed form they took within the book format. The book successfully preserved, established, and disseminated certain narratives while leaving out others, and thus created demand for a certain kind of book-based narrative. Preserved in the form of the book, certain narratives might then take on classic status or other forms of enduring influence.

Meanwhile, the book pins these narratives down. It orders, numbers, binds, encloses and protects them, and yet also gives them 'wings' as the book becomes a vehicle that enables a story to travel far and wide via multiple, identical copies, and perhaps internationally in considered translations. In these ways the book-bound story is unlike the less consistent, less reliable, though no less beguiling tales told by itinerant storytellers, as celebrated by Walter Benjamin in his essay *The Storyteller*.[5]

We could argue that Don Quixote's very absurdity lies in the fact that he takes his books too 'literally'. He insists on living as and like the characters and narratives fixed in the form of the books he has read. It is therefore the encumbering influence of the fixed form of the book that disables Don Quixote from enjoying and adapting – in any way that might prove more fluid, pragmatic, and in-tune with real life and changing times – the influence of the stories and of the past that he finds contained within books.

A certain kind of modernism is thus inaugurated with the technology of the book, as both art and ideas thereby come to be preserved, archived, mobilised, and shared in new ways. The wave of populism, so worrying to established democracies due to its largely right-wing nature, may nevertheless bare some comparison with the roots of what could be described as the current middle-class hegemony, instigated in part by the first print boom and associated café society, wherein a wider range of more or less informed opinions came to be newly voiced and exchanged. Today's own technologically aided political turn might then mark the close of that previous politico-print era and the end of its particular sense of progress and revolution, while heralding a newly disruptive political epoch based upon the ascent of a newly vocal (albeit otherwise unempowered) public.

But how far back should we trace the origins of the book, and what, after all, would precisely define or determine a book? As Walter Benjamin implies in his *Storyteller* essay, a narrative that is merely memorised, spoken spontaneously, and which is thus malleable, nomadic, and alive, clearly differs from a narrative fixed in a printed and bound form.[6] One distinction is that the bound and printed story might be perceived not only as a new technology but also, and soon, as an old story, in that it is fixed, monumentalised, revered and preserved. Meanwhile, the spoken tale, though possibly more ancient, its roots lost in time, is renewed and rewritten by the tongue of every teller and every telling. Thus, the new technology of the book paradoxically ages its contents by preserving them in fixed form, while the more ancient art of live storytelling delivers the story anew in every rendition.

While the model of the book can be compared with the older art of storytelling, Benjamin also compares it with the even more modern phenomenon of the rise of 'information', which he associates with journalism.[7] The book is thus historicised in terms of both a precedent (live storytelling) and an antecedent (journalistic information). These historicising 'bookends' may help to clarify the book's specific form and contributions. However, here we can also see how technology invariably cuts history both ways, apparently unfolding our future while simultaneously immersing us in the past.

The apparently new also serves to make us more conscious of the passing of time and of the instantaneous passing of the new into history. Furthermore, new technologies, be they books, karaoke machines, movies or computers, inevitably exacerbate our tendency (and simultaneously increase our capacity) to archive, and thus continuously and increasingly immerse ourselves in the past, even by means of what appears to be our most futuristic machines.

Books, stories, popular songs, and perhaps all historical objects, may acquire an example of the aura that Benjamin attributed to a constant condition of distance, as soon as they fall into the past and lose their place in the present. Reverb, as used so lavishly in pop music, is thus a gauche amplification of the auratic effects of modernism and its accelerated sense of history. Today, classic status, attributed as readily to a pair of sneakers or a designer lemon squeezer as to a popular song or

Doric column, can be established in minutes, hours, weeks or months, rather than in decades or centuries, as classic status awards its every recipient a seat in an ever-expanding popular pantheon.

We can return now to one of our first examples, from Part 1 of this essay above. George McCrae's *Rock Your Baby* was a worldwide hit in July 1974. It was innovative, inspired, and also prescient, as it might be seen as heralding the coming wave of disco which had its apotheosis circa 1976. Disco newly glued dancers to dance floors using a more technologised means than ever before, and may have culminated, as a genre, in Giorgio Moroder's linking of its famous, skipping, hi-hat rhythm to relentless and intoxicating electronic beats synchronised with inexorably pulsating synthesiser basslines.[8]

George McCrae's multi-million selling song may have had the power and persuasion of a burgeoning music industry behind it, but we could also argue that the existence of some more mysterious power of persuasion – something other than economic strength, well-financed promotion, and the might of supportive media – also contributed to its success. Did hundreds of thousands of people hear, like, dance and sing along to, and ultimately go out and buy copies of this record only because they heard and saw it promoted, heavily plugged, and played repeatedly by DJs, at 'drive time', in their tea break, etc.? If so, did those pluggers and DJs think it was more likely than other contemporary records to succeed? Did they think it was a special record, more deserving of airtime, because it was, in their critical, informed, and experienced opinion, excellent?

If so, we might want to probe further and deeper, perhaps delving back into the origins of the record, e.g., asking why the record company cut it, investing a significant sum while gambling on the hope of making a profit in return? Why did the band use expensive studio time to record it? Why did the songwriter write it up from an original sketch and then resolve it? Just what is – we might ask – the aesthetic and critical value and criteria pertaining to pop, funk, rock, reggae or disco music? How is it evaluated and critiqued, or how can it be?

To answer these questions, we could once again follow in the footsteps of Walter Benjamin and try to carve out our own mode of appreciation, utilising an appropriate vocabulary to create an evaluation that is intrinsic to these innovative, undeniably modern, highly technologised art forms and genres. We could also trace the value of George McCrae's song back to its source in some creative inspiration; a riff, a rhythm, a melody, lyric or chord sequence, later structured into a complete song. But we could also try to trace the success of the composition forwards in time, to the affective moment of someone hearing it, perhaps on a radio, at a fairground, while driving to work, while at work in a factory or an office, or perhaps while dancing at the week's end. If we recall our own experiences of this kind, we might be inclined to agree that a strangely familiar, perhaps even uncanny experience attends our appreciation of any piece of pop music.

Liking a new pop song involves a complex feeling that this music is not only excitingly new but also somehow familiar from the outset. Liking pop music means knowing it and owning it. Liking it means that it becomes in some way ours. It is possible of course that its very ubiquity (due to commercial promotion) means that we might absorb a new song subliminally on several occasions prior to any conscious acknowledgement. Advertising and other forms of promotion often aim to work on us in this subliminal way. However, our ultimate appreciation of the song is also linked to some other form of recognition. Thus, the new and the old, novelty and the familiar, become strangely intertwined. Meanwhile, songs and songwriters may be involved, not only in the crafting of time but of history, weaving echoes and traces, perhaps even of an ancient past, into their innovations.

If we think for a minute here of the implications of the Romantic philosopher Nietzsche's theory of 'eternal return', and of the crepuscular scenarios contrived by contemporary video and installation artist Elizabeth Price (see Chapter 24 of this book) where old clips of young singers create a haunting atmosphere, we might note that the strange familiarity of popular music, or music in general, may be rooted in the fact that it is always a form of return or refrain, an echo or reminder of something that has already been, a repetition, echo or return, even when it is also fresh, new and innovative. The singer, musician or composer seems to us to have unearthed something that always was, already is, and that we always knew, and we applaud, sing along, or move in response to the resulting feeling of recognition.

One way in which this recognition might operate is in relation to a certain tradition, i.e., even a pop song like George McCrae's 1974 hit *Rock Your* Baby is liked and appreciated as something we can readily add to our own canon or archive of previously liked songs; and liked partly because of similarities and marks of influence they bear, and which together amount to a tradition. It may therefore be important to assert the value and power of tradition as it operates within popular culture, even as we might tend to associate popular culture with the new and with innovation.

To return to the strange familiarity involved in the liking of a pop song, is it not possible, in light of the foregoing, that while we simultaneously delight in the novelty of a brand new, supposedly throw-away or ephemeral pop song, what allows us to like, or indeed to love it, is its new illustration of certain traditional values and its triggering of apparently new passions or emotions that are nonetheless indicative of a history of emotions.

There may be occasional innovations, so new and influential that we could call them 'genre-busting', but for the most part the pop song purports to be an innovation or novelty within the context of, and in relation to, a familiar genre. Even if we don't know the new song, we *do* know the genre, the context, the history, the instruments, the notes and chord sequences, the breaks, the references (which in sampled music become direct quotes) and the tendencies. And perhaps this is what makes the song valuable to us, in such a way that, even on first hearing, it is both likeably novel and likeably familiar.

We absorb and retain a song's emotional structure in an instant, then carry it with us as a secret and intimate companion, until such time as we begin to hum, sing, or whistle it out loud, then perhaps confess our love for it to others, obtain a copy of it, and play it repeatedly and as loud as possible.

To further support these points, later generations of popular musicians, perhaps most notably Hip-Hop composers, began actively seeking out citations in the form of 'breaks', sampled and looped, that purposefully play upon and entertain their audience's knowledge of the history of the genre. In this case, new recognitions of what might be called 'traditional' figures and values, lie at the heart of Hip-Hop, perhaps the most innovative and modern of all modern musics. Once again, the theme of reverb is not difficult to feed into our argument, as in Hip-Hop, the past habitually lends its aura to the new.

Even a cursory glance through the oeuvre of a classic pop act like The Beatles would quickly reveal quite explicit forms of dialogue with history. The Beatles initially built their reputation on assimilations and reproductions of emerging American music, but having conquered the American market and media they began to parody it and fuse it with influences from different eras, including Paul McCartney's strangely successful penchant for what John Lennon disparagingly called 'granny music'.[9]

Popular culture and newly technologised culture are, in these ways, no less traditional than any other culture. While they innovate, almost by definition – the popular being invariably commensurate with the modern and the new – they ingratiate themselves to us as a kind of reassuring evidence of a perpetuation of a tradition, and of tradition per se, i.e., not just a tradition of and for what popular songwriter Jarvis Cocker ironically referred to as 'common people', but a wider tradition, the ancient tradition of art itself.[10]

Not all pop songs are concerned with love, but a piece of pop music that we love might seem like something we were destined to encounter. Our encounter with the song is a kind of rendezvous, reunion or return. Even as the song's melody, delivery, and lyrics might be romantic in the more obvious sense, our relationship to the song is not unlike a love affair. We may, after all, fall in love with pop songs, with their images, reflections, and narratives of love, while falling, or hoping and waiting to fall in love for real. Pop songs thus become a rehearsal for, a parallel to, or reminder of love; a nursery for the heart where various feelings and narratives can be tried-out in safety.

We might then use popular songs as models for lost, anticipated, promised, or pending emotional experiences. The new pop song that, on first hearing (at first sight, as it were) we soon or immediately love, perfectly fits a pre-existing receptacle in our consciousness and sensibility. In encountering, liking, and soon loving a particular new pop song among the millions available to us at any one time, we soon become aware that it will constitute a milestone along the way of our most intimate narrative, the story of our life or romance with our self, thus becoming part of our archival identity. It is, and will henceforth always be, a precious part of us, even though we will never adequately describe or articulate the passionate and precious connection we have to it.

Furthermore, in being a popular song, our own, apparently intimate and personal love affair with it, is, by definition, also and simultaneously shared by millions of others admirers, each of whom might justifiably feel that they value the song on equally personal, intimate terms. We are therefore both excited and legitimated by the aura or 'reverb' awarded to the song by its widespread popularity or hit status.

These thoughts coincide to some extent with the aesthetic theories of the 18th-century philosopher Immanuel Kant, but perhaps only as much as with those of Sigmund Freud whose theory of *The Uncanny* explicitly draws into its speculative net our modern age of mechanisation and compound repetition.[11] Freud's thought and writings refer to a modernism infused with new mechanisations, along with new subjectivities, new liberties, and a new permissiveness, all further informed by an accompanying modern rejection of repression and established orders.[12]

Modern machines promise to, or appear to ease our burdens and bring us a cornucopia of gifts and leisure, but in doing so they also encroach on our humanity, intimacy and self-worth, often becoming all-too lifelike and thereby threatening, hence the timeliness and enduring success of Mary Shelley's most famous creative invention.[13] Mass production may engulf or overwhelm our individuality through a 'doppelganger' effect, as we are increasingly pursued by, and simultaneously pursue, stimulated and concocted tastes, prescribed desires and passions, aided by the eerily similar and strangely familiar mechanisations and repetitions intrinsic to a mass-manufactured, simulacral and commodified modern experience.[14] All of this may well be applicable to pop songs.

When we register that we like a popular song it might seem significant that we feel unsure as to where or whether we have heard it before. It arrives replete with auratic cultural 'reverb' as well as more literal and liberal use of the ubiquitous reverb sound effect. Cultural reverb may, as we have said, be caused by a heavily technologised, mediated, and marketised environment in which we may have previously, albeit subliminally, heard brief snatches of the song without being conscious of doing so. We hear so many brief snatches of 'heavily rotated' (or streamed) songs (each of which is also in some way an echo of all others) that we are immersed, from cradle to grave, in a sonic environment filled with musical echoes and ricochets.

However, it is also true that any sense of uncanny recognition fits almost too neatly with the innate repetitiveness of pop music itself, with its typically steady beat, almost identically formed and repeated verses, chants and choruses, use of repeated riffs or looped samples, all compressed into a few minutes. We can then add to this list of repetitions the electronic reproduction of the recording process and mass reproducibility of vinyl records, CDs, downloads, or streamed files. And then there is the aforementioned 'media rotation', as well as the vinyl record's own literal circularity and potentially infinite prolongation through the repeated mixing of two identical records using twin record decks, or the emulation of the same when using a looped sample.

All of this compound mechanical repetition, reproduction and 'cultural reverb' returns us to those copious amounts of actual reverb effect used in popular music recordings; a sonic effect that suggests a lingering presence and in turn implies a form of built-in historical grandeur, a concocted and exaggerated sense of a song's instantaneous historical value, designed to be felt, not only after many years of popularity and success but on first hearing.

Repetition and reproduction thus infuse almost every aspect of a popular music that clearly speaks of and for modernism, and that provides a more or less ambient anthem for similarly repetitious modern lives. Just as much as we might love a song's, a singer's, or a band's unique sound and style, our love of pop music is inextricably bound up with a love of repetitions and echoes, choruses and chants, reproductions, copies, and reverberating auras. Rhyme too provides us with a satisfying sense of recognition and return, as if in rhyme words are finding each other again, as familiars, acknowledging both a sonic similarity and a shared kinship after a period of separation.

Reverb does not only make a sound or a singer appear more important, it also suggests that they exist as, and have already existed as a historical phenomenon, and that therefore and henceforth they will continue to do so. Benjamin's awarding of historical importance to fleeting experience, and to the most banal of modern phenomena, comes to mind here, as if he were willing to award an auratic halo or cultural 'reverb' to any event that rose up and appealed to him for inclusion in the apparently infinite pantheon of his modern perception of history. Reverb is history (or is at least a 'history effect'), and vice versa – history is reverb.

Notes

1 The term 'karaoke' is a compound of the Japanese words for 'empty' and 'orchestra'.
2 Here, the 'classic', 'vintage', and 'retro' come to mind.
3 Cervantes, M.de. (1950).
4 We could also invite consideration of the more recent phenomenon of 'Auto-Tune' here.
5 Benjamin, W. (1968) pp. 83–110.
6 Benjamin, W. (1968) pp. 83–110.
7 Or (to be more specific, and truer to Benjamin's argument) 'the novel'.
8 'Repetitive beats' was a phrase notoriously used in legislating against the phenomenon of nomadic, peripatetic. and relatively spontaneous mass dance parties (or 'raves') by the 1980s Tory-led UK government. I have encountered references to the waltz as also and perhaps equally influenced by the machinic rhythms and technologies of its own heyday.
9 See, for example, the 'middle-eight' of the Beatles' *Back in the USSR*, which is a friendly parody of The Beach Boys. The Beatles (Lennon, J. & McCartney, P. writers) (1968). Interestingly, Simon Reynolds, in his book *Retromania*, discusses ways in which West Coast American hippies began raiding history for old dresses and bits of military uniforms that became part of the hippie style and look, alongside more modern loon pants, T-shirts, etc. The Beatles' costumes for *Sgt Peppers Lonely Hearts Club Band* may have been an extension of this vogue. Reynolds, S. (2011).
10 Blur (Cocker, J., Banks, N., Doyle, C., Mackey, S. & Senior, R. writers) (1995).
11 *The Uncanny* in: Freud, S. (1985) pp. 335–376.
12 We might here consider relationships between Vienna, the waltz, and the possibly *haute bourgeois* officer class.
13 Shelley, M. (2003).
14 TV playwright Dennis Potter alluded to this in one of his final pieces. *Karaoke* features a playwright, not unlike Potter himself, eerily encountering echoes of his writings within the real world that he is attempting to represent. Potter, D. (Amiel, J. Dir.) (1986); Potter, D. (2004) (Haggard, P. Dir.); Potter, D. (Rye, R. Dir.) (2010).

Bibliography

Benjamin, W. (1968) *Illuminations*. New York: Schocken Books.

Blur (Cocker, J., Banks, N., Doyle, C., Mackey, S. & Senior, R. writers) (1995) *Common People* (music recording). Universal Music Publishing Group, Island Records.

Cervantes, M.de. (1950) *The Adventures of Don Quixote*. London: Penguin.

Freud, S. (1985) *Art and Literature – Jensen's Gradiva, Leonardo da Vinci and Other Works*. London: Penguin.

Potter, D. (Amiel, J. Dir.) (1986) *The Singing Detective*. London: BBC.

Potter, D. (2004) (Haggard, P. dir.) *Pennies from Heaven*. London: BBC.

Potter, D. (Rye, R. Dir.) (2010) *Karaoke*. UK: Acorn Media.

Reynolds, S. (2011) *Retromania – Pop Culture's Addiction to Its Own Past*. London: Faber & Faber.

Shelley, M. (2003) *Frankenstein – Or the Modern Prometheus*. London: Penguin.

The Beatles (Lennon, J. & McCartney, P. writers) (1968) *Back in the USSR* (music recording). Northern Songs Ltd, Sony/ATV Tunes LLC.

28

A SELFIE STICK IN THE CHARITY SHOP

History and the self, photography, video, and technology as extensions of man

A few years ago, I came across a selfie-stick in a charity shop. It made me pause and think of the event as a possibly historical moment. This was because both the selfie and its stick have relatively recently been regarded as a vibrant sign of the present and the current. And so, seeing a selfie-stick relegated to this second tier of consumerism, the realm of the used and pre-loved, of Oxfam and Gumtree, seemed to signal that, despite its once cutting-edge *cache*, we have now collectively moving-on as a culture, from the selfie era.

I didn't feel any great desire to obtain the selfie-stick, cheap as it no doubt was, but maintaining a certain distance from it in this way rendered it all the more strongly as a symbol. It nevertheless provoked a certain sense of empathy, after all, deep down we all fear an inevitable day when we too will become demoted from the spotlight of contemporaneity, and jettisoned even by those who once found us *de rigueur*, in order to make necessary physical and cultural space for someone or something more *en vogue*.

Nevertheless, Walter Benjamin in his 1929 essay on Surrealism noted that the Surrealists were invested in what he called 'the outmoded'. Far from seeing these objects and aspects of modern life as merely disempowered by the effects of aging, falling from grace and out of fashion, the arch *avant-gardists* saw 'revolutionary' forces within them.[1]

But how can this be so? The selfie-stick, lying there in the charity shop, among the piled-up fallout from rampant consumerism, tells us, in some undeniable, material, symbolic, and rather convincing way, something about our specific society, times, and culture; about the ways in which we are changing. It shows us, in a way that neither the museum nor the art gallery can do, what we have recently been but are no longer, and it therefore perhaps infers where we might be going.

The content of the apparently benign charity shop thus has the capacity to unnerve the present, haunting those brand-new wares proudly displayed in adjacent

DOI: 10.4324/9781003230632-31

retailers, all nervously hoping that they will be sold before being deemed unfashionable or replaced by the next season's stock.[2]

Despite the relatively youthful hubris of the latest fashions, the charity shop's contents are a constant reminder of fashion's necessary, inevitable, and almost immediate redundancy, its proud *cache* evaporating almost as quickly as the potency of a perfume (which is perhaps the short-lived commodity *par excellence*). As such, the used, 'pre-loved' and outmoded, the charity shop and the flea market, all constitute – for the 1920s Surrealists and still for us today – a slightly uncanny realm within, and yet also outside, the main economy of consumerism, modernism and capitalism that we tend to take for granted as an unalterable paradigm. However, where there is something potentially outside, there lies the potential for alternatives, and any alternative to an apparently unalterable paradigm therefore becomes 'revolutionary'.[3]

Of course, stocked as they mostly are with defanged bric-a-brac, bags of wool, and well worn sweatshirts it seems unlikely that revolutionary ferment is quietly brewing in our benign and anodyne charity shops, but the fact that, in gentrified areas at least, some are becoming more *chic* in their selections, displays, and prices, may point to the fact that they are an alternative to the main thrust of consumerism that may no longer be allowed to disrupt the market place. They must therefore be brought out (and bought out) of the margins into the fold of the main high-street economy.

If the uncanny nature of the charity shop and its contents suggests a certain disruptive ambiguity (or 'intellectual uncertainty', to use Freud's phrase) due to the fact that it resides both inside and outside the main thrust of consumerism, then we are likely to find this disruptive of any complacent vision we might have of how our culture, society, and economy operates.[4]

The selfie-stick in the charity shop is about as banal and uninteresting an object or image as we can muster, and yet, if viewed and interpreted in the appropriate manner it can, simultaneously, be poignant, powerful, meaningful and historical. Billions of these devices must have been built in a rapid boom, only to be soon discarded. Along the way they also helped 'revolutionise' an entire generation's relationship to self through photography and social media. Thus – setting Benjamin, Freud, and Surrealism aside – the selfie-stick in the charity shop might suggest something about our relationship with our self, or about the long history of ways in which our self may have engaged with and been changed by, art and technology.[5]

The selfie-stick is surely a kind of prosthesis, and today we might readily apply the term 'prosthesis' to a false limb, a wig, or a glass eye too, but we can also understand *all* technologies as extensions of the body, and as augmentations of human potential and abilities. Marshall McLuhan, the maverick mid-20th century academic, responsible for presciently predicting a globally networked 21st-century society, and for coining the influential phrases 'global village' and 'the medium is the message', called his influential 1964 study: *Understanding Media: The Extensions of Man.*[6] The subtitle here seems to imply that technology is never other, or never

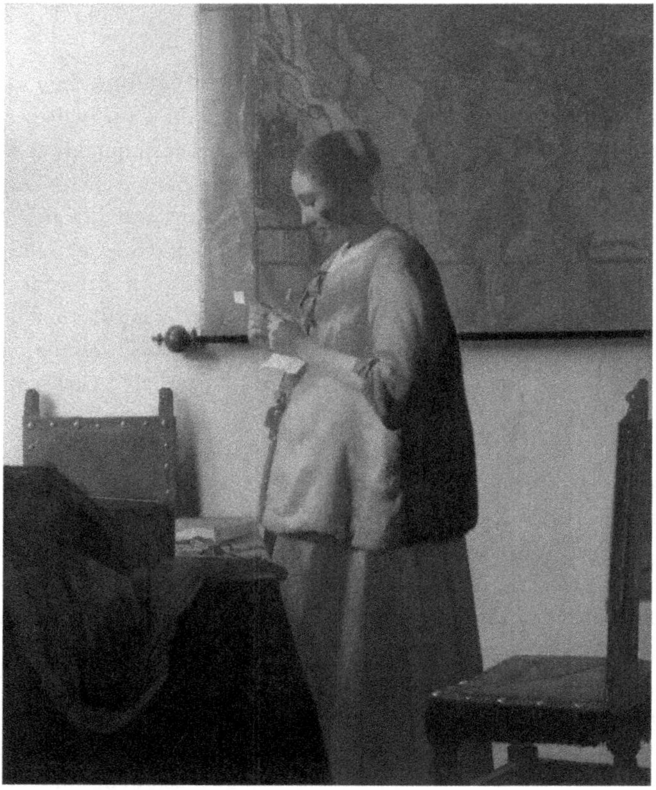

FIGURE 28.1 Johannes Vermeer, *Woman in Blue Reading a Letter/Woman Reading a Letter* c. 1663. Courtesy of Rijksmuseum, Amsterdam.

wholly other to the human, the subject, or the self, but always in some way continuous with, or an 'extension' of that humanity, subjectivity, or self. We might like to think of ourselves as somehow essentially natural, and of technology as somehow other to our natural self, and thus *un*natural, but it may also be true to say that we are technology and technology is us.

In several of his paintings, the 17th-century artist Johannes Vermeer depicted a woman reading a letter.[7] Three hundred years later, artist Tom Hunter re-enacted this gesture for an equally carefully contrived photograph. However, in Hunter's version the woman is a squatter and (like one of Vermeer's subjects, who might be pregnant) she is also responsible for a baby.[8] Neither in Vermeer's nor in Hunter's image can we read the contents of the letter that the woman is reading, however, Hunter's figure is purportedly reading an eviction notice and therefore preparing to possibly lose and leave her home. This narrative element adds a layer of pathos and political or cultural drama to Hunter's image that may also be present within, but is less overtly apparent in Vermeer's painting.

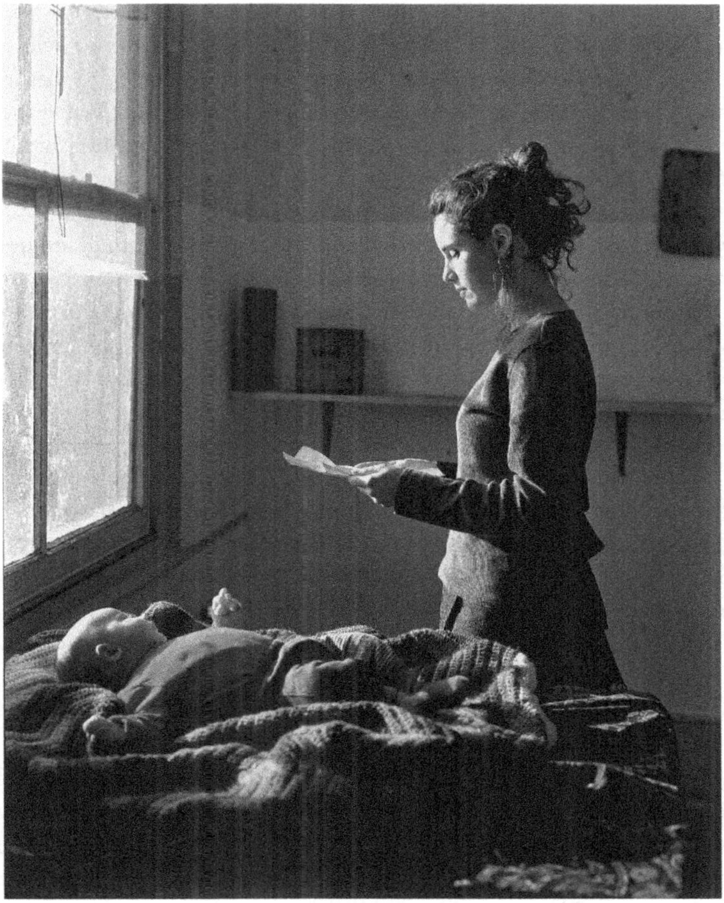

FIGURE 28.2 Tom Hunter, *Woman Reading Possession Order*, 1997, from the series *Persons Unknown*, © Tom Hunter. Courtesy of the artist.

While Hunter might have deployed some of the best photographic technology available in his times, Vermeer also utilised the latest techniques of his own time and place in the world, along with his own innovations, for making oil paintings,. These include a special and personal deployment of lenses to aid in the scrutinisation and accurate depiction of figures, objects, light, spaces, and distances.

Hopefully it can be seen here that, in tracing certain historical continuities across long periods of time and apparently distant places, cultures, and practices, we are able to historicise our own cultural moment, including such apparently banal things or events as our current relationship with the self-as-selfie; or, for that matter, our current relationship with an isolated subject, a person alone in a photograph, in a painting or a room, rendered as an image and created by a mixture of techniques, cultures and technologies.[9]

In our life-long, complex exploration of identity, and our search for a real, true, individual or authentic self, we might need to be aware of, and to acknowledge the tools, techniques, technologies and assumptions that we bring to that search, as these might deflect, skew, or otherwise determine what we find. While the search for the self may be an adventure, the sensitive and uncertain relationship between the self as searcher and the self for whom the self presumes to search, might be justifiably framed as a form of romance, or possibly folly.

As we have said, the contents of the letters in Vermeer's paintings are unknown, they are part of a secret world that we can witness only from a distance of hundreds of years, while always positioned outside the magical world of illusion and representation created by the painter, by the painting, and by the painting's frame. However, we are nevertheless invited and even encouraged to imagine and speculate upon the contents of those letters.

Seventeenth-century Holland was one of the world's leading maritime, trading nations, and therefore many families, couples, and lovers would have been routinely separated for long periods by the international travel and global commerce that made 17th-century Holland wealthy, and that in turn made it able to construct an unprecedentedly layered, structured and modern society. The same period and culture saw both an exponential rise in the qualities and quantities of new optical lenses, and a proliferation of new forms of printed matter. Holland was a new protestant republic and the Reformation had placed scripture closer to the centre of Christian belief, not least by increased access to translations and thus the democratisation of the Catholic, Latin text. As a result, many other 17th-century Dutch paintings depict people, often women, avidly reading, letters, books, and bibles.

Reading, in 17th-century Holland, appears to have meant something special, contemporary, and worthy of being recorded and celebrated in these paintings. In today's terms we might consider it as the revolutionary technology of its time, arising from a combination of lenses, printing, translation, and from improved forms of commerce and distribution. Not only do such paintings of people reading represent the latest, current, or fashionable activities in an emerging modern life (perhaps akin to a portrait made today of someone scrolling a phone and wearing headphones), they might also be considered a kind of cultural propaganda, hype, or advertising, encouraging a viewer to read – maybe to read scripture in particular, or simply to read as much and as widely as possible.

We can also note here the way in which the act of reading draws any individual into a peculiarly solipsistic experience, making them seem not only peculiarly alone in the space they occupy but also more detached from that same space.[10] They are mentally disconnected from their physical environment and have entered what we might call the 'realm' of reading, which is, furthermore, partly an internal dialogue, a cultivation of the self with the self. Today, when we bemoan the prevalent image of ourselves as zombie-like smartphone scrollers, we should perhaps historicise, and thereby relativise any overly harsh self-judgement by comparing our current experience with the enthusiasm seen in 17th-century Dutch paintings for rapt and avid attention to the 'screen' of the printed page.

In Vermeer's paintings we also see the influence of new lenses and admire the invitation that they offer us to enter the painting's space and attend to tiny details, while appreciating the artist's enthusiasm for nuanced light, spatial optics and sense of aerial perspective. Paintings at this time, produced in far greater numbers than ever before, and in guilds (to maintain standards and profitability), also became smaller, more mobile, and thus more marketable, and all these combined factors may have encouraged a way of interpreting these paintings in a more technical, democratic, popular and modern way that went beyond established 17th century interpretations based on iconography, allegory, and connoisseurship.

Aided by the combined technologies of the book, of spectacles and other lenses; as well as the significant technologies of more accurate maps and faster, stronger, more reliable ships by means of which to deliver people, goods, and correspondence all around the world, we might also imagine that the very idea of a human subject is technologically 'extended' as it is subjected to these various kinds of modernism and as the modern subject is born in dialogue with these technologies.

We may have begun to blur boundaries between technology and the self, but there could also be another division emerging here between the self and the human. Perhaps it is the human rather than the self that forges the intimate and interwoven relationship with technology described above, while the self remains capable of observing all of this (perhaps inhumanly) as if in the role of a non-participating observer.

It could be possible, after all, that the self is no more or less than this observer, no more or less than our capacity to observe and reflect on our own experience. Perhaps this explains our fascination with the many ways in which the self and reflection interplay. For example, self-reflection introduces us first to a non-productive narcissism which, if multiplied, leads on to a secular form of infinity in which we glimpse a vertiginous and ecstatic loss of any human grip, perspective, and position. So, it may be that while the self finds satisfaction in reflection, it finds ultimate satisfaction in infinite reflection, which leads beyond the human, beyond nature, beyond technology, and beyond the self.

Aside from the special photographic and cinematic effects and processes that interested Walter Benjamin, the relatively simple technology of still photography had already created an existential, or perhaps some other form of crisis, both for the human subject and the self. If we turn to Louis Daguerre's celebrated image, *Boulevard Du Temple* (seen in Chapter 25 of this book), we can see the first recorded photograph of a human being, inadvertently and indexically marked out by history, apparently as he lingered to have his boots polished.[11] The crowd of shoppers buzzing around him 'disappeared', we might say, 'to' the lens of the camera, because of their restless activity during a necessarily, and of course relatively, long exposure.

A new age of the human subject begins in that place on that day, during those few minutes, within this image. The subject's figure becomes an unwitting graphic monument to its own event. That is because here photography made and makes us newly aware of the human subject *as* a self, even reconciling a certain dilemma or dichotomy we perceive between the two.

The 'human subject' is an abstract notion that is universally applicable. The self however is, by definition, unknowable to anything or anyone other than itself, and so is less accommodating to the objective and universally recognisable notion of *a* self. Rather the self might always be *the* self or *itself*.

Photography – as the exponentially proliferating phenomenon of the selfie will eventually confirm and compound – is able to draw the self (knowable only as and to *its*elf) out into the wider world of objectivity, and correspondingly draw the objective realm into the necessarily reflective and self-reflective experience of the self. The small dark room of the 'camera' and its lens might therefore perform not only an inversion of the image but a turning inside-out of the encounter between self and world.

One compulsion that the self might feel when confronted by Daguerre's famous image is to associate with the only figure the self finds therein, a figure who might reliably be akin to the self. In an *ur* form of 'facial recognition' the self seeks another self, which, to that other self, is also *the* self. Photography's special indexicality allows us to consider this empathy in a new way or to a new degree. It newly convinces us, as a kind of 'evidence' (to use Benjamin's term) regarding the experience of others and the existence of historical experience. Thus, with this image, and with the inauguration of photography, we seem able to *see seeing* (our own and that of others) anew, even for the first time, and to *experience experiencing* (our own and that of others) in a new way too, i.e., to see our existence, our humanity, our presence in time and in place, and also our relative animation or stillness. In this way we become newly, and differently aware of life and of living, not necessarily in a philosophical or spiritual manner, but in a *photographic* manner, becoming newly aware of life in terms of a new nexus of light, time, lens, chemistry, and the medium's other attendant tools, processes and materials.

Similarly, Gilles Deleuze argued that the invention of cinema, just as much as the formation of crystals, may offer us new ways of thinking about, measuring and representing time.[12] A photograph of the human subject, however beautiful, banal, awkward, or ugly, is always evidently and undeniably a point on a journey from a birth to a death. Photography makes the very fact of our life more real than, and different from, ways (technologies, processes, epistemes and paradigms) in which it had been hitherto considered. Correspondingly, the self develops a reciprocal, new, modern and particularly *photographic* relationship with the human subject; with humanity and with life, in which an apparent or supposed nature is, once again, extended by technology.

Let's consider the carefully contrived street portraiture that brought artist-photographer Philip-Lorca diCorcia to international prominence.[13] In a world flooded with photographs of streets, people and faces he managed to capture something quintessentially 'photographic' about faces, lives and journeys that enter inadvertently into his image-making, like innocently passing creatures falling into a trap that they are neither aware of entering into or (a fraction of a second later) escaping from. His portraits might be historic however, in that they capture, with unusual

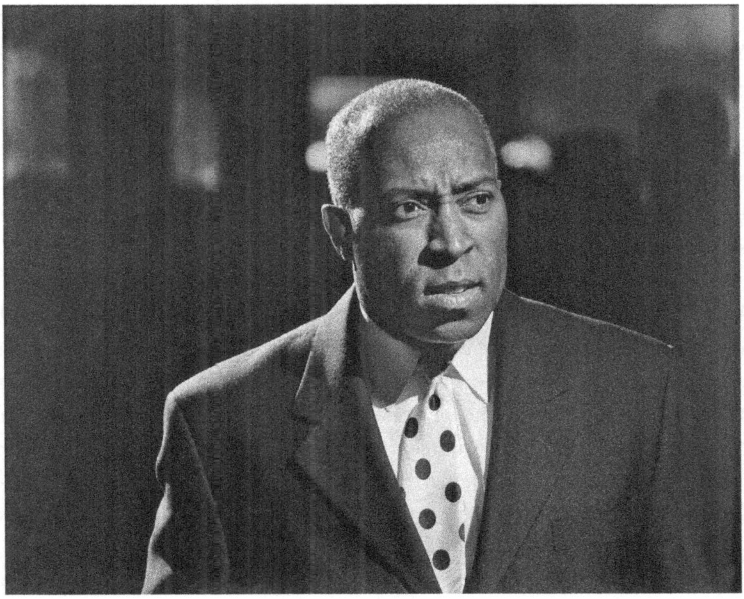

FIGURE 28.3 Philip-Lorca diCorcia, *Head #1*, 2000. Chromogenic print mounted on plexiglas. Sheet (sight) (120 7 cm × 150.8 cm). Image (sight) (120.7 cm × 150.8 cm). Promised gift of the Fisher Landau Center for Art. Inv.: P.2010.305. Whitney Museum of American Art, New York, USA. Scala.

specificity and clarity, the spirit, beliefs, and motivations of the people of his own time, place and culture.

For our purposes here, perhaps we could claim that it is within their particularly photographic rendering that we can discern the historicity of their lives and consciousness. They may have stumbled inadvertently into the artist's photo-trap, but in their moment of capture they have entered an archive, and thus history. Of course, this happens and has happened every time these people are photographed, but here the artist has managed to show us the difference between walking along a street and being singled out of passing time by photography to enter and add to history.

Mark Wallinger achieved something similar in his video artwork titled *Threshold to the Kingdom* (2000).[14] Here, a combination of video, slow motion, and an emotive musical soundtrack causes us to consider the humanity and spirituality of everyday people doing everyday things, like simply passing through an airport, and yet taking on a wonderous and sublime presence as a result of the particular process and influence of the effected video image.

The still photograph is not just another mirror to the self, nor is it the kind of unfixed natural reflection found in any shining surface with which (pre-photography) the human subject had previously had a relationship. Photography's fixed, enduring, captive, and indexical image of the self makes us newly other to a self that we also are, thus multiplying subjectivity and causing further confusion as to who or what is the real me – and just at the moment when, and in the place where we think we might, find clarification, confirmation and / or simplification.

Photography *extends* our idea of who and what we are, and as such may have always been a kind of 'stick' by means of which the self is measured, distanced, seen, and set apart from the self, viewed anew and viewed from elsewhere, 'there'; and then further set apart as it is cast into an archive and /or entered into some form of dissemination.

If we assume that photography is something more than and other to a mere mirror or reflection, then portable or 'home' video – which had become ubiquitous at a popular and amateur level by c.1980 – introduced us into a potentially permanent 'live' field. Now life became not merely a fixed or moving image but potentially a broadcast, once the preserve only of televised people and events but now celebrating our own importance. Previously, most of us would have appeared in a video broadcast only as extras or bystanders, as those who are unintentionally included in the frame, those who do their best to bring attention to themselves, or simply aim to disrupt the broadcast image.

Video Acts, a 2002 retrospective held at The Institute of Contemporary Arts (ICA) London, gathered numerous examples of the very first uses of portable or 'home' video cameras, monitors and recorders, made by artists and art students of the 1970s.[15] The majority of the works in this show involved the artist turning the early video camera upon themselves, as if relishing the challenge of this new 'live' field. The artists enthusiastically explored the technological crossfire in which they newly found themselves and which seemed to provide an unprecedented spatio-temporal context. Being between a video camera, monitor, and recorder is a little like being on stage, and yet strangely placeless, ghostly, dematerialised. If video is theatrical, it nevertheless consists of a theatrical atmosphere minus the theatre.

What video art is most like is, of course, TV, on which the video art generation grew up passively digesting thousands of hours of dramas, movies, sports, news, advertising, chat shows, repeats, cartoons, etc., with most including close-ups and what were originally called 'slow motion action replays' of sporting moments. For the artist in a studio that had recently acquired video equipment, everything that occurred in front of a video camera (and that could be simultaneously viewed on a monitor, recorded for posterity, played back as a moving image, paused, etc.) was instantly revalued and re-valuable, as was the self and the human subject under the scrutiny of this new technology. Artists soon sensed both the novelty of this experience and the fact that, like photography, the technology of video is capable of telling us something more, new, and different about ourselves. Consequently, the ICA's *Video Acts* logged numerous artworks that consist primarily of simple, repeated gestures and small events, including many monologues (Vito Acconci looms large in my memory of the show).

During the post-World War II period, artists like Claude Cahun, Francesca Woodman, Duane Michals, and Cindy Sherman remained loyal to the still photograph, but nevertheless tended to bend it in the direction of moving-image technologies, dressing up and posing, making film-like sequences, or creating 'stills' from movies and TV shows that never existed. Together they have come to extend and accumulate a strangely new and intense catalogue (a catalogue which, we might argue, begins with Dauguerre's figure, in 1838, standing in *Boulevard Du Temple*) of the modern human subject intensely examining itself according to photographic technologies, within newly private spaces that seem to be derived from or analogous to the camera itself, in that they too are rooms ('cameras'), private boxes of secrets containing a wellspring of magic, illusion, transformation, possibilities, questions, and surprises. The self-reflexive images of these artists often appear intimate, quiet, and internal, and yet were always destined to eventually be seen by a public – and many have now become world famous.

The modern subject, growing up in dialogue with lenses and cameras, may itself have become a kind of sealed enclosure, carefully releasing only those facets of the self that, in our world of torrential communications, it wishes to be exposed and shared. Certainly, the modern subject is a photographic subject, a psycho-photographic subject perhaps.

Cindy Sherman's work is today so prominent and successful that it may almost have come to be regarded as *clichéd*, and yet the recent 'selfie' boom, along with associated investigations by artists like Petra Cortright and Erica Scourti exploring the possibilities of our self-reflexive online personae, seems to bear out Sherman's precocious hunch (she began her famous series while still an undergraduate) that postmodern lives are marked out and moulded as a form of ruptured subjectivity or traumatised identity that is constantly playing catch-up with the plethora of technologised models, examples and images with which it is surrounded; images that enthral it and by which it is challenged.[16] The world of globalised media and capitalist consumerism now provides a constant kaleidoscope of reflections in which the subject can only ever see itself in multiple, fragmentary, and ceaselessly shifting terms.

Artist Theresa Hak Kyung Cha, who worked mainly on a North American West coast campus before dying tragically young, now appears prescient and precocious in the way her practices involved performances, documented as both still photographs and videos, plus video works incorporating monitors, performances using microphones and speakers, slide projections, transformed spaces, and also ways of speaking, writing, and bookmaking that repeatedly show her playing with language as yet another of the 'technologies' that appear to define us; and all the while questioning and extending our supposed nature and self.[17] In her many word works, including the renowned experimental book *Dictee*, Cha seems to turn the tables on language and treats it as a material and a process that we can manipulate and determine in return for the way it defines and determines us.

We may now seem to have travelled far from the seafaring and trading society of 17th-century Holland where our essay began, and far from the meditations of the Dutch woman reading a letter perhaps sent from a loved one abroad. However, when thinking historically we should never cease to extend an unbroken line that connects ourselves and this moment, this society, and its technologies, even this reading and this particular use of lenses and language, here and now, as we connect to that woman and her time, her society, technologies, etc.

The 17th-century Dutch protestant Republic is regarded by many historians as the birthplace of the modern, federal, nation state, as well as the birthplace of modern capitalism and global trade. We have already noted how the lenses and enhanced possibilities for distanced communication, which have become the focus of our 21st-century society, were significantly developed in and by 17th-century Dutch society, thereby possibly provoking new questions about the human subject and the self. Today the highly technologised 21st-century subject loses itself anew in transfixed scrolling, in statuesque concentration on mouse, desk and screen, while networked and newly dispersed in the virtual space of an apparently empty street, boulevard, or the so-called 'superhighway' that is nevertheless virtually teeming with online crowds. Each human subject thus becomes both a processor and a prosumer, contributing constant correspondence in word and image, either still or moving, using language and lenses, and mutually exploiting and being exploited by the 'attention economy'.

We are more eventful, more displaced, more photographed, more fragmented, more networked, more distributed, and more extended than ever before, and it is our technologies as extensions, augmentations and prostheses that show us this, revealing what Walter Benjamin called a 'new' or 'different' nature, in which the subject and technology are neither distinct nor in contention but each extending the other and therefore becoming ultimately indistinguishable.

And yet somewhere within all of this there still seems to reside a self, unreached, untouched by, and unknown to technology and even to *it*self. The modest and short-lived selfie-stick may have only pushed that self a little further away from us, allowing us a slightly new perspective on our self, a perspective that is a little more distant but yet not so far away as to be other to the self, as we pass on, beyond the selfie-stick's brief heyday, and leave it, outmoded, to the charity shop, perhaps one day to history and the museum, and yet also to landfill and thus to geological entropy, whereby it might lose all its cultural meaning and value in some distant future, to one day become material for a Robert Smithson and George Kubler-inspired piece of land art.

Notes

1 *Surrealism, The Last Snapshot of the European Intelligentsia* in: Benjamin, W. (2000) pp. 225–239, quote 229.
2 Echoes here perhaps of Kazuo Ishiguro's novel *Klara and the Sun*. Ishiguro, K. (2020).
3 Mitchell, W. J. T. *Revolution and Your Wardrobe – Fashion and Politics in the Photography of Jane Stravs* in: Stravs, J. (2002) pp.79–82.
4 *The Uncanny*, in: Freud, S. (1985) pp. 335–376.
5 See also a valuable update and further historicisation of these themes in:Vasey, G. (2013).
6 McLuhan, M. (2001).
7 See www.rijksmuseum.nl/en/collection/SK-C-251.

8 See www.tomhunter.org/persons-unknown/. A 'squatter' is someone who occupies and utilises empty housing without initially gaining permission to do so.
9 See also a valuable update and further historicisation of these themes in: Vasey, G. (2013).
10 Walter Benjamin's *The Storyteller* essay deals with the special solipsism associated with both the reading and the writing of the modern novel. Benjamin, W. (1968) pp. 83–110.
11 See http://100photos.time.com/photos/louis-daguerre-boulevard-du-temple.
12 Deleuze, G. (1986, 1989).
13 See www.moma.org/artists/7027#works.
14 See www.tate.org.uk/art/artworks/wallinger-threshold-to-the-kingdom-t12811.
15 Biesenbach, K., London, B. & Eamon, C. (2002).
16 Cortright and Scourti are both featured in: Vasey, G. (2013).
17 O'Kane, P. (2015).

Bibliography

Barthes, R. (1981) *Mythologies*. London: Granada Publishing.

Benjamin, W. (1968) *Illuminations*. New York: Schocken Books.

Benjamin, W. (2000) *One Way Street and Other Writings*. London: Verso.

Biesenbach, K., London, B. & Eamon, C. (2002) *Video Acts – Single Channel Works from the Collections of Pamela and Richard Kramlich and New Art Trust*. Long Island City, NY: P.S.1 Contemporary Art Center.

Cadava, E. (ed.) (1991) *Who Comes After The Subject?* London: Routledge.

Deleuze, G. (1986) *Cinema 1 – The Movement-Image*. London: Athlone.

Deleuze, G. (1989) *Cinema 2 – The Time-Image*. London: Athlone.

Freud, S. (1985) *Art and Literature – Jensen's Gradiva, Leonardo da Vinci and Other Works*. London: Penguin.

Heidegger, M. (1977) *The question concerning technology, and other essays*. New York: Harper and Row

Heidegger, M. (1982) *On the Way to Language*. San Francisco: Harper & Row.

Ishiguro, K. (2020) *Klara & the Sun*. London: Faber & Faber.

McLuhan, M. (2001) *Understanding Media – The Extensions of Man*. London: Routledge.

O'Kane, P. (2015) *Curating the Legacy of Theresa Hak Kyung Cha*. Third Text (Volume 29, Issue 1–2, pp. 31–46). London: Taylor & Francis.

Stravs, J. (2002) *Jane Stravs – Photographic Incarnations*. Ljublana: Scientific Research Centre of the Slovenian Academy of Science and Arts.

Vasey, G. (2013) '*Self 2 Selfie*'. Art Monthly (No. 371, pp. 5–9, November). London.

29

THE INCIDENT AT *MODANE*

What have we learned?[1]

At dawn on 20 April 2010, a rather outmoded sleeper train, packed with anxious holiday-makers trying to return to North Europe and destinations beyond, stood motionless in the dark just on the French side of the French-Italian border. To be more precise, the train stood on the tracks of the main line from Turin to Lyon at a station named *Modane*.

As a passenger on that train, I was unaware at that time of any incident of great historical significance associated with *Modane,* but its position on the alpine borders suggested it might well have been involved in territorial negotiations through centuries of shifting European Geopolitics. Hannibal or Napoleon might have passed this way, ghosts ofVichy France possibly haunt its sidings.

On the date in question, rather than anything worthy of historical record, *Modane* seemed to be playing host to a huge non-event. When I say the train 'stood', I mean motionless, and when I say 'dawn' I mean it stopped at precisely 4.45 a.m. and, after minutes that were expanding into hours, showed no sign of wanting to continue its journey The train had rumbled and clunked to a halt here in pitch darkness following a midnight rush out of Milan, through Turin and across Northwest Italy, with a momentum that had revitalised its previously despondent human cargo. It had then lumbered more ponderously up a series of steep Alpine tunnels before coming to rest as soon as it was in France. The fact that the train's destination was Paris – still 5 or 6 hours distance – with a promised arrival time of 9 a.m., made the prolonged hesitation acutely frustrating for the occupants, who had been gratefully relieved to have this special service laid on to rescue them from a desperate situation.

For the past two or three days their holidays had been disrupted by the eruption of a volcano in faraway Iceland. They had endured anxiety bordering on panic, suffered repeated frustrating setbacks, negotiated compound obstacles, and put up with ignominious discomfort. Their privileged status as 'first world' tourists had

DOI: 10.4324/9781003230632-32

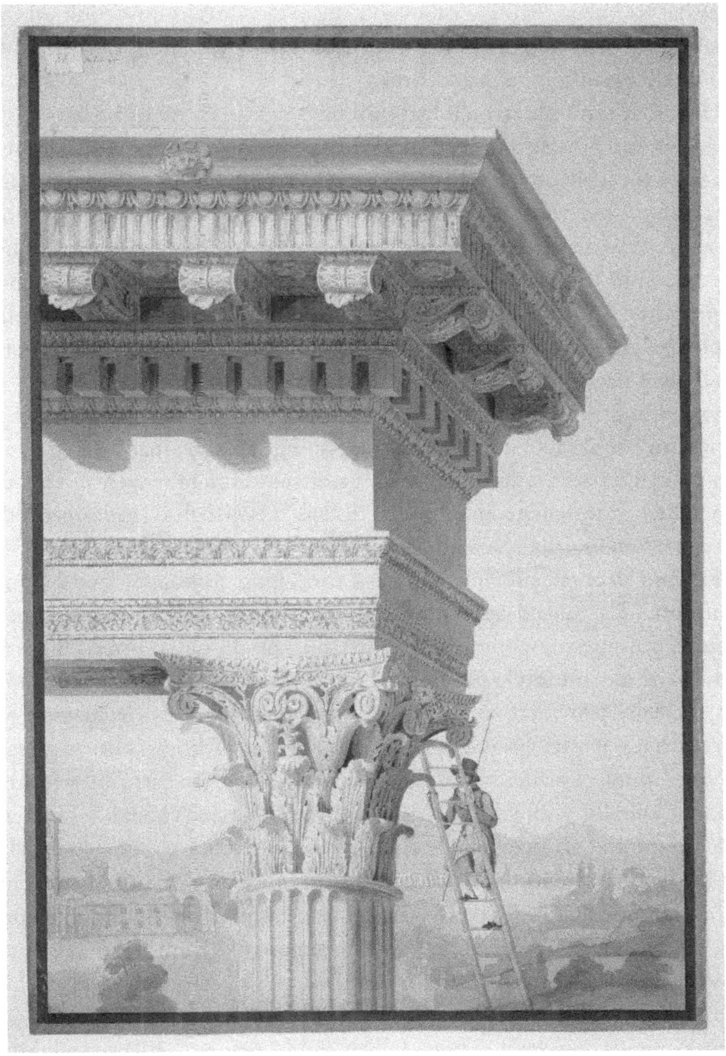

FIGURE 29.1 Henry Parke, detail of undated drawing made to illustrate one of John Soane's lectures as Professor of Architecture at the Royal Academy, showing a student on a ladder with a rod measuring the Corinthian order of the Temple of Jupiter Stator (Castor and Pollux), Rome, pencil, pen, and watercolour on paper, 940 mm × 634 mm, by courtesy of the Trustees of Sir John Soane's Museum. © Sir John Soane's Museum, London. Photographed by Ardon Bar Hama.

turned turtle, casting them instead as refugees deprived of the power of consumer choice and denied compliant, affordable services.

Unexpected changes to travel plans meant that holidays originally made excusable and triumphantly celebrated as 'bargains' had morphed into full-price equivalents costing sums many of these travellers would not regard as within their means. What had been thrifty escapes and cheap city-breaks now took on the magnitude of a far *grander* tourism as the truly aristocratic aspirations of their adventures ate alarmingly into their bank accounts.

The fact that this train, which had promised deliverance from a havoc of blocks and obstacles, had now succumbed in its turn to inertia, did not provoke the uproar one might expect. Most of the passengers were physically exhausted, spiritually resigned and coated with an ironic patina of the kind one acquires when things that have gone wrong have only got worse, and worse, despite every rational and irrational attempt to improve them. They had railed against injustice, become first theological then scatological in their invocations, and having exhausted their mainstay expletive: 'unbelievable', finally acclimatised to an unfamiliar reality for which they really had no words.

Thwarted and silenced, the travellers accepted the futility of their indignation in response to a sublimely indifferent force issuing from the inaccessible depths of a volcano – of all things – a thoroughly unreasonable, undemocratic, and un-modern volcano which, though geographically distant, nevertheless confronted them at every turn, extending its reach to all points of the globe, animistically taking the form of closed airports, enormous queues, shrugging consulates, multiplying hotel and transport bills, missed appointments, small spaces shared with strangers, fear, uncertainty, powerlessness, and most infuriating of all, call-centres whose inanely spooled *muzak* glued mobile phones to enraged and insulted ears.

This specially provided and very crowded train had been a magnet for desperate returnees at various stages of a wide variety of homeward routes, so that one couple, mildly ashamed of their difficulty in merely returning from Venice to London literally rubbed shoulders with suntanned Thailand–trekkers who tried to ignore and sleep-off their rude awakening from paradise behind airline eye masks decorated with logos of companies who, on hearing of the European cloud, had dumped them back in Asia leaving them with an almighty problem. And so, a rare collection of global and continental adventurers now sat, stuck, gently snoring or silently seething in *Modane,* a place to which none had ever planned to take a trip.

Peering out of windows where Italian fields, pylons, and moonlight had all recently flashed past, all we could now make out was a glum unchanging scene. It was as if an exciting action movie had resolved itself into an unusually grim still photograph. A few empty platforms and uninspiring buildings vaguely asserted their shapes and tones in the dim dawning light, while the station's name – 'M O D A N E' – in letters barely bolder than their background, provided the signature for the image. Much as one might wish for the scene to change, and for this train to do what trains should do, and move, for the time being this world refused to comply with our desires.

Our post-industrial age of largely mouse-bound virtual skills makes it unlikely that any of the passengers were experts in the mechanics of train locomotion, and this blissful ignorance ensured that, though curious about our uneventful drama, we were wholly unaware that the Italian engine driver who had heroically hauled us up here from Milan, had, without any announcement, rather unheroically separated his engine from the train immediately after arriving in *Modane* and powered off back towards Turin and his comfortable bed. The passengers were also unaware that, on 20th April 2010 *all* train drivers on the French side of the border, who might have been expected to liaise with and replace the Italian driver, were very much on strike.

As the small hours of 20th April stretched themselves across the slowly coming morning, barely anyone stirred on the un-stirring train, but after almost two hours of this strange waiting, some confused and jaded creatures, blearily encountering each other on the way to crude and inadequate toilet facilities, broke the code of distance and privacy one adopts when travelling in greater style than this and began to share observations and information, more like grumpy guests of a disappointingly cramped hotel.

Shelving their longer tales of woe, they compared immediate distress and confusion regarding the excessive halt, in particular objecting to the complete lack of information given by any employee of the train company. One nervy young American, acutely aware of our 'rights', pointed out the lack of drinking water on a train presently restraining what he estimated to be eight hundred people within its heavy steel carcass and behind centrally locked doors. This observation momentarily raised the level of collective alarm from bleary-eyed anxiety to paranoid probing, and potentially embroiled us in a historically infamous tragedy that, along with numerous other spin-offs from the main volcano story, might just feature in the next day's newspapers.

However, this was *not* to be an event of historical magnitude, it would not merit a Twitter trend nor a news flash on Yahoo, nevertheless I am retelling it here and suspect it was significant enough to all those who directly experienced it to sear its way into our memories. Though local and particular, this story probably did re-emerge, all over Northern Europe and in destinations beyond Paris to which passengers were travelling on, told and retold up to at least 800 times as an after-dinner tale or episode in an odyssey transmitted by telephone from a sofa.

My partner and I had been forced to find alternative routes from Rome to London and had reluctantly abbreviated our trip to the 'eternal city', fulcrum of a Grand Tourist tradition that we now approximated only poorly in our pathetically postmodern plight. A few days into a well-deserved break we had been riding into Rome's centre from our cheap accommodation on the periphery, when, on a crowded morning metro we were suddenly confronted with a hundred volcanos, paraded as front-page news pictures by the seemingly choreographed row of commuters seated opposite, each brandishing an identical copy of a give-away morning newspaper. The banner headline and accompanying full-page picture spoke clearly; smoke spewed from a mountain overlaid with two enormous words 'VOLCANO EUROPA!'

Perhaps because of our deep-felt desire not to spoil our longed-anticipated trip, or possibly due to an over-educated degree of hermeneutic sophistication, we managed to brush aside this emphatic omen, interpreting it as a crass tabloid's editorial device that merely invoked the *image* of a volcano as a *metaphor,* and referring perhaps to imminent economic 'eruptions' between Europe's member states. Anxious to maintain the vacationer's bubble of unreality and, saturated in the pleasure-seeking principle that intoxicates all hope-filled tourists, we simply couldn't link this grim announcement to any real, ruinous volcano, partly because – we rapidly theorised – no actual volcano could ever be described as 'European' according to such an imprecise location. And though we had at certain times in our lives also considered visiting Sicily and Pompeii, the words 'Vesuvius' and 'Etna' flitted only briefly across our minds before we blithely turned our attention back to the day's plans.

It is testament to the enthusiasm with which Rome grips a first-time visitor that for several days we did manage to avoid being sucked into those unpleasant concerns with which the workaday world is relentlessly oppressed by media and its insatiable thirst for attention. However, as we gradually came to accept that we had become embroiled within the news headlines it seemed odd that a natural disaster so far from this dreamy city could reach out and exert its influence over us. But Rome is a city where the miraculous appears on every blessed corner, and no place to focus on banal pragmatics, and so, even as we begrudgingly allowed our rich sensory environment to be tainted by bad news, we insisted on exploring the city in the way we had so long intended.

We had looked out at sunset from the grounds of the gorgeous Villa Medici, home of the French Academy and historic haven for artists, sharing the haughty overview of Rome once enjoyed by the Napoleon who had resided there and protected the academy from revolutionary forces. At the Trevi Fountain and Colosseum we ducked and twisted to avoid being caught in a crossfire of iPhone operatives making mini-movies of themselves amid a stampede of tourist trainers treading in the footsteps of 18th-century gentry, who, prior to the invention of digital film and photography, bought prints here by Piranesi, Fuselli, and Clerisseau as equivalent proof of their own visit.

More professional and academic 18th-century specialists had tended to take home lumps, chips and casts of almost everything they witnessed, thereby providing the rapidly growing taxonomic institutions of their North European homelands with a cornucopia of haptic ghosts and textured traces of the lost Mediterranean civilisations against which they compared themselves with extreme deference. To illustrate this condition, one drawing by Fuselli shows an overwhelmed artist or architect, dwarfed and perhaps weeping at the scale and skill of the ancients. Meanwhile, Henry Parke, a contemporary, drew a tentatively ascending toff gripping an inadequate looking ruler as he climbs an enormous capital, like a lower form of life in a land of giants.

Classicism, knowledge, and culture; discovery, adventure and exploration; along with the expanded mind, broadened taste and seasoned character of the traveller, are all condensed within the image of the Enlightened 18th-century Grand Tourist, on whom – we might suggest – so much of the bourgeois-centric gaze still depends today. What separates and defines the empowered middle classes of Northern

Europe has always been their ability to *acquire* and evaluate – or more specifically to acquire and evaluate culture, capital, and commodities.

On the long, evolutionary ascent of Western man to realise the pinnacle of its achievement in the form of postmodern, city-breaking tourists, some form of Neo-Classicism has repeatedly provided a kind of 'fuelling station' or plateau at which to regain orientation and self-belief by means of reverential reference to the past. At crucial intersections on the road to consumerist supremacy, the past and learning became inextricably linked and simultaneously enshrined as virtuous. Indeed, history itself, as popularly consumed, is invariably valued as an efficacious fusion of 'learning' with 'the past'. Notwithstanding its obvious metaphysicality, 'the past' is habitually invoked as a kind of ballast used to balance the shaky trajectory of an inherently progressive modernity, while also associated with values of education and wisdom.

The lessons of the past can and must be learned wisdom can and must be gained by encountering and considering the past – if possible close to hand enough to absorb it directly into one's flesh or breathe it in. The original document in the archive, the displayed relic and its humble cousin the souvenir, all fetishise our link with the value of the past even while such over-determination of accessible material objects suspiciously suggests an attempt to compensate for the unacceptable inaccessibility of the immaterial 'past itself' to a culture which is, as we have said, above all acquisitive.

To apply a Freudian term here, 'screen memories' might provide an appropriate model for the way in which the demands of the present necessarily and imperceptibly distort the truth of the past, thus making our ability to 'learn' or 'gain' from the past a matter of mere delusion The great loss and evaporation that is, or might be the 'past itself', and which, more than anything, determines experience and shapes life, is unfortunately *not* accounted for amid the serial secular revolutions that supplanted primitive, irrational worldviews with the sacred and superior spirit of bourgeois desire (an eternal flame now burning at the heart of every power-broking institution).

If the past, unlike its material relics, does not, by definition, exist, how and why should or can we learn from it? True, its images and evidence may steer us away from repeating its mistakes; we place coals into a fire fully expecting them to burn, and our hands into the same fire (un)safe in the knowledge that pain will be our only gain; yet all too often we avoid one mistake only to make others. Despite our magnificent hubris, modern mankind can, it seems, only avoid error by means of modest and prolonged procrastination, but this too can prove fatal, merely providing a further illusion that we are in control of temporal forces acting upon us, and which might just have wills of their own.

The figure of Walter Benjamin and his inter-war Frankfurt School colleague Siegfried Kracauer perhaps inevitably appear at this point, dubiously privileged as they were to be all-too aware of the errors into which men could lead themselves and might soon lead themselves again. Visiting Italy, Benjamin chose Naples and not Rome to write home about, just as he always insisted on gifting the secondary, overlooked, marginal, and accidental with all the dignity normally afforded to the presumptuously primary. Benjamin applied this method in search of the true, underappreciated lesson that history is in fact never more or less than a thoughtful 'snapshot' of the present, a reverie envisaged and interpreted (to invoke Freud once again) both subjectively and fleetingly in the constant dawning of the now.

Against the grain of that more awe-struck form of history coined by 18th-century academics, and by *aristos* trailing in their wake, Benjamin, like his contemporary Proust, productively enriched the academic, accepted, and established relationship between past and present by making it far less clear to what extent we could expect to gain or learn anything of dependable value from history. It might be our greatest folly to trust in the past as our guide, and perhaps wiser to attend forensically and critically to examining our current *approach to* the past as just one more aspect of all that is new, emerging, empirical and current, meanwhile accepting and asserting that *this,* and only this, can honestly be what we today refer to as 'history'.

As long as we measure cave paintings in millimetres or weigh pharaohs in kilos, we must accept that anachronism and incongruity rule the so-called science of history, and only then can we proceed, safe at least in the knowledge that, while we learn little we nevertheless create much. And surely this, possibly Nietzschean (perhaps equally Freudian) thought seeks to protect us from the enthusiastic hubris of a dubious Enlightenment, as well as from any headless or headlong modernism.

Under the influence of the particular kind of history that produced and encouraged what we know today as tourism, all that is considered of importance becomes self-consciously so. The originally dynamic emphasis on 'discovery' is countered by the equally archaeological emphasis on 'site', which encourages a kind of importance that becomes itself immobile and compounded; 'important' in that some particular phenomenon is repeatedly wrapped in layers of a particular valuation that increasingly renders its worth invisible by its very familiarity, or uninteresting precisely because of the increasingly unimaginative interest taken in it. Meanwhile, the apparently insignificant and overlooked might just retain and reveal unexpected secrets that cast the past in today's own light, exposing the qualities and motivations of today's perspectives. Thus, given the opportunity, the past reveals the present in a charming and essential symbiosis.

Still, we shouldn't call this 'education', as any discovery *by* the self is simultaneously a discovery *of* the self, and the least grand of tourisms – i.e., our everyday *flaneurie* – is most likely to teach, inform, and place us in communication with something true about the past that iconic monuments only disguise or deny, precisely because didacticism is *avoided* in any process of self-discovery.

Thus, it may be that Rome's Colosseum is purportedly the most important of the city's attractions, proving as it does the ancient Romans' theatrical fascination with spectacular combat and contest. However, for an unapologetic Benjaminian like myself, the past lurches up unexpectedly in multi-dimensional sound and colour all around these colourless husks that we feel so dutifully obliged to admire. For example, the fact that, just around the corner from the Colosseum I stumbled across a tiny, bizarre emporium making and selling only comically outsize men's shoes in every fashionable style, opened my imagination to think in unexpected ways about where I was (particularly offering an oblique perspective on the scale and pervasive masculinity of my ancient surroundings). Meanwhile, the comprehensive didactic packaging of the Colosseum's all-too-obvious self-importance seems to have drained it of any inspiration that it may have provided for Rome's original tourists, or indeed the ancient Romans themselves.

To give another example, concerning a more modern historical interest, at an early stage of our complex protestations and enquiries regarding cancelled flights home my partner and I found ourselves pressing the brushed aluminium buzzer of the city's only British Airways office, located remotely in an almost suburban area of Rome which I gradually came to recognise as the fascistic proto-utopia named Esposizione Universale Roma (EUR), commissioned in Mussolini's heyday and used as the discomforting setting for Michelangelo Antonioni's classic 1962 movie '*L'Eclisse*.[2] Here, far from the huddling, colourfully washed walls of the classical city, unmitigated sunlight and the failure of our mission soon beat us into dejection, as we pounded the dusty verges of wide roads lacking all shelter in this De-Chirico-like zone marked by the inhuman atmosphere that pervades all 20th-century developments built primarily for the automobile and with only seemingly reluctant regard for pedestrians.

But what Benjamin, his colleague Siegfried Kracauer, and Marcel Proust surely sought was precisely such unexpected, personal, political, and historical profundity, latent within the banalities of the present, that we pass-by a thousand times until, in some privileged moment, unexpectedly unearthing its value for history in the sense that we have attempted to determine it above, i.e., the maintenance of a vigilant and prophetic perspective upon all possible consequences of present phenomena. According to this scenario, far from the *end of history* proclaimed by certain theorists of postmodernism and Neoliberalism, we today inhabit *nothing but* history; history is immanent, our default environment, from which we escape only temporarily, on brief holidays from history, while enjoying the delusion of deliverance from time itself; time which (reversing Proust's famous title) appears to have *found* us.

It is noteworthy that, while we can readily associate Benjamin, Kracauer, and Proust with early modern urban environments, we simultaneously distance them (as they seem to have done themselves) from academia. To learn *per se* might fall outside the undirected structures and elusive forms evolved and evoked by these creative thinkers. For these thinkers – open to influence as much by Bergson as by Hegel – intuition, fragmentation, passage, duration and becoming are all more credible than any debatable, standard educational presumption that we should gain or learn in any measurable, progressive, or reliable way from the past.

In a scene from Peter Bogdanovich's 1971 movie *The Last Picture Show* that the preceding thinkers might appreciate, a teenage boy, restless in a summer classroom, is unable to concentrate on a teacher who strives to inspire him with 'great' English literature.[3] Bogdanovich uses angles and cuts to show the boy's attention is instead taken by dogs rutting in the school grounds, seen through the classroom window. In this moment cinema makes us aware of the overwhelming eruption of 20th-century subjectivity, displacing the assumed authority of the objective and classical, while perhaps defining the modern itself as a kind of distracted, searching, desirous adolescence that no longer necessarily appends the value of the present to that of the past.

To take these thinkers one at a time, Kracauer's tone (important to distinguish from Benjamin's) is biting; necessarily reliant upon a healthy scepticism and suspicion towards the all-too-knowing mechanics of modernity, which in 1920s Germany are gearing up to produce the extremist machinery of 20th-century nationhood, monopolising and carving up modern power between economic engines and the state apparatus. We could argue that Kracauer's Swiftian satirical distance insists that, far from assuming we learn from the past and its mistakes, it is better to acknowledge the ways in which we revel blindly in the past and its errors to such a degree that man's folly – if not armed at least with such a sufficiently vigilant and sceptical facility – is to ignorantly exchange error for error while intoxicated by mirages and delusions of right, righteousness, and progress.

The form and effects of Proust's most famous literary experiment offer us little chance of gaining in any way practically from the past, as the past's lessons and gifts surrender themselves only at the least expected and perhaps least useful moments. Even if time can, by Proustian means, be somewhat 'regained' (the ultimate dream of a bourgeoisie affronted by any denial of its voracious acquisitiveness), its *un*availability to 'use' is precisely what renders such memories primarily aesthetic. Regained time is beautiful precisely in that it cannot be pressed into any service other than the sensual, nor kept for long. Meanwhile we might store up acute and beautiful observations if only so that the tragedy of our ailing futures might be decorated with, or denied within folds of sensual memory.

Walter Benjamin's 'Angel of History', who necessarily 'progresses' facing backwards, marks itself so strongly on our image of Benjamin's cavernous thought because it thwarts a simplistic popular notion of progress (fostered perhaps by our habitual, physical perambulation) that we consequently come to suspect by appreciating the real, multi-directional and/or non-directional complexity of experience.[4] Benjamin's clumsily moving angel seems for us to be a more responsible messenger than any forward-thinking personality cultist confidently trying to lead a people into an imaginary future about which the would-be leader claims privileged information. While such 'leaders' pretend to see into the future, we must look instead directly at our world as history, and there and therefore (sic) see with more reliability and responsibility our very own glimpse of glinting prophesy.

But to return to our tale just in time to conclude: the traumatic disruption and unexpected return journey from Rome inexorably usurped the city's intended historical and aesthetic glories, and so, of the pile of memories I brought back it was that mundane and uncomfortable non-event of waiting patiently in the liminal non-place of *Modane* that found its way to the top and remains there to this day. However, months later, as I prepared this text, whatever consumer indignation and tourist blues that myself, my partner and many others experienced back there and then was put into perspective when I discovered that a certain eerie hunch I had felt while staring hopelessly into the dawn gloom beyond that train's windows was in fact correct: *Modane* is indeed the site of a significant and very well-known historical event; the worst train crash in history.

On 12 December 1917, a pig-headed attempt to ferry war-weary troops back to France via Turin for Christmas, using dangerously overloaded trains and an inadequate engine, led to the deaths of 800 young men, half of whom couldn't be identified due to the severity of the crash and the ensuing fire. On the insistence of a belligerent officer, and under threat of military discipline, an unwilling civilian driver and his engine had been forced to pull excessively loaded carriages on precisely the same route we had taken, across Italy and up through the alpine tunnels to the height of *Modane,* at which point we might imagine the returning soldiers might have cheered and revelled to be on home soil, soon to be free of their professional restraints. But after passing *Modane*, on the long and steep descent into welcoming France (that we ailing tourists spent hours longing to attain) the engine's brakes were unable to control the train's excessive weight and consequent downhill speed; they glowed white-hot and quickly caught a fire which spread along the train's undercarriage before the carriages piled off the tracks and into one another, slamming young lives temporarily reprieved from war into the unforgiving rocks of the beautiful alpine landscape. The whole then rapidly erupted into an uncontrollable inferno.

When I learned this, I learned, and learned again of the eerie palimpsests of history, where diverse events of relative fame or infamy are overlaid on and in places whose names remain unchanged by the events that take place within them. Why not believe in ghosts, and even 'witching hours', when every day we unknowingly walk in dead men's shoes, and even while doing so add trails of our own that those in future times will innocently blur or compound in their turn.

At 7.45 a.m. on Wednesday 20 April 2010, with the sun glinting brightly on mountaintops glimpsed beyond *Modane* station's buildings and yards, we finally heard the central locking of our train's thick doors click open and the public address system cough into action A French man's voice spoke hesitatingly in broken English to the battered and confused passengers:

> Ladies and gentlemen, I am the driver. We will continue to Paris. Depart 20 minutes. Now, I will be standing on the platform with a bottle of water.

The final nouns had clearly and comically lost their plurality in translation, as a single bottle of water would, after all, be of little use to 800 passengers eager to quench their thirst and freshen up, so I momentarily feared for the driver's safety, imagining him helplessly inundated with furious demands, questions, and complaints.

We later learned that it had not been possible for French strikers to predict and account for this specially provided emergency train coming up from Italy, and that when it arrived before dawn at a driverless *Modane* some panic had ensued among managers who wanted to be seen internationally to be doing their best for Europe's stranded tourists. They had in fact made numerous nocturnal enquiries and even physical forays into the dark in search of a driver willing to work on this sacred day of righteous protest. Eventually the driver who would now take us onward had been dragged unexpectedly from his bed to save the honour of France and of all consumerist Europe, perhaps with a strike-breaking promise of some extra financial reward.

After a further half an hour, during which our hearts and hopes were lifted by the sound of a throbbing engine, the train suddenly and effortlessly eased itself into motion like a young bird overcoming the fear of flight, and almost immediately our faith and patience were rewarded by a long, steep downhill train-ride through a glorious alpine landscape, bright with dew under a crisp new sun, with reflections of the sky's crystal blue subtly tinting the snow on the rugged crags and peaks, above which wheeling eagles dramatically hunted for breakfast.

Notes

1 This is a slightly edited version of an article published in Third Text. O'Kane, P. (2011) pp. 269–279.
2 Antonioni, M. (Dir.) (1962). See www.imdb.com/title/tt0056736/?ref_=nv_sr_srsg_0.
3 Bogdanovich, P. (Dir.) (1971). See www.imdb.com/title/tt0067328/?ref_=fn_al_tt_1.
4 The 'Angel of History' is a motif used in Benjamin's *Theses on the Philosophy of History.* Benjamin, W. (1968) pp. 253–264.

Bibliography

Antonioni, M. (Dir.) (1962) *L'Eclisse.* Cineriz.
Benjamin, W. (1968) *Illuminations.* New York: Schocken Books.
Bogdanovich, P. (Dir.) (1971) *The Last Picture Show.* Columbia Pictures.
O'Kane, P. (2011) *The Incident at Modane.* Third Text (Vol. 25, Issue 3, May). London: Taylor & Francis.

30

CONCLUSION

What have I done?

I always admired and enjoyed the artist Douglas Gordon's witty title for what seemed quite a precocious retrospective for a young artist who had achieved so much and so rapidly. Held at London's Hayward Gallery (Nov 2002 to Jan 2003) '*What Have I Done*' lacked a question mark for some reason, but seemed to transmit the right message I think, i.e., that our achievements as artists and writers are best, and safest, when we are not quite sure what they are, when we are not sure quite what we have achieved.

If our chapters have now been written, re-written, edited, read, and reflected on, what, we might perhaps ask, is or was the history of this book, and of all these combined histories? Is there any way to tally-up these collected speculations, each of which, after all, may have come to their own tentative conclusions? What, in short, have I done, what have the chapters done, what have they done to and with each other, and what have we done together as writer, writing, and reader?

There is perhaps no single history or story of the assembled glimpses of history told and shown above. Rather, this final pool of reflection can only draw us back into a newly informed consideration of the content, motives, and experiments to be found or rediscovered in this book. Simply writing about that which has come to pass may at least begin to evaluate the whole, as well as some details, and this may be the best that can be done at this moment to 'write a conclusion'. Of course, readers may draw their own conclusions too, despite what I write here.

Looking back at our essays we can see that each, like a pebble dropped in water, has created ripples starting from a seemingly arbitrary point which go on to expand, overlap, and soon suggest an infinite field of historical enquiry that we can never hope to encompass or exhaust. Hopefully, however, these essays, thoughts, words, and images may have raised some questions, inspired some new thoughts, made some interesting connections, and perhaps even provided some answers, signposts,

DOI: 10.4324/9781003230632-33

or suggestions regarding how contemporary art and culture might illustrate or extend our image and understanding of history.

It may be helpful to briefly recall some of the artists, ideas, works, and histories of which and of whom we have spoken: *Country Life*, Jimmie Durham, Walter Benjamin, Gilles Deleuze, Folkert de Jong, New School Hip-Hop, Dark Horses and Hollow Men, Cao Fei, Yu Hong, *O Xiangxue*, *Platform*, Tradition, Robert Smithson and George Kubler, Tacita Dean, Sigrid Holmwood, Pablo Bronstein, Wade Davis, Folk-Tales and Fairy-Tales, The Outmoded, Memories, Reverb, Johannes Phokela, Chloé Zhao, Kazuo Ishiguro, and others.

Then we could perhaps take just one example at random from this list and briefly reflect on the historical nature of, e.g., folk tales and fairy tales. It might strike us that, despite being collected in volumes like those by the Grimms or by Italo Calvino, the tales are presented as discontinuous and apparently arbitrary. Fairy tales are largely without layers and deprived of flashbacks or back stories. They therefore lack much of the guile, the porosity, the complex narrativity and cohesive attributes found in novels, screenplays, or modern short stories.

In their relative simplicity of form, folk and fairy tales retain a resilient innocence (complimenting the fact that they are often read and read repeatedly to children). They thereby constitute what Walter Benjamin suggests might be the childhood of all storytelling, and thereby the childhood of socialised man, who, by deploying stories, becomes able to live with myth's fear and uncertainty.

Studying such tales now, as adults, and reading them more critically, they may allow us to peer into the origins of story as the root of history. Like a story told or a fairy tale read aloud, history invites us to imaginatively inhabit a different and other time and place. But perhaps – as this book has hopefully shown, and always wanted to show – history also invites us to savour our own time and place, while asking, with a special historical sense of responsibility and traction, who, where, what, and how we are; as well, crucially, as asking how we *became* who, where, what, and how we are.

History may seem to concern itself with all that is over, with events (like those referred to by Douglas Gordon) that are apparently 'done', and yet history itself is never done, and despite the fact that this little word 'done' might look increasingly inviting and important to our conclusion, history is a special kind of presence, perhaps a haunting one, but never done and never gone. It may be a 'last continent to be explored' as expressed by Nicolas Bourriaud (with perhaps inadequate regard for the colonial perspective conjured by his image), and it certainly seems like an environment we can inhabit, even if we slip in and out of it while barely realising that we do so.

Today, each of us fields a barrage of supposedly important communications. We are also producing and attending to manifold archives. 'New' or 'Hi' Technologies harry us along in thrall to an urgent sense of presence, contemporaneity, and futurity. But the 1920s and 1930s, when Walter Benjamin wrote his *Theses on the Philosophy of History*, his essays on *Surrealism*, *Storytelling* and *Mechanical Reproduction*; and when Walter Ruttman made his movie *Berlin, Symphony of a Great City*, may have been times when people felt similarly harassed by modernism into a combined and constant state of distraction, attention, and emergency. It's worth remembering that Benjamin closed his essay on Surrealism with the image of 'an alarm clock that in each minute rings for sixty seconds'.[1]

This image leads me back to an image of my own, documented in the book above, the image of my adolescent self, late for school, hovering on the threshold of my home, trying to listen to the fading choruses of Gladys Knight's pop song, while caught up in the subjective importance of that event (something possibly formative that I am still writing and thinking about 40 years later), and feeling the traction of savouring that event, along with an emerging sense of responsibility – even if that is only responsibility for a pop song (someone *has to* listen when Gladys sings).

And this image, in its turn, leads me back to another encounter, at the start of this book, which may in a way have inspired the entire book, i.e., my 1990s encounter with an edition of *Country Life* magazine, wherein a slave brand, sold as *objet d'art*, seem to divert my life and career and draw me deeper into what I now think of as historical responsibility. For me, this is history, and this shows that the way into history is always via the now, given a heightened state of presence which comes from without, but requires something within us to respond to.

The content that has now been presented here is not, and never was intended to give a thorough overview of an academic field (which is not only beyond my personal reach but also impossible in the case of history as a subject). Nor did this content ever aim to be synthesised into a singular enquiry that stakes a claim for a specific theory. Rather my primary aim – always working as an artist writing *in* history, as much as a seminarian, lecturer, and researcher – has been to make a book that emulates, complements, and does justice to the experiences from which it arose, the life experiences, encounters with artists, works and texts, as well as seminars, students, and students' responses.

I don't expect here to have shaken or questioned the realm of professional historians, but I do hope – despite my slightly wayward approach, in following hunches and intuitions, to destinations of varying value but hopefully also of a rich diversity – that I have managed to interest, engage and inspire some artists, students, and other readers to pursue these ideas in their own ways, or pursue their own ideas using some of my own ways. If so, that is a satisfactory and sufficient outcome. I hope this book offers a thought-provoking, accessible, and enjoyable resource that can be used, returned to, built upon, referred to, cited, and challenged in the special ways that only books can be.

Having finally arrived at this concluding point, after negotiating some sorry troughs deprived of perspective, and many positive peaks filled with possibility, I hereby bring this book to a close while looking forward to opening it to the world as something more or less 'done', in the best traditions of art; art that, it seems, is always concerned with doing and with doing our best. This little contribution to history is then, for the time being, 'done', as finely and as artfully as I can, but not, of course, as I would.[2]

Notes

1 Benjamin, W. (2000) p. 239.

2 Echoing the words *Als Ich Can*, that Jan Van Eyck inscribed on his *Portrait of a Man (Self Portrait?)*, 1433. Painted in Greek letters on the upper frame, the words are an abbreviation of a Flemish saying and a pun on Jan's name: 'as I[ich/Eyk] can [but not as I would]'. The lower inscription is in abbreviated Latin and says, 'Jan van Eyck made me on 21 October 1433'. (National Gallery, London).

Bibliography

Benjamin, W. (2000) *One Way Street and Other Writings*. London: Verso.

SOME ESSAY QUESTIONS FROM THE SEMINAR ON WHICH THIS BOOK IS BASED

1. Is there a difference between History and 'The Past'?

   If so, how might artists, writers, and theorists demonstrate or suggest this difference?

   You might recall the quote from L.P. Hartley: 'The past is a foreign country, they do things differently there', or from Nicolas Bourriaud who described history as 'the last undiscovered continent'.
2. Italo Calvino has collected 'fantastic' Italian Folk Tales for us. How might these help us, as contemporary artists, researchers, writers, and theorists, to conduct and orientate ourselves in a 'magically technologised' era that is sometimes referred to as 'post-truth', and in a world in which the word 'fake' has taken on a new political power and currency? Write an essay referring to Calvino, to Walter Benjamin's '*The Storyteller*' essay, and to contemporary art and thought (Simon O'Sullivan's book *Fictioning* might also be useful).
3. Walter Benjamin's '*Theses on the Philosophy of History*' are intricate critiques of presumptions we might have concerning history's form, purpose, etc. Write an essay responding to just one of Benjamin's theses, using additional reference and citation, including artist's works and other thinkers' words to demonstrate your interpretation.
4. In Walter Benjamin's '*Theses on the Philosophy of History*', we can find two well-known statements (deployed in Chapter 1 of this book). One reads:

   > There is no document of civilisation which is not at the same time a document of barbarism. And just as such a document is not free of barbarism, barbarism taints also the manner in which it was transmitted from one owner to another.

The other states that: 'every image of the past that is not recognised by the present as one of its own concerns threatens to disappear irretrievably'.

Write an essay using your own examples of such 'documents' or such 'images' drawn from contemporary art and life in order to show that Benjamin was right, or perhaps wrong, when he made these statements (Olivier Assayas' movie *Summer Hours* might also be useful to watch.)

5. Jimmie Durham and Folkert de Jong both address history critically, artfully, humorously, and yet very seriously too, in terms of their own culture and its dark history. Write an essay using the work of other contemporary artists who achieve something similar.
6. In Walter Benjamin's essay '*The Storyteller*' he compares the particular values of the oral tradition with 'information' and 'the novel'. He also talks about the 'usefulness' of stories and storytelling. Write an essay that shows your understanding of Benjamin's thoughts regarding use, information, storytelling, and the novel. Discuss how these ideas might relate to contemporary life and use examples of contemporary artists who might draw upon the storytelling tradition.
7. Contemporary artists – like Tavares Strachan, Cameron Rowland, Cao Fei, and the classic short movie *La Jetée* by Chris Marker – all use memory, personal or cultural, as something mysterious and mercurial. In this way they might echo the writings of Frances Yates ('*The Art of Memory*'), Marcel Proust, Sigmund Freud, or the theories of the scientist and philosopher Henri Bergson (who influenced philosopher Gilles Deleuze). Explore the work of some of the artists and thinkers mentioned here and find your own examples of contemporary artists who might be working in the field of memory. Write an essay that draws these artists, writers, and theorists into play, asking: 'What can art and artists bring to our understanding of memory?'.
8. In Walter Benjamin's paragraph on 'the outmoded' (from his essay on Surrealism), he lists various everyday objects and experiences that he claims Andre Breton invested with revolutionary potential, explosive qualities, and 'revolutionary nihilism'. Write an essay discussing if and how Benjamin's ideas still relate to 21st-century life and art. Create your own lists of objects and experiences that might serve as equivalents to those listed by Benjamin. You might also take the last sentence in the paragraph on the outmoded, and answer Benjamin's own question there about popular music.
9. Write an essay that explores the current value of, and approach to tradition in contemporary art and life. Use Azoulay's texts and/or similar texts (e.g., Trin Minh Ha's writings in '*The Narrative Reader*') to show how contemporary artists might deploy tradition as a 'progressive', anti-Imperial force of resistance.
10. Write an essay that explores the monument through the eyes of Contemporary Art. What and who should be monumentalised today? If we still need monuments, what forms or processes should they involve? Choose some

examples of contemporary artists working with and against the monument tradition and come to your own conclusion about the relevance, currency, or anachronism of monuments and monumentality (you might refer to W.J.T. Mitchell's book '*Art in the Public Sphere*'; read Robert Smithson's article on the monuments of Passaic New Jersey, and/or look at Marina Warner's '*Monuments & Maidens*').

11. The short story titled '*O Xiangxue*' subtly reveals how historic forces shape the lives of individuals and societies. Similarly, the movie *Platform* (2000) directed by Jia Zhangke notes these historical and cultural changes as something that the characters in this film seem barely aware of. Meanwhile, the artist Yu Hong, who featured in the Lisson Gallery (London) exhibition titled *After Image: Dangdai Yishu* (2019), shows more explicitly how personal biography and personal history run in parallel with national or 'big' history. Write an essay, using one, two, or all three of the examples given above, and bringing your own examples too if necessary. Discuss the ways in which national, personal, and cultural histories evolve more or less consciously and explicitly, or unconsciously and implicitly, in our lives. Describe how artists represent, or might represent, the relationship between ('small') personal experience and ('big') 'History'.

FURTHER READING

Further reading (general)

Agamben, G. (2007) *Profanations* (J. Fort, trans.). New York: Zone Books.

Allende, I. (1987) *Stories of Eva Luna*. London: Penguin Books.

Barson, T., Campany, D. *et al* (2006) *Making history: art and documentary in Britain from 1929 to now*. London: Tate.

Baudelaire, C. (1992) *Selected writings on art and literature* (P.E. Charvet, trans.). London: Penguin Books.

Baume, N. (2005) *Getting emotional*. Boston, MA: Institute of Contemporary Art.

Benjamin, A. (1968) *Illuminations: essays and reflections* (H. Arendt, ed.) (H. Zohn, trans.). New York: Schocken Books.

———. (1973) *Charles Baudelaire: a lyric poet in the era of high capitalism* (H. Zohn, trans.) London: NLB.

———. (1978) *Reflections: essays, aphorisms, autobiographical writings* (E. Jephcott, trans.) New York: Schocken Books.

———. (1985) *Moscow diary* (R. Sieburth, trans.) (G. Smith, ed.). Cambridge, MA: MIT Press.

———. (1999) *The origin of German tragic drama* (J. Osborne, trans.). London & New York: Verso.

———. (2000) *One-way street and other writings* (E. Jephcott, & K. Shorter, trans.). London & New York: Verso.

———. (2002) *Walter Benjamin and romanticism*. London: Bloomsbury.

———. (2003) *The arcades project* (H. Eiland, & K. McLaughlin, eds.). USA & England: The Belknap Press of Harvard University Press.

———. (2004) *Walter Benjamin: selected writings: volume I, 1913–1926* (M. Bullock, & M.W. Jennings, eds.). USA & England: The Belknap Press of Harvard University Press.

———. (2016) *The storyteller: tales out of loneliness* (S. Dolbear, E. Leslie & S. Truskolaski, trans. & eds.). London & New York: Verso.

Berlin, I. (2000) *The roots of romanticism*. London: Random House.

Boyer, J. (ed.) (2013) *This me of mine: self, time & context in the digital age*. London: XLIBRIS.

Bronstein, P. (2017) *Pseudo-Georgian London*. London: Koenig Books.

Brook, T. (2009) *Vermeer's hat*. London: Profile Books.

Buck-Morss, S. (1989) *The dialectics of seeing: Walter Benjamin and the arcades project*. Cambridge (MA) & London: MIT Press.

Breton, A. (1987) *Mad love* (M.A. Caws, trans.). Lincoln (NE) & London: University of Nebraska Press.
———. (2007) *Nadja*. Paris: Gallimard.
Burley, R. (2013) *The disappearance of darkness: photography at the end of the analog era*. New York: Princeton Architectural Press.
Cadava, E., Connor, P. & Jean–Luc, N. (eds.) (1991) *Who comes after the subject?* London: Routledge.
Canetti, E. (1992) *Crowds and power* (C. Stewart, trans.). London: Penguin Books.
Caygill, H. (1998) *Walter Benjamin: the colour of experience*. London & New York: Routledge.
Cervantes, M. de. (1950) *The adventures of Don Quixote* (J.M. Gohen, trans.). London: Penguin Books.
Clare, J. (2007) *John Clare: poems selected by Paul Farley*. London: Faber & Faber.
Clark, T.J. (2003) *The painting of modern life: Paris in the art of Manet and his followers*. London: Thames & Hudson.
Coleridge, S.T. (2006) *Samuel Taylor Coleridge: poems selected by James Fenton*. London: Faber & Faber.
Costelloe, T.M. (ed.) (2012) *The sublime: from antiquity to the present*. Cambridge: Cambridge University Press.
Coyne, R. (1999) *Technoromanticism: digital narrative, holism, and the romance of the real*. Cambridge, MA: MIT Press.
Crane, D., Hebron, S. & Woof, R. (entries) (2002) *Romantics & revolutionaries: regency portraits from the National Portrait Gallery London*. London: National Portrait Gallery.
Danow, D.K. (1995) *The spirit of carnival: magical realism and the grotesque*. Lexington, KY: University Press of Kentucky.
Deleuze, G. (2003) *The logic of sense* (M. Lester, trans.) (C.V. Boundas, ed.). London: Continuum.
———. (1995) *Negotiations, 1972–1990*. New York: Columbia University Press.
Deleuze, G. & Guattari, F. (1996) *A thousand plateaus: capitalism and schizophrenia* (B. Massumi, trans.). London: Athlone Press.
Diamond, J. (2012) *The world until yesterday*. London: Penguin.
Dillon, B. (ed.) (2011) *Ruins*. London: Whitechapel Gallery & Cambridge (MA): MIT Press.
Doyle, J. (2013) *Hold it against me: difficulty and emotion in contemporary art*. Durham (NC) & London: Duke University Press.
Edgerton, D. (2008) *The shock of the old*. London: Profile Books.
Edensor, T. (2005) *Industrial ruins: space, aesthetics and materiality*. Oxford: Berg.
Eliot, T.S. (1981) *The waste land, and other poems*. London: Faber & Faber.
Foucault, M. (1990) *The history of sexuality vol. 3. The care of the self*. London: Penguin Books.
Freud, S. (1990) *Art and literature: Jensen's Gradiva, Leonardo da Vinci and other works*. London: Penguin.
Gleber, A. (1999) *The art of taking a walk: flanerie, literature, and film in Weimar culture*. New Jersey: Princeton University Press.
Goethe, J.W.V. (1994) *Elective affinities* (D. Constantine, trans.). New York: Oxford University Press.
Hanssen, B. & Benjamin, A. (eds.) (2002) *Walter Benjamin and romanticism*. New York & London: Continuum.
Hart, S.M. & Ouyang, W.-C. (eds.) (2010) *A companion to magical realism*. Woodbridge: Tamesis.
Harrod, T. (2015) *The real thing: essays on making in the modern world*. London: Hyphen Press.
Hatherley, O. (2010) *A guide to the new ruins of Great Britain*. London: Verso.
Heidegger, M. (1977). *The question concerning technology and other essays* (W. Lovitt, trans.). New York, London, Toronto & Sydney: Harper Perennial.

Hell, J. & Schönle, A. (eds.) (2010) *Ruins of modernity.* Durham (NC) & London: Duke University Press.

Holmes, R. (2009) *The age of wonder: how the romantic generation discovered the beauty and terror of science.* London: Harper Press.

John Eakin, P. (2008) *Living autobiographically: how we create identity in narrative.* USA & London: Cornell University Press.

Jonscher, C. (2000) *Wiredlife: who are we in the digital age?* London: Anchor.

Kant, I. (1987) *Critique of judgment* (W.S. Pluhar, trans.). Cambridge, IN: Hackett Publishing Company.

———. (1991) *Observations on the feeling of the beautiful and sublime* (J.T. Goldthwait, trans.). Berkeley, Los Angeles & London: University of California Press.

Kittler, F.A. (1999) *Gramophone, film, typewriter* (G. Winthrop -Young & M. Wutz, trans.). USA: Stanford University Press.

Kracauer, S. (1995) *The mass ornament: Weimar essays* (T.Y. Levin, trans. & ed.). USA & UK: Harvard University Press.

———. (1998) *The salaried masses: duty and distraction in Weimar Germany* (Q. Hoare, trans.). London & New York: Verso.

Krause, L. & Petro, P. (eds.) (2003) *Global cities: cinema, architecture, and urbanism in a digital age.* New Brunswick (NJ) & London: Rutgers University Press.

Kris, E. & Kurz, O. (1979) *Legend, myth and magic in the image of the artist, a historical experiment.* New Haven and London: Yale University Press.

Laing, O. (2016) *The lonely city.* New York: Canon Gate.

Leakey, F.W. (1992) *Baudelaire, Les fleurs du mal.* Cambridge: Cambridge University Press.

Leslie, E. (trans.) (2015) *Walter Benjamin's archive: images, texts, signs.* London: Verso.

Lyons, M.C. (trans.) (2008) *The Arabian nights, tales of 1001 nights, volume I, nights 1 to 294.* London: Penguin Books.

Love, K. (2022) *An affect of an experience, and how I learnt to write about it in the context of Fine Art.* London: Intellect.

Marchand, Y. & Meffre, R. (2010) *The ruins of Detroit.* Göttingen: Steidl.

Marcus, G. (2010) *Listening to Van Morrison.* London: Faber & Faber.

———. (2001) *Lipstick traces: a secret history of the twentieth century.* London: Faber & Faber.

McLuhan, M. (1994) *Understanding media: the extensions of man.* USA: MIT Press.

McQuillan, M. (2005) *The narrative reader.* London & New York: Routledge.

Mumford, L. (1991) *The city in history: its origins, its transformations, and its prospects.* London: Penguin Books.

———. (1934) *Technics and civilization.* London: Routledge.

Nietzsche, F. (2008) *On the genealogy of morals: a polemic: by way of clarification and supplement to my last book, Beyond good and evil.* Oxford: Oxford University Press.

———. (2001) *The gay science.* (B. Williams, ed.) (J. Nauckhoff, trans.) (A.D. Caro, Poems trans.). UK: Cambridge University Press.

———. (1990) *Twilight of the idols and the anti–Christ* (R.J. Hollingdale, trans.). London: Penguin Books.

———. (1969) *Thus spoke Zarathustra: a book for everyone and no one* (R.J. Hollingdale, trans.). London: Penguin Books.

Nochlin, L. (2001) *The body in pieces: the fragment as a metaphor of modernity.* London: Thames & Hudson.

Nye, D.E. (1994) *American technological sublime.* USA: MIT Press.

O'Kane, P. (2017) *Technologies of romance – part 1.* London: eeodo.

O'Kane, P. (2018) *Technologies of romance – part 2.* London: eeodo.

———. (2014) *Where is that light now?* London: eeodo.
Potter, D. (1996) *Karaoke & cold Lazarus* London: Faber & Faber.
———. (1986) *The singing detective.* British Broadcasting Corporation London: Faber & Faber.
Réda, J. (1996) *The ruins of Paris.* (M. Treharne, trans.). London: Reaktion.
Reynolds, S. (2011) *Retromania, pop culture's addiction to its own past.* London: Faber & Faber.
Riesman, D. (2001) *The lonely crowd: a study of the changing American character.* New Haven & London: Yale University Press.
Roman, M. (2016) *On stage: the theatrical dimension of video image.* Bristol, UK: Intellect.
Smith, T. (2019) *Art to come: histories of contemporary art.* Durham: Duke University Press.
Staff, C. (2018) *Retroactivity and contemporary art.* UK: Bloomsbury.
Stafford, F. (2013) *Lyrical ballads: 1798 and 1802: William Wordsworth and Samuel Taylor Coleridge.* UK: Oxford University Press.
Steichen, E. (1983) *The family of man.* New York: Museum of Modern Art.
Steyerl, H. (2012) *The wretched of the screen.* Berlin: Sternberg Press.
Stiegler, B. (2010) *Travelling in place, a history of armchair travel* (F. Filkin, trans.). Chicago & London: University of Chicago Press.
Tronzo, W. (ed.) (2009) *The fragment: an incomplete history.* Los Angeles, CA: Getty Research Institute.
Turkle, S. (1995) *Identity in the age of the internet.* New York & England: Simon & Schuster.
———. (2011) *Alone together: why we expect more from technology and less from each other.* New York: Basic.
———. (2008) (ed.) *The inner history of devices.* New York: Routledge.
Voltaire. (2001) *Candide.* London: Penguin.
Weber, M. (2001) *The Protestant ethic and the spirit of capitalism.* London: Routledge.
———. (1965) *The sociology of religion.* London: Methuen.
Willett, J. (1996) *Art and politics in the Weimar period: the new sobriety, 1917–1933.* New York: Da Capo Press.
Witkin, R.W. (2003) *Adorno on popular culture.* London: Routledge.
Zalasiewicz, J. (2008) *The earth after us.* Oxford: Oxford University Press.

Further reading (moving image and music)

Bacharach, B. & David, H. (Dionne Warwick [1966], Aretha Franklin [1968]) *I say a little prayer for you.* USA: Blue Seas Music Inc.
Bogdanovich, P. (dir.) (1971) *The last picture show* (film) (S. J. Friedman, producer). USA: Columbia Pictures.
Bowie, D. (1972) *The jean genie.* UK: RCA Victor.
Bresson, R. (dir.) (1983) *L'Argent* (film) (H. Jean-Marc, producer). France & Switzerland.
Bruckman, C. (dir.) (2008) *The general* (Buster Keaton) (film). UK: Pickwick Group Entertainment.
Casey, H.W. & Finch, R. (1974) *Rock your baby* (George McCrae). USA: T K Records.
Coen, J. (dir.) (1996) *Fargo* (E. Coen, Producer) (film). USA & UK: PolyGram Filmed Entertainment.
Cline, E. & Keaton, B. (dir.) (1922) *The electric house* (Buster Keaton) (film). USA: First National Pictures.
Cousins, M. (dir.) (2012) *The story of film: an odyssey* (film). UK.
Fei, C. (artist) (2006) *Whose utopia?* (film). China.
Gance, A. (dir.) (1927) *Napoléon* (film). France.
Godard, J.L. (dir.) (2008) *Histoire(s) du cinéma* (film). London: Artificial Eye.

Gomes, M. (dir.) (2015) *Arabian nights* (film). Portugal: BOX Productions.
Gordon, D. (1993) *24 hour psycho* (art video installation). UK.
Grimonprez, J. (dir.) (1997) *Dial H.I.S.T.O.R.Y* (film) (J. Grimonprez, producer). England: Zap-O-Matik.
Kurosawa, A. (dir.) (2012) *Seven samurai* (film). London: BFI.
———. (dir.) (2011) *High and low* (film). London: BFI.
Marclay, C. (2010) *The clock* (art video installation). USA.
Potter, D. (2010) *Karaoke* (R. Rye, dir.) (film). UK: Acorn Media.
———. (2004a). *Pennies from heaven* (P. Haggard, dir.) (film). London: BBC.
———. (2004b) *The singing detective* (J. Amiel, dir.) (film). London: BBC Worldwide.
Price, E. (artist) (2015) *K* (film). London.
Ruttmann, W. (dir.) (2011) *Berlin, symphony of a city (Berlin, die Sinfonie der Grossstadt)* (film). Germany: Film & Kunst.
Tornatore, G. (dir.) (1988) *Cinema paradiso.* Italy: Les Films Ariane.
Truffaut, F. (dir.) (2014) *The 400 blows* (film). UK: Artificial Eye.
Vertov, D. (dir.) (2000) *Man with a movie camera* (film). UK: BFI.
Weatherly, J. (Gladys Knight and the Pips) (1973) *Midnight train to Georgia.* UK: Eric Records.
Wonder, S. (1972) *Talking book* (music album) (S. Wonder, R. Margouleff & M. Cecil, producers). Detroit: Tamla Motown.

ACKNOWLEDGEMENTS

I would first like to thank my Routledge editors Natalie Foster, Jennifer Vennall and Sarah Pickles, and all involved in the Routledge peer-review process, whose encouragement and criticisms I conscientiously responded to and learned much from. Thanks also to Fiona Hudson Gabuya, Priyanka Mundada and everyone at Newgen involved in the subsequent production process.

Thanks to all the students, and ex-students who, over the years have participated in and fed back into my lectures and seminars, bringing their important questions, reservations, updates and segues; their essays, dissertations, research papers, events, and other creative and critical responses; to enrich, challenge, and expand my ideas on this theme.

Special thanks go to Mick Finch at Central Saint Martins, University of the Arts London who pointed me to Routledge and really set these wheels in motion. Thanks to Tom Corby, Caterina Albano and Debi Kenny, also at CSM UAL Research, for so much help, patience, advice, and for crucial funding for images and more. Thanks to Alex Schady for advice at difficult times and for suggesting that Routledge was the next way to go with my book writing and bookmaking. Thanks also to Mia Taylor, and to Paul Haywood, as well as the CSM Fine Art admin team.

Many thanks to all my lecturing colleagues at Central Saint Martins Fine Art, particularly to the Critical Studies BA Fine Art team, and especially to Jon Cairns and Stuart Elliot, and the late and sorely missed Kate Love to whose memory this book is dedicated. The Critical Studies team, as well as keeping me (as much as is possible) on my critical toes, has always been inspiring, supportive, encouraging and understanding regarding the necessary ambition of my writing and publishing journeys. My Critical Studies role has provided invaluable opportunities of lectures and seminars with which to develop many of my ideas. Thanks also to Louisa Minkin, Alex Landrum, Marc Hulson and Erika Tan for giving me invaluable and unforgettable opportunities to work and develop these ideas with Central Saint Martins MA Fine Art students.

Thanks also to Professor Michael Newman of Goldsmiths, and Dr. Maria Walsh at Chelsea, and others who have allowed me to experiment with my seminars over the years. Thanks also to Matthew Murphy and all colleagues and students at SOAS where I have been fortunate to develop my 'Art of the World in London' summer course.

Special thanks to artists Tacita Dean, Pablo Bronstein, and Sigrid Holmwood with whom I had helpful telephone conversations, and many thanks to all the generous, friendly, and helpful galleries and institutions, and to all the artists, particularly Folkert de Jong, who promptly supplied images of their work along with permissions to use them.

Thanks to all the inspiring lecturers at Camberwell Art History c. 1992, and all at Goldsmiths Visual Cultures c. 2000, and particularly to my inspiring professor and PhD supervisor Howard Caygill. Thanks also to all the friendly, creative and spectacular thinkers who participated in Howard Caygill's's formative 'Contemporary Thought' seminar at Goldsmiths, c. 2000–2007.

Thanks to Richard Dyer and Nicola Gray at Third Text, to Patricia Bickers and the Art Monthly team, and all to editors who have regularly, or occasionally published my writing and thus 'raised my game'.

I am forever indebted to my wise and supportive partner, the artist Bada Song, and to all the friends, family and colleagues who have helped and encouraged me to carry out this project. My elder brother Mike O'Kane was especially kind in sharing hard-won wisdom regarding life, the universe and academic publishing.

Thanks to Rob Prewett for first opening the door to teaching for me, and for being a great friend and teacher with whom I have laughed a lot and learned even more over the years, and whom I thank more specifically here for his advice about bronze casting and the Cellini reference.

Thanks to Barnaby Lambert, Catherine Dixon, Scott house and Tony Yard for their magnificent help with the *eeodo* books that were in many respects forerunners to this book.

Thanks to colleagues around the world in the Association of International Critics of Art (AICA) for opportunities to develop and share ideas on an international stage, with the most critical of audiences, and particularly to Marjorie Allthorpe-Guyton, Henry Meyric Hughes, and Danièle Perrier, and also to Sacha Craddock, Ingrid Swenson and Laura Tomlinson at AICA UK, all of whose support, advice and encouragement have helped so much.

Thanks to my music business friends from back in the day (and even earlier): Rob, John, Nick, Owen, Cesare, Richie Rich, Jon and all at Gee Street Recordings; as well as to Mark McDonald, a newer friend and supporter who is making his own book on 1980s British Hip Hop.

Finally, thanks to everyone who cultivates possibility through creativity, and to the many more people whom I know I should have also thanked here, but whom, in meeting my deadline, I have omitted from this list – thank you.

AUTHOR BIOGRAPHY

Paul O'Kane is an artist and writer who lectures on histories and theories of art and culture at Central Saint Martins (CSM), University of the Arts London (UAL), and at SOAS, University of London. Paul completed a PhD (writing as an artist) in History at Goldsmiths College in 2009.

Paul's research and writing is always informed by a historical model and always comes from and returns to Fine Art. However, Paul's thinking invariably visits a range of historical, cultural, and popular themes and issues, alluding to capitalism, modernity, technology, and popular culture.

Paul's own artworks have focused on anachronistic and atmospheric uses of visual imaging technologies to draw the contemporary into a seamless dialogue with history.

Paul's long-running CSM seminar '*Technologies of Romance*', and recent books of the same name (published in two parts by *eeodo*, London, 2017/2018), encourage the contextualising of 'new' technologies in accordance with an unbroken history of technologies and their significant influence on the development of art.

Paul is a long-standing member of the International Association of Art Critics (AICA) for which he has presented several papers at international congresses and has written extensive reports for the same.

With his partner, the Korean artist Bada Song, Paul also translated, for an AICA publication, the anthologised writings of the revered Korean art critic Lee Yil. Paul also edited the English version of the transcribed papers for the AICA conference in Berlin 2019 on 'Art & Populism'.

Paul teaches '*Art of the World in London*' at SOAS and has hosted seminars at Goldsmiths College and Chelsea College, on titles including '*Uses of History in Contemporary Art*', '*A World of Stories*', *Rêve Générale*, and '*Walter Benjamin*'.

The pandemic and lockdown also pushed his recent research interests in the direction of '*Small Worlds & Short Stories*' a title under which Paul began writing and lecturing during 2020 before moving to consolidate his history seminar as '*A Thing of the Past?: History, Story, Memory & Tradition in Contemporary Art*'.

Paul has published over 200 professional pieces, including reviews, catalogue essays, articles and art writing, featuring a series of articles for *Art Monthly* and regular essays and reviews for Third Text's referee and online journals, and other refereed journals.

Paul's current publications and research interests are wide ranging. In addition to the themes outlined above he has been writing a series on pop, popularity, populism, carnival, and the mask, culminating in an emerging piece titled '*On Mask-Ocracy*'.

INDEX

Note: Page numbers in *italics* indicate figures in the text.

Lightning Source UK Ltd.
Milton Keynes UK
UKHW020856131022
410399UK00016B/176